The Illustrated History of
WHISKY

James Darwen

HAROLD STARKE PUBLISHERS LIMITED

For M.

This English-language edition first published 1993
© Harold Starke Publishers Limited 1993
adapted from *La grande histoire du Whisky*
© Flammarion Paris 1992

Graphic design: Marc Walter
Editorial direction: Ghislaine Bavoillot
Colour reproduction: Colourscan France
Typesetting: The Five Castles Press Limited

ISBN 1 872457 15 0

Harold Starke Publishers Limited
Pixey Green, Stradbroke, Eye, Suffolk IP21 5NG, England
and 203 Bunyan Court, Barbican, London EC2Y 8DH, England
Printed in Italy

CONTENTS

The Fashion
for Whisky

*U*isce beatha . . . *aqua vitae* . . . the water of life . . . whiskey . . . whisky . . . In the soft Celtic twilight, when the sky is ablaze with purple, pink and gold, and when the birds are stilling their song, the man of taste places a shining crystal glass on a silver tray before him, and musingly mulls over the stalwart line of malts standing ranged in their bottles, reflecting back the orange glow and warmth of the fire. He pauses.

Should he opt for a Highland, with its rich fruity notes, a calmer elegant Lowland, a rare and sophisticated Campbeltown, or an Islay with its boisterous hints of peat and of the mists coming up off the sea?

A log slips in the fire sending sparks up the chimney.

Or should he take up an old and trusted blend? A Bell's, a Black & White, a J. & B., a Clan Campbell, or The Famous Grouse . . .? And there are many others . . .

The breeze sings gently in the bare trees.

Or should he cross the Irish Sea and pay homage to the men of Power's and of Jameson?

It is a moment of calm, of decision.

He takes a bottle and pours, sagely, but, be it said, generously.

The whisky glows in the glass, a golden light dulling the embers in the fire . . . it is a deep gold, perhaps, with reddish tones . . . or with the echo of the ruby . . . or a gold with the deep brown tones of a cello . . . a clear forthright yellow like condensed distilled primroses . . . a pale misty dream shot with the dying rays of a northern sun.

He adds a touch of clear cool water. Gentle vapours rise. He raises the glass to his nose. What hints of glen or strath are there here? What notes of heather and flowers, honey, autumnal grasses,

of mint and hedgerow berries? Is that the hint, perhaps, of the sea dashing high against the rocks, or of the clean vapours born of sun on the icy deep waters of the loch? . . . or a memory of a peat fire sending its white plume into the sky? A malted touch of the barley?

He takes a little in his mouth. The flavours develop, expand subtly. They betray vocabulary, being higher than mere words. But is there a touch of almonds, of nuts, of citrus, of hay, perhaps, and is that chocolate, raisins and cream?

He swallows. A fugitive sweetness passes and leaves behind it an astringent hint of invigorating bitterness. And the flavours linger on, echoing out in pools of warmth, changing, a moiré effect of hundred flavours.

He swallows deeply and the subdued fire warms him, down from his throat to his innermost being. He looks at the golden glow in his glass. They call it whisky. It is the water of life.

Across the hills comes the sound of the pipes or a high Celtic lament. The man of taste breathes in the aroma again, and sips, and savours and drinks. There is a faint drum beat and his feet begin to tap gently. He holds his glass against the dying light of the fire and smiles. He sips the whisky yet again, as his father did and his grandfather before him, and all his forebears stretching back in time . . . the men of taste. Had it always been so?

The golden glow of a measure of whisky in a shining crystal glass, held up against the light filtering through the grey skies, became the comforting ideal for the man of taste in the gritty 1940s and grim early 1950s of a war-torn Europe facing the pessimistic horrors of George Orwell's *1984*. This shining golden glow of

Queen of Scots

Highland Queen
SCOTCH WHISKY
Established 1893
MACDONALD & MUIR LTD. DISTILLERS LEITH SCOTLAND

whisky was the warm remembrance of things past, the traditional accompaniment to the friendly handshake of hospitality. It was the sign that things could be getting back to normal, that the horrors and deprivations of war were coming to an end. It was and, most gloriously, is the smiling *vade mecum* of tradition and joy.

Tantalizingly, films from the United States

A tricksy camera angle from Orson Welles in his *A Touch of Evil*. Beautiful legs do very little to distract Bourbon lovers from their rich amber nectar.

had Chandler's or Hammett's dashing, quick-quipping heroes, as incarnated by Bogart or Cagney, sipping a glass of the golden nectar as they gazed out from a mellow cluttered office to the slanting rain outside. This glass held the very essence of cherished warmth against a harsh and brutal world. The glass seems to glimmer in bright colours against the monochrome of the screen. As the tough private detective held up his glass in greeting, grown men in darkened cinemas felt their hands twitch and swallowed at dried throats and remembered whisky.

Whisky was in short supply in war-ravaged Europe. Wartime Scotch whisky producers had been exporting it to the States to bolster flagging revenues. Churchill, no mean man of taste himself, had declared, "On no account reduce the barley for whisky. This takes years to mature and is an invaluable export and dollar-producer. Having regard to all our other difficulties about exports it would be most improvident not to pre-

serve this characteristic British element of ascendancy." We echo his growl.

This was certainly a civilized and farsighted view in a world crushed by the debris from falling bombs and where hope was hamstrung by a puritanical insistence on utilitarian norms.

If things had been dire enough in the mellow smoking-rooms of the London clubs where gentlemen sucked at their empty pipes, and held dead cigars in bored fingers, if things had been dire enough in the pubs where the meagre rations mocked the silver-bright pre-war advertisements etched on the dusty bomb-cracked mirrors, and if things had been dire enough in the country houses where the bottle kept against better days was growing alarmingly low, up in Scotland and the Isles during the war the whisky drought had been bitter and cruel.

Here, as Compton Mackenzie describes in his *Whisky Galore*, the lack of whisky, in decent dram-size glassfuls, practically stopped all civilized intercourse . . . no weddings could be held, no contracts signed, no greetings could be given, no creaking joints eased . . . old songs echoed joylessly, empty glasses gathered dust. There was no whisky in the bars, nor in the manse.

Until, that is, a ship ran aground laden with

"Johnnie Walker, born in 1820, and still going strong" goes the advertising legend. Below: Johnnie strides out with a well-heeled post-war couple, hinting that things would soon get back to normal.

GIs posted to post-war Europe brought whisky back over in their kitbags, like this sailor lover of Lola, the cabaret chanteuse in Jacques Demy's 1961 film (with Alan Scott and Anouk Aimée). Here we see whisky as the symbol of good times.

whisky for their kinsmen across the Atlantic . . . then, smiling blissfully in the dark, the islanders ventured out at night and brought back the wooden crates with their clinking bottles, and life joyfully took up again with a salvaged dram in the hand, a wink of complicity and a smile of welcome.

Civilization was threatened. The foe was implacable. The Luftwaffe bombed Edinburgh and Glasgow. Bonded warehouses went up in flames sending a fleeting whiff of the amber joy

to the noses of lairds and workers alike. Though later the Germans claimed it was all a sorry mistake, the Füehrer directed his bombs more savagely. In 1948 a Junker 88 aircraft dropped its payload on the Inverboyndie distillery in Banffshire, that sleepiest of small counties. Peterborough in the *Daily Telegraph* takes up the story ". . . after the attack the local fire brigade was quickly on the scene and emptied [!] the stocks of maturing whisky into the Boyndie Burn to stop the fire spreading. But a herd of cows

Whisky Galore, the 1948 film from Sir Compton Mackenzie's book based on the true story of the SS *Politician* which ran aground on the Hebrides coast with 2000 cases of Haig whisky. The whisky salvaged by the islanders allowed them not only to take up their normal social life but also to cock a snook at Westminster.

grazing downstream drank the whisky-enriched waters. They toppled over, poor dears, and their milk had to be thrown away for several days until it had returned to its normal proof. [. . . Oh the madness of war!] Ducks and geese were also affected and were found wandering on Banff Links in a confused state."

On the night of the attack, the Nazi propagandist William "Lord Haw-Haw" Joyce came on the air on Reichsender Bremen Germany to claim that the Third Reich had destroyed "an important ammunition dump in north-east Scotland". Important ammunition indeed, and a

telling and powerful argument, *faute de mieux,* for the beneficial qualities of roast beef and goose *à l'Ecossaise,* and of whisky and milk punch. They were desperate times.

Europe was dry of whisky at the war's end. And then the Americans were streaming into Europe, with jazz, food, soft cloth uniforms and an eagerness to have a good time. GIs fresh from the States quickly learnt, as they had equally quickly learnt back home, the gentle qualities of whisky, and the undeniable fact that a bottle of whisky from the PX was a most acceptable visiting card to even the staidest of European families.

Whisky, the symbol of peace, of pre-war plenty and good generous living, crept timidly back to a great welcome and eagerly outstretched hands. But, with gathering strength, and quick-

Bogart listens and Sam plays "As Time Goes By" in Michael Curtis's Second World War film *Casablanca.* Whisky was the fashionable drink at Rick's Café – rendezvous for friends and foes alike (opposite).

The whiskey bottle is Ray Milland's fiancée's deadly rival in *The Lost Weekend.* Jean Tulard in his definitive cinema guide reports that an important whisky group offered Paramount 5 million dollars to destroy the negatives (left).

Some Like It Hot, Billy Wilder's 1959 film, parodies the gangster films of the 1930s. Its brilliant opening takes place in a speakeasy (an illegal bar) and its main characters get caught up in the St Valentine's Day Massacre before making the acquaintance of singer Marilyn Monroe (opposite) who hides a flask of whiskey in her stocking top.

Some Come Running, Minelli's 1959 film. Long nights with a deck of cards and a bottle of whiskey. Professional gambler Dean Martin gulls demobbed writer Frank Sinatra (left).

1947 – 2,500,000 bottles of whisky are unloaded at Brooklyn Docks, exported to to shore up Britain's trading deficits. As for the harbour guard (right), he sticks to coffee . . .

ening hearts, with returning prosperity, peace and developing wealth, in the pubs of London with their Dickensian charm, at the sophisticated bar of the old Crillon in Paris where journalists filed their stories, and in the bars of Dublin with their wild haunting music and talk of books, men of taste could once again call for the amber glass of the water of life, *uisce beatha* . . . whiskey . . . whisky.

Once again was heard, in the words of the Irishman James Joyce, "the light music of whiskey falling into a glass . . . a most agreeable interlude". It was a symbol not only of relaxation regained but also of

Britain, which had been prepared to stand alone; of traditions to be admired, of a gentlemanliness unsullied by the smears of collaboration and defeat. It went with the idea of everyday luxuries, of good leather and fine horses, of bespoke tailoring . . . and of walking along gentle sunny streets to the club without having to look up to the sky for black-crossed bombers.

And then through the decades of the 1960s and 1970s, with the development of appreciation and taste, the connoisseur started to discover the massed range of the simple blends, the aged more mature bottlings, all those rare

A London pub (right and opposite) caught by British photo-journalist Bill Brandt in 1939. During the war much of the whisky distilled was reserved for the troops or exported, and barley fields were given over to food production.

and various single malts . . . all the full broad kaleidoscope of that mysterious, beguiling elixir which is the water of life.

The Celts of Ireland and Scotland and down through Wales had long known the amber golden glow and cherished it for themselves. It had not always been so south of the border.

French brandy and wine, very good in their own way, had been the drinks of London high society in the early nineteenth century. French food was on the table and French wine was in the glass. But there was a worm in the apple. *Phylloxera vastatrix* hit the vineyards of France. Between 1858 and 1863 the phylloxera beetle

ravaged the vines. Vineyards were destroyed, plants uprooted . . . a cold wind blew across the dusty barren soil. The French breathed in deeply and rolled up their sleeves. American strains of vine resistant to the deadly phylloxera beetle were planted and the long, long process of growing, nurturing and maturing had to start again from the beginning.

And as the wine and, above all, the brandy supplies dried up, the great houses of London went thirsty. But there was salvation just round the corner in the Lowlands and up the purple heathered glens.

With the development of blended whiskies

The library of the Travellers' Club, London, comfortable meeting place for the English gentleman home from arduous foreign travel, with its deep armchairs and a glass of whisky to hand (right).

using grain spirit from a Coffey still which provided a continuous distillation, and with better transport – using, paradoxically, the roads that General Wade had built to quell the Highlanders after the 1715 Rebellion of the Old Pretender – together with the grouping of certain Scotch whisky interests into the Distillers Company to create a vigorous marketing approach and thrust, whisky was ready to fill the gap. Whisky, blended whisky, served with water started to appear on the tables of the highest in the land. Whisky was drunk before meals, during meals, and after meals as a digestif.

Habits were completely overturned . . . and very quickly at that. What the Scots and the Irish had known for a long time up in the hills

and braes of Scotland and under the gentle rain of Ireland – that good whisky in moderation is very good indeed was taken up by high society.

The tartan banner was raised to the glory of whisky and the *titres de noblesse* of the northern distillation were reinforced. Now it was found in the smoking-rooms of the great London clubs and the libraries of noble houses. The success of whisky, not simply as a stop-gap but as a noble

Advertisers have never been slow to link the better aspects of high society and sport to their product: polo (left) and golf (opposite top).

drink in its own right, underlines something very special in the magical, mystical qualities of what the early Irish monks with their first Celtic distilleries had called the "water of life" . . . *uisce beatha*.

The upper crust of London was not alone in discovering that what had hitherto been considered an amusing, fortifying though particularly idiosyncratic northern drink had certain qualities of warmth and pleasure.

From the tables of London, so recently laid bare by the beetle, whisky was taken up across the world to wherever the fleets of Britain traded and to wherever the drums of the Empire beat.

Spike Hughes in his witty *Compleat Imbiber* brings forth evidence from the world of opera, "The only 'hard' liquor of any consequence to be mentioned by librettists appears to be whisky. Whisky is the staple diet of everybody in Puccini's *La fanciulla del West*, where the first act is set in the Polka Bar and orders for drinks all round are accompanied by cries of '*wisky per tutti.*' The hero of the piece, Johnson, makes a considerable impression all round by ordering water with his 'wisky'. Though Puccini did write one opera with a setting in the British Isles, he kept his whisky exclusively for his American characters. So in the first act of *Madama Butterfly* we find Lieutenant Pinkerton offering the American Consul a choice of 'milk punch or wisky'."

Sharpless, being no fool, chose "wisky", thus proving without question that the Scotch whisky trade was a flourishing dollar-earner more than fifty years ago. At least I presume it was Scotch and not one of those remarkable Japanese brands

"as supplied to HRH King Victoria". *Wisky per tutti* indeed.

Though there were certain low points such as when the francophile Prince of Wales, later to become Edward VII in 1901, reintroduced the champagne habit, during a time when the whisky trade had run into some difficulties of its own, English gentlemen of the old school stuck to whisky with their meals. Did not Colonel Race in Agatha Christie's novel *Death on the Nile*, set

in the 1930s, healthily drink whisky at table while Belgian Hercule Poirot was laid low by an adulterated wine? The British Ambassador to Paris, Sir Ewen Fergusson remembers, "My Scots father-in-law always had a decanter of whisky at his elbow at table as late as the 1950s, which he would drink in preference to wine."

It is salutary and most heartwarming to note, as did the *Daily Telegraph* in April 1955, that Edward VII's great-granddaughter, the Commodore of the Sea Rangers section of the Girl Guides and Colonel-in-chief of the Highland

Lieutenant Pinkerton of the US Navy and the Consul in Nagasaki drink a toast to Pinkerton's American wife-to-be (near left). Madama Butterfly dies, distraught at the news. With Puccini's work of 1904 whisky makes its first appearance on the stage of grand opera; with his *La fanciulla del West* (1910) the cry "Wisky per tutti" rings to the rafters.

"The Queen's View" over Loch Tummel, not far from Edradour – Victoria's favourite view when she was discovering the charms of Scotland and making her first distillery visits (pages 22–3).

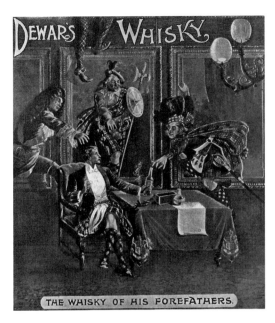

THE WHISKY OF HIS FOREFATHERS.

Light Infantry, knows the real thing when he sees it: "At the glittering champagne reception thrown by the British Ambassador to Hungary . . . Princess Margaret was in danger of having a dry run. A royal aide pointed out to the diplomats that she favours whisky and water rather than a glass of bubbly. A discreet gentleman from the Foreign Office thereupon gallantly smuggled a bottle under his dinner jacket into the building to rescue the parched princess."

But well before the shake-up caused by the ravages of phylloxera, whisky had indeed impinged joyfully on the consciousness of men of Lord Randolph Churchill's stamp north of the border. In 1848, the romantic young Queen Victoria visited Scotland with her beloved Prince Albert. They discovered the charms of Scotland, and fell

in love with it. Prince Albert was stolidly reminded of his native Thuringia; the Queen was enchanted by the wild and beautiful scenery. They stayed at Balmoral, in Deeside, later to be rebuilt as the Queen's "dear paradise". She wrote in her journal: "It was so calm, so solitary that it did one so much good as one gazed around; and the pure mountain air was most refreshing. All seemed to breathe freedom and peace, and to make one forget the world and its sad turmoils." The Queen looked, felt the trembling of her heart, decided, set the tone and others followed. Things Scottish became something of a fashion, a rustic fashion – to the uncharitable, reminiscent perhaps of Marie Antoinette and her dairy – but a royal fashion nevertheless . . . tartan was the fabric, the Scottische the dance, the skirl of the pipes in the heather and the caw of the wild eagle in the sky the leitmotif . . . and the taste, the savour, in the mouth was whisky, that very essence of the glens, the peaty elixir.

Frederick Ponsonby, courtier, remembers whisky at Balmoral: "In Queen Victoria's reign whenever anyone went stalking, a whole bottle of whisky was given out, and whatever the guest did not drink became the perquisite of the stalker. It was quite common for a stalker to come to the castle and drink off a glass of neat whisky before he started. Of course, if he went out stalking no harm was done, but when the weather was impossible and the mist came down he retired to his house and started the day slightly intoxicated."

Whenever the Queen went out driving, a bottle of whisky was put under the coachman's seat, supposedly to provide a stimulant to anyone who had an accident. It was said that early in the Queen's reign a poor man had been found at the side of the road in a state of exhaustion and that

Queen Victoria and her ghillie, John Brown, painted by Charles Burton Barber. She remained devoted all her life to things Scottish. The stuffier of her courtiers were often shocked by the uncouth ways of the Highlander when he had taken whisky, but even today the royal family is attached to the Highlands – the present Queen is woken in the early morning by the skirl of the pipes.

The Prince of Wales and the young Prince Alfred in Highland garb (below) – a watercolour by Queen Victoria. The royal children visited the distillery of Lochnagar, near Balmoral. (The distiller remembered: "HRH The Prince of Wales was going to carry the glass too quickly to his mouth. I checked him, saying that it was very strong, so he did not but take a very small drop of it.") Shortly afterwards the distillery obtained its first royal warrant.

Her Majesty had remarked what a pity it was that no one had any stimulant to revive him. The order went out that no royal coach should travel without a bottle of whisky for just such an eventuality.

And where the Queen had led, her people followed. The habit developed of members of society coming to Scotland in the autumn for the stalking, shooting and fishing. The north of England with its magnificent landscapes had already been almost completely spoiled by the Industrial Revolution, and the new rich, too, went further north to the charms of the Highlands and the clear open air, and they drank whisky.

The sportsman in Scotland soon discovered in that often rude and wet climate the importance of a dram to keep out the cold and to keep up the spirits. Indeed, a decent dram between casts is the essential of many fishing stories, if not the *raison d'être*, of the sport itself.

Mr Jones offers his ghillie a dram by the riverside. A tiny dram. Macdonald looks at it with a sniff.

"What's the matter, Macdonald? Don't you like it? It's a twelve-year-old."

"Twelve-year-old, do you say? Well, it's awfu' sma' for its age."

From Ireland, its fine old whiskeys still not eclipsed by the Troubles or by the Scotch whiskies blended with grain spirit, there is a more direct whiskey fisherman's tale. Jones was fishing with Paddy. They were using worms. Jones was catching nothing. Paddy, using the same worms, was catching really quite a lot. Jones noticed that Paddy was dipping his worm in whiskey.

"Is it that the fish like whiskey?" Jones asked.

"No," came the laconic reply, "but with a little whiskey in him, the worm just ups and grabs hold of the fish and pulls him out by the throat."

Though whisky was still not yet to become common in the smoking-rooms of men's clubs, Victoria favoured it all her life. After Albert's death she kept herself rather to herself, staying in Windsor Castle and appearing little in public, but she maintained her links with Scotland where she and her dear Albert had so enjoyed themselves.

Much to the Court's chagrin one of the links that she maintained with Scotland was the royal ghillie, John Brown. A simple man with a natural brusqueness, he treated Her Majesty and her courtiers with a certain rough Highland lack of respect. He naturally brought other things from the Highlands with him. Tyler Whittle records, "Brown had a primary appetite . . . for whisky. When he was young, and living an active, out-of-door life, his drinking made very little difference. Brought indoors with next to nothing to do, whisky began to affect him."

Clearly the Queen enjoyed her whisky and drank it neat, or in her tea, or with Apollinaris mineral water. (Doubtless her mind was on something else at the time, but the astonished Gladstone once even saw her lace a very repectable claret with some of Begg's best.) Though she did not drink very much herself, long custom had rather made her come to expect it of her beloved Highlanders, and she was especially indulgent to her friend Brown. One day at

Balmoral, Brown was tipsy and stumbled and fell flat. The Queen looking round in some surprise instantly announced that she, too, had felt "an earth tremor". *Noblesse oblige*. But then Queen Victoria was not the first member of the royal family to have discovered Scotland and, indeed, its most famous elixir.

In 1822, King George IV, in a great conciliation celebration became the first English King of Scotland since Charles II to visit Edinburgh. The visit was orchestrated by the writer and antiquarian Sir Walter Scott, and the King arrived at the nearby town of Leith and proceeded to the capital. Outlawed, after the 1745 Rebellion, the Scottish kilt, the use of which had lingered on in the Highland regiments and which had been restored only some years earlier, gave Scott, whose romantic Scottish novels basically rewrote much of Scotland's history, the opportunity to set up a "tartan extravaganza", in the words of Alastair Campbell of Aird, of almost Hollywoodian fantasy.

An excess of enthusiasm in the royal party give rise to some smiles. The Lowlanders, who had never taken to the kilt since the Dark Ages, looked aghast at the carnival, as the rotund King in

shin-length kilt and fully accoutred Highland dress appeared with the equally tubby Lord Mayor of London, who wore a kilt reaching almost down to his ankles. Even Lowlanders knew that the kilt should not go down further than the very top of the kneecap. But the sly smiles apart, George did get one thing right. He was if nothing else a man of taste; indeed he was the man who re-established the royal family's art collections after a period of studied philistinism. George tasted whisky and then tasted whisky again.

Elizabeth Grant of Rothiemurchus, the daughter of one of His Majesty's hosts, tells the story, "This autumn King George the Fourth visited Scotland. The whole country went mad. The Clan Grant had quite a triumph, no equipage was as handsome as that of Colonel Francis Grant, our acting chief, in their red and green and gold. There were processions, a review, a levee, a drawing-room, and a ball. Lord Conyngham, the Lord Chamberlain, was looking

everywhere for pure Glenlivet whisky; the King drank nothing else. It was not to be had out of the Highlands. My father sent word to me – I was the cellarer – to empty my pet bin, where was whisky long in the wood, long in uncorked bottles, mild as milk, and the true contraband taste in it."

What is interesting here is not only the King's desire for a particular kind of whisky, The Glenlivet – and he chose well – but that, during these last days of the struggle between excisemen and the smaller, illicit distillers, the King, himself, actually preferred, and asked for, some of the contraband elixir.

This was the true Highland hospitality. Sassenachs, those from the south, often make fun of the supposed Scottish meanness. With money perhaps – in that rural society there was need for little as such – but with whisky . . . never. In the eighteenth century, Samuel Johnson, finally enveigled up to Scotland by his amanuensis, the Scot James Boswell, noticed this dram-giving in the Hebrides, this essential part of the daily life of the northerners. "They are not a drunken race but no man is so abstemious as to refuse the morning dram." And, telling Boswell, "Come, let me know what it is that makes a Scotchman happy!" he drank it and declared soundly, if somewhat confusedly, that it was "preferable to any English malt brandy".

The writer John Macullough is more precise on this Highland hospitality: "In all the wilds I ever visited, I never yet entered the blackest hut without having what was to be given, the best place by the fire, the milk tub, the oatcake, the potatoes . . . and a glass of whisky . . ." It was the drink of hospitality, at meeting and at parting.

Sir Archibald Geikie, travelling in the Highlands, passed a funeral: "As soon as I came in sight two or three of the mourners at once made for me, carrying a bottle, glasses, and a plate of bits of cake. Though I was a stranger

George IV (left), who reigned from 1820 to 1830, a man of taste and a great aesthete, built the oriental Brighton Pavilion and particularly appreciated the Glenlivet, which he drank to celebrate – among other events – his meeting with Sir Walter Scott on board the royal yacht. His name was later used for a blend.

The Macphersons (opposite). The clans were oppressed by the English; the wearing of the kilt and the bagpipes were forbidden in the eighteenth century. Clandestine distilling – and a Macpherson was one of the practitioners – was for the Scots one of the best ways of asserting their Gaelic identity and of getting back at the "foreign" parliament in London. In the words of the poet Robert Burns, "Whisky and Freedom gang the gither."

Dunrobin Castle, midway between Clynelish and Balblair. The sycamore-panelled library, with its paintings by George Romney and Thomas Lawrence, is the place chosen by Lord Strathnaver for that evening moment of peace when a glass of whisky is the best companion to a quiet read (right).

to them and to the deceased, I knew enough of Highland customs and feelings to be assured that on no account could I be excused from at least tasting the refreshments. The halt of a few minutes showed me that much whisky was being consumed around the ruined kirk."

Whisky and funerals seemed to go well together. A minister, the Reverend Charles Rodgers, noted "the funeral expenses of Hugh Campbell of Calder in 1616, amounted to £647 16s 4d. This expenditure included a charge for whisky equal to one-fourth of the amount." Sometimes things did get out of hand. Another minister reported, "At funerals four rounds of whisky were considered due to wounded affection and departed worth, and respect was shown to the dead by the intoxication of the living." If funerals and whisky went together, death did pose some problems . . .

Alexander Hislop writes, "A clergyman was administering consolation to a dying Highlander when he was shocked by the patient asking him if there was "any whisky in heaven". Half apolo-getically he added, "Ye ken, sir, it's not that I

care for it, but it looks weel on the table." Well on the table, well in the shining glass and well on the lips.

Others were to praise the genus, whisky. Peter the Great of Russia on his visit to London drank Irish whiskey which was more common there in

Evan Cattarach, distillery director and great opera buff – pictured left with the six stills of his Cardhu distillery – declares that the perfume of the newly distilled spirit gives a sparkle to his voice.

28

those days, and declared, though with a certain inaccuracy, "Of all the wines, whiskey is the best." The great Queen Elizabeth I of England also enjoyed whiskey from Ireland; and, no doubt, on advice from her apothecary, she used it to cure her raging toothaches and enjoyed it. Perhaps she had heard of it from Sir Walter Raleigh, who on one of his voyages of discovery to the Americas stopped off in County Cork to take on some whiskey, noting appreciatively the "supreme present of a 32-gallon cask of the Earl of Cork's home-distilled *uisce beatha* . . ." Was this the first export to the Americas of that nectar that came so happily back in force to the war-torn Europe of the 1940s and 1950s?

Through the shredded veils of history, through the Celtic mists of Scotland and of Ireland, from the rude huts and bothies of the north to the clubs of the Indian Empire, from the bars of Paris, and the faded mahogany brown London gentlemen's clubs, to the laser-flashing Karaoke bars of downtown Tokyo and Kyoto, from the filtered light of New York bars, the

sophistication of grand hotels and embassy receptions, to the carefully hoarded bottle in some far away atoll where an English flag once flew, whisky has a special place in the hearts of men of taste.

That whisky was made well, in the north, where in Boswell's words, there was whisky "in order to supply by art the want of that genial warmth of blood that the sun produces." In this north, it was the daily drink of health, of life and fellowship; it was the smiling peaty companion of lazy evenings by the fire; it was the laughing, singing guest of friends together in the warmth of shared reminiscences of hunt, river and hard riding; it was the firm handshake at the sealing of contracts and the saying of adieu; it was the golden bowl that dispersed clouds; it has all those mystic magical qualities that the monks who first distilled it, in Ireland and then across the narrow waters in Scotland, attributed to it . . . their *uisce beatha* . . . their water of life; it is simple, compounded of barley from the earth, fire and clean sparkling water; it has something inherent that no other drink, however noble, can give; quite simply, it tastes very, very good. All this has contributed to its being the drink, the golden companion, of the man of taste.

The brute will look at beauty and find ugliness, and then will drink and grow drunken and raging. But in whisky, the "sovereign liquor", the man of taste will find friendship, warmth, quiet and health.

Gently, Ivor Brown wrote, "Whisky, properly savoured and not grossly gulped, is essentially a pensive and philosophic liquor." With hand on hip in full literary flow, Oliver St John Gogarty, smiles, "There is no such thing as a *large* whiskey." Wise as his Father Brown, G. K. Chesterton whispers:

A cargo of whisky from Scotland arrives in New York in the 1940s (right).

Prohibition: a fashionable hotel organizes a wake for the much loved and lamented whisky (left).

The Hôtel Palais d'Orsay, photographed by Henri Cartier-Bresson (opposite). Built in 1900, the reception rooms are now the restaurant and cafeteria of the Museum. Under the great clock, the bar offers clients a selection of the best and most fashionable blends.

Michel Serrault as Léo Malet's detective, Nestor Burma. "Marc Covet, the journalist, contemplates a misty glass in which ice cubes gently clink" (*Corrida aux Champs Elysées*).

"If an angel out of Heaven
Gives you something else to drink
Thank her for her kind intention
And pour it down the sink."

And we, smiling, with John Ryan, ambassador *extraordinaire* of whiskey, we raise our glasses to the old Irish toast:

"Health and long life to you
Land without rent to you
The woman (or man) of your choice to you
And may you be half an hour in heaven
before the devil knows you're dead!"

But before you feel John O'Sullivan's "torchlight procession marching down your throat", let the wit and writer Patrick Campbell, Lord Glenavy, an Irishman, educated at Rossall in England, living long in the sun of France, sum it all up: "Whisky is, whenever gentlemen are met together . . . an elegant drink, a mannerly one, not to be rushed at or otherwise abused and a good talking drink that stirs the imagination."

Gentlemen, men of taste, hold up the golden glow in the shining crystal glass against the grey light . . . and savour its warmth and delights gently with a smile . . . the water of life . . . whisky.

THE WATER OF HEALTH . . . IF IT BE ORDERLIE TAKEN . . .

Not for nothing was the distillation of fermented barley called the "water of life" by the early monks. Combining pleasure with prudence, we can read a British Medical Association report of the 1930s which tells us that the equivalent of four single whiskies per day can offer protection against heart disease.

Clearly, though some drinkers have devotedly ensured that, whatever they will die of, it certainly will not be of heart disease, this is no call to excess. Nor should the quibble that the British Medical Association of the time was ruled by Scotsmen be taken as a disclaimer. Could it not be that having been brought up with a drop of whisky about them, this encouraged them to pursue a medical career of practical healing?

Even earlier devotees were ready to press whisky's claim as the true water of life as well as a pleasant golden *vade mecum* in the rude climate of of the heathery glens. The English writer Tobias Smollett in 1771 reports that he found it "an excellent preservative against the winter cold which must be extreme on those mountains . . . I am told that it is given with great success to infants as a cordial in the confluent smallpox."

Jeanne Moreau and Monica Vitti in Antonioni's *La notte* (1961). Whisky, the drink of the Roman smart set, encourages the breaking down of barriers and the telling of secrets (left).

Men of taste, finding something mysterious and delightful in whisky that other coarser distillations cannot give, insist on its beneficial qualities. The Great Scottish poet Hugh MacDiarmid, a man of many principles, writing of deaths due to disease in the Salonika campaign in the First World War states, "The principal causes were dysentery, blackwater fever and malaria. It was noted that when there was whisky in the officers' or sergeants' messes there were very few recurrences of malaria, but when whisky was not available the recurrence rate went up at once."

In 1827 John Wilson, Professor of Moral Philosophy, attributes to James Hogg, the Ettick shepherd, the glorious words, "The human mind never tires of drinking The Glenlivet . . . if a man could find oot the exac' proportion of and quantity that ought to be drunk every day and keep to that, I verily trow that he might leeve for

Brendan Behan (left), the hard-drinking hard-talking Dublin poet and playwright, has this to say of poteen, the illicitly distilled spirit: "It is just murder. It's the end, you can take it from me, for I have wide enough experience of it."

The American film *Her Man* (1930) expresses all the poetry of the sailors' bars. The whore and the handsome matelot who tries to tear her away from her immoral life are brought together by the joys of whisky (pages 34–5).

ever, without dying at a', and that doctors and kirkyards would go out of fashion."

Perhaps, again, in view of the opinion shifts of modern medical science towards the claims of the more aggressive drug companies and the ranting killjoy anti-drink lobby which is once more raising its bitter pallid head . . . despite the pure truth in that old sovereign cure for the common cold (Take a toddy of whisky to bed, put a bowler hat at the foot of the bed and drink until you see two) . . . these claims to support the therapeutic benefits and pleasures for the connoisseur may possibly seem just a slight touch exaggerated, nay old-fashioned. However, in the letter column of the very serious *Daily Telegraph*

the distinguished Sir Eric Franklin of Cambridge could write as late as July 1991, ". . . our work in the Pakistan Secretariat (1947) involved very long and arduous hours in the humid climate of Karachi, with the result that quite a number of senior officials were struck down in their offices by coronary attacks. All of them were Pakistanis. When we were talking about this one night after dinner in my home, the Begum Sahib, the wife of a very senior official whose intelligence matched her beauty said, 'Our British officers work just as hard as our own men, if not harder, yet not one of them has had a heart attack. I put it down to this: at the end of the day, the British officers relax with a couple of pegs of whisky and soda at

The Milroy brothers, Wallace (left) and Jack (right), two great whisky buffs. The former writes sagely on the water of life while the latter runs Soho's famed whisky mecca.

The art of the master blender remains unchanged over the years. He relies on his nose rather than his taste buds in his work.

a very familiar bottle which, though it was labelled on one side 'Cholera Mixture: a wine-glassful to be taken every two hours or *oftener* as required', had upon the other side the well-known label of a firm of Scotch whisky distillers whose name modesty requires me to suppress."

Thus this idea of health in the good taste and the even mellow glow of a dram of the water of life serves medicine, the man of taste and good living and the contrabandist alike, in a direct line down from the early earnest recommendation by the chronicler Raphael Holinshed in 1564, who must have the last word, writing of Irish whiskey, the forefather of the genus. He encapsulates it all –

Whisky . . .

"*being moderately taken,*
it cutteth fleume,
it lighteneth the mynd,
it quickeneth the spirits,
it cureth the hydropsie,
it pounceth the stone,
it repelleth the gravel,

the Sind Club or at home, whereas our men just come home, sit down and go on worrying about their office problems. If only they would relax with one or two pegs of whisky like the British.'"

Ah! And have not the medical benefits of whisky been the saving of many a man of taste in more barbarous and cruel societies? Thomas Dewar, scion of the great whisky family, set out across the world to sell his whisky. He visited over twenty-six grateful countries. "While travelling in the 1920s through a prohibition state (in Canada), I tried to get some whisky from the conductor of the train but without success. However, he eventually advised me to try at a store at the next stopping place, and this I did.

"'Do you sell whisky?' I asked.

"'Are you sick, mister, or got a medical certificate?'

"'No.'

"'Then I can't do it; but I reckon our cholera mixture'll about fix you. Try a bottle of that.'

"I did, but to my great astonishment received

Whisky is good for the health, at least according to the British medical lobby, which is dominated by Scots. Here the virtues of a small dram are extolled (below left).

it puffeth away ventosite,
it kepyth and preserveth
the eyes from dazelying,
the tongue from lispying,
the teethe from chatterying,
the throte from rattlying,
the weasan from stieflying,
the stomach from womblying,
the harte from swellying,
the belie from wirtching,
the guts from rumblying,

the hands from shivering,
the sinews from shrinkying,
the veynes from crumplying,
the bones from akying,
the marrow from soakying,
and truly it is a sovereign liquor,
If it be orderlie taken."

The man of taste raises his glass and reminds us that he had known all along.
    Good Health! . . . indeed.

A pub on Islay (opposite), where locals taste their own characteristic peaty brew, with a half-pint of beer on the side – a custom not without its charms. The murals are by the well-known local artist Sean O'Leary.

Eilan Donan, one of Scotland's most romantic castles, on the road to the Kyle of Lochalsh, and the ferry to Skye, home of the gingery Talisker malt (page 40).

The tam o' shanter and the kilt are the essential elements of the dress of the Highlands – the birthplace of so many great

malt whiskies, whose distilleries are temples to the ancestral art of distillation.

Thirteen Centuries of Whisky

When exactly whisky was first distilled is not known any more than when the first wheel was invented.

What is known in the matter of distillations is that around 800 BC arrack was being distilled in India, and that Aristotle, who was born in 584 BC, wrote of distilling in his *Metereology*.

At some point here, a Sinologue usually claims that the Chinese were distilling two thousand years ago, or was it thirty thousand years ago? Either way it does not matter unduly as whatever they produced has left little mark on the development of noble distilling in the Western world, nor has there been a particularly headlong rush of men of taste to sample the stuff.

The argument that there are, today, along the old Silk Route in mid-China, people distilling a form of *eau de vie* with primitive makeshift apparatus made out of bamboo serves only to underline man's need and pleasure in a water higher than water, even if it does lag far behind its highest and most developed form, whisky.

The earliest delights and uses of whisky, too, are undocumented, however Neil M. Gunn, in his perhaps rather fanciful *Whisky and Scotland*, puts forward his theory:

"The Celt, in the season, flails and winnows his barley. Left happily in water the barley ferments. It is boiled and by happy chance the steam is condensed against some cold surface . . . and lo! this condensation of the steam from the greenish yellow fermented gruel is clear as crystal. It is purer than any water from any well. When cold it is colder to the fingers than ice. A marvellous transformation. A perfect water. But in the mouth. What is this? The gums tingle, the throat burns, fire passes down into the belly, and thence outward to the fingertips, to the feet, and finally to the head. The man was a bit tired, exasperated a little, for things had been going wrong (how often they must have for the primitive experimenter!), and for the rest – or he wouldn't have been at the job – not a little weary with the dullness of social life, including the looks of women and the ambitions of fools. And then – and then – the head goes up. The film dissolves from the eyes; they glisten. He abruptly laughs and jumps to his feet; as abruptly he pauses to look over himself with a marvellous scrutiny. He tries the muscles of his arms. They are full of such energy that one fist shoots out; then the other. A right and a left. His legs have the same energy. He begins to dance with what is called primitive abandon. Clearly it was not water that he had drunk . . . it was life . . ."

Perhaps, indeed, this is what happened, perhaps . . . What we do know is that far back into history the Egyptians had used distillation to produce fards, aromatics and perfumes. Above all, they produced kohl to underline the eyes and make them sparkle. This gave rise to the name *al kohl*, thus alcohol, from their *al ambic*, alembic.

Early Christian monks set up monasteries in Egypt where the ground in those days was, curiously, suitable for growing a form of barley, and here alcohol was produced. Apparently, at first, they had little official use for alcohol, except for rubbing into the stiffened joints of their mules.

Later they used it on their human patients, externally . . . and then internally . . . ah the happy chance and the benefits of finger licking. And, oh brother, was it this that made the mountains to skip like rams and the hills like lambs?

In those days, of course, monasteries were not only centres of religion and prayer. The monks kept libraries, infir-

The Cork countryside not far from Midleton. Here Saint Colman built a cathedral in the sixth century; it was the monks who brought the art of distilling from Egypt to the green land of Ireland.

The Cork countryside not far from Midleton. Here Saint Colman built a cathedral in the sixth century; it was the monks who brought the art of distilling from Egypt to the green land of Ireland.

maries, and centres of commerce. Self-contained and self-suppporting, they drew in those from outside to learn, to pray, to trade and to be healed . . . to be healed of all those ailments which later Holinshed so diligently enumerated for us.

Certainly there must have been outpatient departments where the sick were sent on their way with a jug of the water of life to be taken four times a day to stop the "the weasan from stieflying and the stomach from womblying". Equally certainly some of these outpatients must have gradually discovered that they had developed a chronic problem of the stiefying and the womblying.

The monks spread northward to the Celtic lands, with their evangelizing zeal, their books, their goods and their equipment for supplying potions to the infirmaries, including large black pots and curious coils of copper. They came to the northern Celtic lands, lands with barley and peat, heavy rains and a cold climate.

There is always heated partisan discussion between the two Celtic cousins, the Irish and Scots, whenever a bottle is opened, as to who first invented *uisce beatha*, the water of life.

But all evidence points to Ireland.

In AD 432, St Patrick, whom the Scots, as their consolation prize, are quick to point out was a native of Scotland, was sent to County Wicklow in Ireland as a missionary. He baptized the heathen in the clear streams of this green land, was reputed to have banished all snakes for ever from the Emerald Isle . . . healed the sick and built monasteries.

The monasteries flourished in this Celtic land

Below: an engraving from John French's *The Art of Distillation* (1664), a treatise on the making of whisky.

where the tradition was not the Roman one of urban development, but was essentially an agricultural tradition, with semi-nomadic groups or clans, rival or not, coming together in designated areas once or twice a year for trading.

The quickly developing importance of the new monasteries, with their stability, in this absence of urban settlements, as centres of life, learning and trade – and distilling – established quite clearly the happy knowledge that this water of life could do a great deal to heal aching limbs and shivering teeth. Also, with a psalm on their lips, monks moving out to preach to the heathen, ensured the rapid propagation of pot stills and distillation around the country.

The Irish Celts were not slow in improvising ways of making whiskey for themselves without the help of the monks. Was not a still in essence only a kettle with a long neck and a coil of metal, or worm, for condensing?

In those early days travel across to England was hard, but the distance between the Giant's Causeway, near the Old Bushmills Distillery of today, and the Mull of Kintyre, home of the still very similar triple distilled Campbeltown whiskies – and just next door to the Lowland whiskies of similar production – was hardly the leap or even the step of a giant even if he was carrying a cask of whisky on his back.

And both countries had the same basic essentials: barley, peat for heating, fresh clear water and a climate that needed more than a little of the art of distillation to put some sunshine into it.

The fact that a distillation of spirits was known early on among other Celts – the Welsh – is supported by the *Mead Song* of the Welsh Bard Taliessin in the late sixth century.

". . . Mead distilled sparkling, its praise is everywhere."

It was not until the Anglo-Norman King Henry II of England invaded Ireland in 1170 that his roistering soldiers and England first discovered *uisce beatha*. They saw that their Irish enemies drank it and became fierce in battle, and full of song in victory. Not being able to get their tongues round the word, the English called it first *uisce*, then *fuisce* and then . . . and then finally *whisky*.

THE RISE AND FALL OF IRISH WHISKEY

"If his mother had raised him on whiskey he'd have been a suckling babe all his life."
    Old Irish Saying

With the developing sea trade between Ireland and England, and, no doubt, the often repeated folk stories of giants in strength and singers of wild songs, handed down from Henry II's men, it was at first Irish whiskey that held a dominant position in the taverns of London.

The Scots with their difficult overland route over, at best, the decayed remains of Roman roads in the south, distilled for themselves and, as good Celts, tried to have as little to do with the upstarts south of the border as possible, let alone give or even sell them their water of life.

The reputation of Irish whiskey stood firm.

In 1750, Samuel Johnson, admittedly a man not, at first, very well disposed to things north of Hadrian's Wall, has in his *Dictionary* the entry: "Usquebaugh . . . it is a compounded distilled spirit, being drawn on aromaticks; and the Irish sort is particularly distinguished for its pleasant and mild flavour. The Highland sort is somewhat hotter . . ." Irish whiskey prospered from the early days of the great monastic development

The Irish Still by the Scottish painter Sir David Wilkie (1785–1841), National Gallery, Edinburgh (right). This is very much the same type of still used in Scotland today.

and expansion during Ireland's first Golden Age (AD 620–740) when it was known as the "island of saints and scholars" and, by the end of the eighteenth century during Ireland's second great Golden Age, when Dublin's artistic and intellectual life rivalled that of London or Paris there were more than two thousand known stills in production.

Official stills that is. Licences for stills had been introduced at the beginning of the seventeenth century.

Old Bushmills on the northernmost tip of Ireland is credited with being the world's oldest known licensed distillery.

The King's Deputy of the Plantation of Ulster was authorized to grant licences. This he promptly did – to himself – at Bushmills.

Then in the 1660s Charles II hit on the idea of imposing an excise tax on whiskies at fourpence a gallon.

The whole history of whisky in Ireland, Scotland, and later over in the United States, is dogged by the imposition of taxes on home-produced spirits. At best, it developed the great whisky houses; at worst it was a direct attack on traditional liberties, on a traditional way of life. Wherever whisky started to flourish there was an exciseman somewhere in the bushes ready to impose a tax. Was there a direct tax on bacon, on barley cakes, on honey, on woven wool or on cattle hides? Had there been it would have met with almost as much fierce resistance. Almost, but then a tax on whisky was also a tax on pleasure.

Both the distillers and the customers were hit by the vile intervention of tax.

Poteen (*poitin*) spirit from illegal distilling was rife.

It is estimated that in 1806 out of 11,400,000 gallons of spirits made in Ireland, 3,800,000 were made on illicit stills. Some of this illegal whiskey, poteen, was possibly palatable enough. Some people indeed preferred it. But most of the men, hidden huddled away in the boggy hollows, produced, on their primitive stills, such a fiery potion that to drink it was to court a lingering death from blindness or madness or both.

The tales of leprechauns, giants and magical apparitions of various grisly sorts, and indeed the Loch Ness monster in Scotland with its haunted castles, and towns appearing from nowhere out of the mist, can quite probably be laid at the door of an over-enthusiastic indulgence in these raw spirits. Against the proliferation of illegal stills in Ireland, hordes of excisemen, backed up by the army, attacked the country with cruelty and corruption. Rebellion was in the air . . . and poteen was in the beaker.

A communal fines system was set up in 1783. A town or parish where a still or parts of a still were found was subject to a fine. There was no defence. The very presence of the evidence found, or said to be found, was proof enough. There was no appeal. In face of such patent injustice the communal fine system was abolished for a few years but then, of course, reintroduced, when it was seen that the poteen men quite happily regarded this as an unofficial licence to distil.

Even more stringent fines were imposed, half of which would go to the excisemen who found the booty – not so much a reward as an

inducement to take even more heavy-handed measures.

Finally, an Act was passed in 1823 imposing a new, more just, tax on the amount of whisky distilled in the United Kingdom. This gave an impetus to legitimate manufacturers in Ireland and, as we will see, in Scotland, and encouraged them to reorganize their industry on a better, more solid footing. To some extent, it also eliminated the poteen men, who, nevertheless, lingered on, even in recent times, producing their thunder-and-lightning distillations.

These poteen men were astute and cunning in hiding their tracks. Malachy Magee, in his *1000 Years of Irish Whiskey*, tells of one such incident between poteen men and the exciseman: "Repeatedly the official saw the peasant figure leading his horse across a lonely stretch of ground at dead of night. A substantial sack was flung over the horse's back. But as the official watched, both man and horse seemed

Poteen distillers in Ireland (1952) with their makeshift apparatus. Officially the practice has now been stamped out; unofficially its adepts can still taste its fleeting pleasures and experience the blinding headaches of the morning after.

Power's, Jameson's great rival. The two makes, started in 1780 and 1791, still dominate the Irish whiskey scene.

A whisky fountain (centre right). The unscrupulous landlord's habit of diluting or adulterating whiskies led to the introduction of sealed bottles.

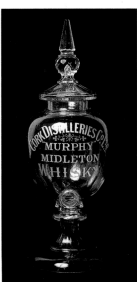

suddenly to disappear in the darkness. One moonlit night the determined official followed his quarry at a safe distance. But again the disappearing trick took place. The lawman made a careful note of the spot, and early next day, with military assistance, he set out for the mysterious rendezvous. He found everything serene and silent, with not a clue to the mystery. The ground appeared to be unmarked. But, as his eyes searched anxiously, he saw some brambles scattered loosely around. He kicked through them and found some loose sods underneath. As the men pulled away the sods they came upon a trap-door. This led to a small cavern at the bottom of which the party saw a complete miniature distillery, supplied by a subterranean stream. Further excavation revealed a winding tube which conveyed the smoke from the still to a house some distance off where it was funnelled into the chimney."

Another, much happier, tale is told of two young policemen in the west of Ireland who happened upon a hidden cask of poteen. They took it back to one of their houses and bottled about half of it for their own use and filled the cask up with water and then took it to the police station and proudly claimed their reward. Their sergeant congratulated them, and then he, in his turn, invited a fellow sergeant from another station to come and do some surreptitious home bottling. This they did and duly topped up the cask with water. The sergeant then left to find his officer, and in the meantime the two original policemen came back for some more urgent bottling of their own and added further water. Finally, the officer arrived and, a hardbitten teetotaller, congratulated the young policeman and righteously emptied away the watery contents.

But the legal trade developed. In Dublin two names stand out: Jameson and Powers. John Jameson set up his distillery in 1780 during the golden age of Irish whiskey in Dublin, then the second city in the British Empire. In 1791, his great rival John Powers established his distillery south of Dublin's river Liffey. Both were men of considerable business acumen, with energetic sales approaches and were sticklers for quality in their products – the best production methods, the best cereals. Their sales empires grew; the excellence of their whiskeys became a byword. Both used a triple distillation of their whiskeys, as is the case still today in Ireland. Both, as

today, kilned their barley and cereals in closed kilns without that infusion of peat which is such a salient feature of the single malts of Scotland. The peat infusion, the Irish claimed, hid some of the true qualities of the pure whiskey.

Then came a turning-point, which was to leave the Irish at a disadvantage and open the door to the Scots. In 1832 the Jamesons and the Powers were approached by Aeneas Coffey, himself a retired Irish exciseman. This Coffey had produced an improved variant of the Scot Robert Stein's patent still, which had been patented in 1826. Briefly, the patent still is a method of making spirits from grain – barley, wheat or others – on a continuous system. Sceptical, the Powers and the Jamesons tried Coffey's newfangled device. After tests, they agreed that it did make spirit very well, a very pure spirit but, even after maturing, this spirit seemed to them to be "silent", in other words tasteless. It was not for them. They would continue distilling their whiskey in their time-established and proved and much lauded way . . . using barley and a triple distillation in huge pot stills of up to 20,000-gallon capacity and over. Perhaps, they politely suggested, Mr Coffey could take the still to Scotland. After all, the idea for it seemed to have come from there in the first place, and did not the Scots, who were lagging behind badly in the trade figures at the time, seem to be having a certain amount of difficulty? (Apart from the Campbeltown and Lowland whiskies perhaps – and they were to the Irish mind rather light and lacking in taste – many of the Scotch whiskies were suitable only for transporting to London for rectification into gin.)

Unabashed, Aeneas Coffey showed his still in Scotland, where some people started to look at it very hard indeed. Irish whiskey was still selling

In 1859 Andrew Usher (left), the father of the modern blends, hit on the idea of blending over-characteristic malts with bland grain whisky to create a cheaper and more readily enjoyed whisky for the general public.

Advertising for the old Cork distilleries, formerly second in importance to those of Dublin. It is near Cork, now, that the most modern distillery complex in the world is sited.

Casks of whiskey are moved from the old distillery of Midleton (now a museum) to the maturing sheds (below).

49

well in the pubs of London, where in fact many Irish labourers had gone to build the canals, and contruct the railways . . . to dig in the streets for gold . . . And then, in 1853, the Scot Andrew Usher, an influential and prominent spirit and wine merchant, produced the first true blended whisky. In essence there was basically nothing very new in this. For as long as people could remember, whiskies, with off-notes or with a tang rather difficult to market, had been treated with herbs and heather to make a more palatable drink. Whisky produced in Wales today still goes through a process of filtration through herbs.

But this time Usher had made a blend using grain spirit from a Coffey still and a rather pungent Highland whisky that he had found difficult to get rid of. Just as, much later in the 1960s and 1970s, when blenders found that they were able to develop their art to produce, say, a light whisky for the American on-the-rocks trade or a less pungent whisky for the Japanese taste and style of adding 80 per cent water to their whisky, so blenders could produce a whisky similar in flavour and colour to the rather bland but subtle Lowland whiskies which the English were beginning to favour, and which had hitherto been very similar in production methods to the Irish whiskey.

The potential for output using Coffey stills was enormous. Then in 1877 the Distillers Company Ltd (DCL) was formed by whisky merchants with common interests. In the same year John Haig founded his company; in 1880 Johnnie Walker set up a London office; in 1882 Whyte & Mackay was founded; two years later the flamboyant James Buchanan set up in London with the blend "Black & White". A whisky boom was well under way.

The Irish started to face

serious competition from the canny Scots.

And then the First World War broke out. All trade was disrupted. Crops were diverted away from whisky production and into foodstuffs, despite claims that this was an agricultural nonsense. As early as 1813 a report states: "The grain consumed in distillation is not wholly lost in human food. It has been ascertained that as much milk, beef, pork, or other animal food can be raised from the draff and dreg, after the spirit is extracted, as could have been produced upon the land on which the barley grew."

Though the Scots were under similar restrictions and heavy-handed interference from government, in Ireland an extra dimension muddied the clear

The top-hatted dandy drawn by Tom Browne at the beginning of the century still strides out for Johnnie Walker.

James Buchanan (right), one of the leading Scotch whisky barons, can be deemed the model of true Scottish grit and the Victorian – indeed Thatcherite – ethic of determination and success.

Aerial view of the Jameson distillery in Dublin's Bow Street in 1920. Today there remains nothing of the bustle of the place where the coopers' hammers rang out to the sound of the workers' oaths and curses under the weight of the heavy casks.

sparkle of whiskey production: political turmoil. Violence was in the air.

In the face of years of gross mismanagement from the parliament in Westminster, the Irish had long argued cogently for Home Rule.

This denied, the Irish, that happy welcoming people, full of song and poetry and the charm of the well-turned phrase and the quick smile, turned to stronger measures. Finally, on Easter Monday 1916, after what were seen as more half-kept promises from the Union Parliament, 1,500 men seized key points in Dublin. The brave Irish tricolour was raised at the General Post Office and the Irish Republic was proclaimed. The Irish War of Independence broke out, followed by a bitter Civil War (1919–21), a war as bitter as only civil wars can be, a war that still has sad reverberations in the truncated province of Ulster. A bitter wind blew harsh on the orange flames from the country houses of the Anglo-Irish gentry. A trade war was set up against England in which both countries put up tariff barriers against each other's products. Irish whiskey was thus denied not only the markets of England but also of the whole of the Empire. Irish whiskey could now no longer sell in Canada, Australia, India, in much of Africa nor in many Far Eastern countries.

And in the United States, where Irish whiskey was so popular in Murphy's Bar in New York, where so many Irish had immigrated after the disastrous Great Famine of the 1840s, where men of Irish descent could call for a ball of Jameson or Power's and get the real thing just as good as back in Old Ireland, Prohibition struck!

Killjoy minister to wounded soldier in bar, "Don't you know that whisky has killed more men than bullets?"

Wounded soldier lifting glass, "Aye, but I'd rather be full of whisky than of bullets."

To put it generously, there is a sad tendency among inadequate people following a rather fundamental idea of Christianity, faced with the dilemmas and difficulties of moderation, to fall back weakly and viciously on to an eleventh commandment of their own heretical making: "Thou shalt not enjoy . . ."

For over fifty years in the United States, such bizarre and cranky organizations as the Woman's Christian Temperance Union, the Anti-Saloon League and other groups, all too sadly reminiscent of present-day would-be benevolent woolly puritan movements, had been decrying what they saw as the insidious and evil influence of strong drink. These persons who, in the words of Bertrand Russell, "forgo ordinary pleasures for themselves and find compensation in interfering with the pleasures of others", had been attacking saloons and the purveyors of alcohol with hatchets, screaming biblical texts, misquoted and out of context, and generally trying to mislead the more ignorant newer settlers not brought up in a Celtic tradition: the Swedes, the Germans, and the Dutch.

Whimpering and howling, the prohibitionists besieged Congress and the State legislators in an attempt to impose their own gloomy, tiresome

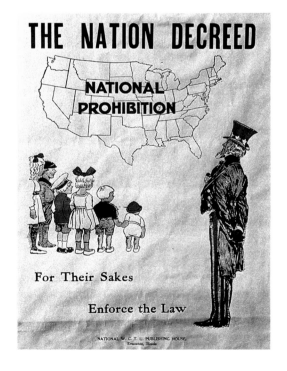

four hundred different brands of Irish whiskey sold in the New York bars before Prohibition), could not compete with the vigorous activities of some of the Scottish retailers who were well versed in their own traditions of contraband. When the supplies of the real Irish whiskey ran dry, to meet the demand the bootleggers created an imitation Irish out of boot polish and rot-gut liquor. The image of Irish whiskey was shattered.

Scotch whisky, filtering in along various devious routes (though here, too, there were imitations brewed in the dustbins of the Bronx), gained the ascendancy in the speakeasies, the illicit bars, of the cities.

Worse was to come in these troubled times. When it became clear to almost everyone that Prohibition, far from making America dry, rather had given it a very healthy thirst, and when it was obvious that Prohibition had to go sooner or later, the industry in Scotland started to wake up. It is said that Joseph Kennedy, the businessman and later American Ambassador at the Court of St James, father of John, Robert and Edward, himself of much proclaimed Irish stock, approached the whiskey distillers of Dublin. Perhaps, he suggested, with an eye to some good business, the time had come to make ready? Admittedly, Ireland was still in the throes of a serious upheaval, but the Jamesons and the Powers, as well as the Cork Distillers Group, said

objective on the people: to make America dry. In the exhausted emotional aftermath of the First World War they succeeded in their bitter tightlipped end. The 18th Amendment to the Constitution passed through Congress and was ratified by the necessary thirty-six states out of forty-eight in 1919.

Over the veto of the President, the Volstead Act was passed. This imposed a ban on the manufacture, transportation and sale of all intoxicating beverages. The nation was to become dry, thus heralding, within the decade, a land for people who would become peaceful and prosperous (ho, hum). Of this, the amendment supporters were sure. They knew the people would obey the law . . . Hearing this, quite a few people smiled very broadly – in Chicago and in New York.

But Ireland was in this way again deprived of the only remaining strong foreign market for its whiskey. Busy with its own serious internal problems, it could not fully join the bootleggers, the modern-day smugglers. Irish whiskey, the market import leader in the States (there were

In the dead of night, smugglers discharge their cargo of of illicit whisky. (From the film *Whisky Galore*.)

in effect that Ireland, as a Free State, had no call to interfere implicitly with the affairs of any other free state. They said "no". The boat was missed.

By the time Prohibition was abolished by Roosevelt in 1933, Ireland was in no position to export quantities of matured whiskey. The Scots

had taken a more realistic and, let it be said, reasonable approach. They were ready, despite the Depression. The Irish distilling industry withered. Irishmen abroad remained faithful but there was a whole new generation of connoisseurs who had never tasted Irish whiskey and for whom the fine nectars of Scotland held a new and mellow warming glow. . . . and, after all, the words "Scotch on the Rocks" had a mellifluous ring to them.

Ireland's *uisce beatha*, the forerunner, remained in the doldrums until 1973, when the five remaining distilleries (remember the two thousand stills at the end of the eighteenth century?) joined forces to form the Irish Distillers Group. Further rationalization led to the concentration of production in two sites. In the Republic, at Midleton, where a fine modern distillery complex was set up near the Old Midleton

Ireland, which had little whiskey to export for many years, and which refused to violate the Prohibtion laws of the United States, started shipping whiskey in the 1930s (left and below).

work needed to get the money to buy it."

Irish whiskey is fighting back.

Men, men of taste, ready to lift their balls of malt, sing and toast:

"Here's to health and prosperity,
To you and your posterity,
And them that don't drink with sincerity
That they may be damned to all eternity."

"May you have warm words
On a cold evening.
A full moon on a dark night,
And the road downhill all the way
   to your door."

"In the New Year, may your right
   hand always
Be stretched out in friendship
   and never in want."

"Here's a health to your enemy's enemies."

"St Patrick was a gentleman,
Who through strategy and stealth,
Drove all the snakes from Ireland,
Here's a toasting to his health,

Distillery, where there are water records for over 150 years, a vital source of information, and up in the North at Old Bushmills, the first reference to which was in 1276 and which tells of the swashbuckling ground landlord of Bushmills, Sir Robert Savage, suitably fortifying his troops with the local potion before going into battle.

In 1988 the Irish Distillers Group, after some little squabbling and in-fighting, was taken under the wing of the vigorous, thrusting international group from France, Pernod Ricard. Sales and true appreciation of Irish whiskey are being developed steadily by those who have learnt the recipe for long life written by Malachi Horan at the age of ninety-four: "Plenty of whiskey and the hard

"All alcohol changes the world, but each changes it in its own way. Whisky brings neither storms nor languor, neither perturbs nor dismays. When it has gone by, the world remains a rational place, but more relaxed and the art of the possible becomes more fluid" (Antoine Blondin). Pub scenes in Ireland: the Irish have made the English pub their very own (left and opposite).

But not too many toastings,
Lest you lose yourself and then,
Forget the good St Patrick and see the snakes
    again."

SCOTCH WHISKY STRIDES OUT FROM THE GLENS . . .

". . . Freedom and whisky gang the gither"
    Robert Burns

The proud men of Ireland, the ghosts of the Powers and the Jamesons may clench their teeth and stamp their feet. The grey lowering skies may well shed their heavy tears over the green land of Ireland. There is no escaping the fact. Scotch whisky, starting out from the same Celtic traditions, with the same holy technical assistance from the monks and with much the same unholy interference from governments, stands firmly at centre stage.

The Scots were no more overconcerned with writing things down than were their Celtic cousins across the Irish Sea. The first historical reference to whisky is to be read in the Scottish Exchequer Rolls for 1494, where we find the entry of "eight bolls of malt to Friar John Cor wherewith to make aqua vitae". (A boll was a Scottish measure of not more than six bushels: 1 bushel = 25.4 kilos.)

And when King James IV was at Inverness in 1506, his treasurer's accounts have entries for "aqua vite for the King" and for "ane flacat of aqua vite for the King". A drink for a king and a drink for the simple man of taste up in the highland bothies. In 1505, true to its healing and medicinal role, a

Title page of Hieronymous Braunschweig's treatise (1519) on the alchemist's art of turning barley into liquid gold (centre right).

monopoly of whisky distillation was granted to the Guild of Surgeon Barbers in Edinburgh. A cup of tea is given to blood donors in England today; perhaps in the Scotland of the time a better practice was adopted after blood-letting. Be that as it may, here we have a first attempt at restrictive practice. But, happily, from the earliest days, whisky distilling had spread up along the glens of the Highlands, where men took little, if any, heed of such edicts. So much so that, in 1579, the Scottish Parliament passed another law restricting distillation to the upper classes: earls, lords, barons and gentlemen . . . for their own use; the fallacious argument so often put forward being that barley for cattle feed was getting to be in short supply. Obviously this restriction suited the upper classes, especially as, among other things, their tenants would pay them in barley for their land . . . barley, the excess of which they in turn could use for distilling.

Again and again, as always when governments see a good thing they tax it. Obviously and sadly, of course, there is no point in taxing something that nobody wants, the revenue would be nil. Clearly, the activities of the stills seemed to be quite a profitable source. In 1644, Charles I passed an Act of Excise "on every pynt of aqua-vytie or strong watter within the country". Despite restrictions, by the end of the seventeenth century several large distilleries had been established, together with some smaller legal one- or two-man distilleries up in the remoter areas, though the now illegal distilling was to remain part of the way of life of the Scot.

In the words of Gordon Brown, the whisky writer, "Whisky makers in the

A romantic landscape (opposite): *Loch Lomond* (National Gallery of Scotland, Edinburgh) by Alexander Naismith (1758–1840), whose pictures, together with the novels of Sir Walter Scott, did much to make Scotland fashionable.

After the defeat of Bonnie Prince Charlie (right) at Culloden, England tightened its grasp on Scotland. The Government at Westminster imposed heavier and heavier taxes on whisky – to the advantage of London's gin distillers.

industry to the necessary beverage of wholesome spirit, whether diluted with water as a grog or taken as a cordial dram to brace sometimes the humid – sometimes the bleak-piercing – winds of the North." Indeed.

In 1777 of the 408 stills said to be operating in Edinburgh itself, it is reported that only eight were licensed. One of these was discovered in the crypt in the Free Tron Church in Edinburgh High Street!

Though the Church was often quick to condemn for its own ranting purposes, this was not always the case.

Alfred Barnard, a London journalist of taste, undertook a grand tour of the distilleries and published a book in 1887. Visiting Highland Park Distillery up in the far north in Orkney, still producing its excellent

Highlands did not *start* illicit distilling; they just did not stop what they had been doing for hundreds of years when a new law, deriving from a foreign capital, meant it became illegal." And smuggling increased. "All", John Grant of Balnagowan sighed in 1798, "that is contended for on behalf of the Highlander is that he should have liberty on moderate terms suited to the poverty of his circumstances to convert the growth of his own soil through his personal

whisky, he tells the tale: "The site whereupon the distillery now stands was the place where the famous Magnus Eunson carried on his operations. This man was the greatest and most accomplished smuggler in Orkney. By profession he was a Church officer, and kept a stock of illicit whisky under the pulpit, but in reality he was a non-professing distiller. This godly person was accustomed to give out the psalms in a more unctuous manner than usual if the excise officers were in church, as he knew that he was suspected and that a party of the revenue officers, taking advantage of his absence, might at that moment be searching his house. A singular story is told of this man. Hearing that the church was going to be searched for whisky by a new party of excisemen, Eunson had all the kegs removed to his house, placed in the middle of an empty room, and covered with a white clean cloth. As the officers approached after their unsuccessful search of the church, Eunson gathered all his people, including the maidservants, round the whisky, which, with its covering of white, under which a coffin lid had been placed, looked like a bier. Eunson knelt at the head with the Bible in his hand and the others with their psalm books. As the door opened they set up a wail for the dead, and Eunson made a sign to the officers that it was a death, and one of the attendants whispered 'smallpox'. Immediately, the officer and his men made off as fast as they could and left the smuggler for some time in peace."

The illicit still was known as the black pot.

"Bless the black pot and nae guid to them that seek it," was a toast that was as common up in the Highlands with that first glass of newly distilled illicit spirit as the equally forthright battlecry, horn beaker in hand, "Here's to us and damn the whisky duty." The hide-and-seek of distillers and excisemen was complicated

In the Highlands the illicit distillers' stills were quickly dismantled at the approach of the excisemen (below and right).

by the need to hide the draff – the barley residue after fermentation. Some could be tipped into the burns but this could lead the excisemen up the stream to the still. Most often it was hauled away up a hill in the dead of night. Then another member of the team would drive cattle from a neighbouring farm to the spot where they would eat the rich malt. By morning the cattle would be back in place on the farm, satisfied and full, with the farmer possibly knowing nothing about it.

Many of the distillers were small-time operators producing a cask at a time. There is the story of the exciseman who, having captured such a cask, took no chances and slept with the cask in the upstairs room of an inn. When he woke the next morning the cask was empty. His later flustered investigations showed that the innkeeper, in cahoots with the distiller, had bored with a drill up through the floor into the cask to siphon off the contents. It would be nice to think that the innkeeper offered the exciseman a wee dram of it the next morning by way of consolation.

Whisky's history and this hero of the battle of Culloden (left) highlight the traditional tension between Scotland and England.

Painting by the Scottish painter Richard Ansdell (1815–1855) showing the drovers' halt with the Isle of Mull, home of the Tobermory malts, in the background. Cattle drovers often lent themselves to the transportation of illicit spirits, which they hid in ankers (small barrels) hung from the cattle.

Another innkeeper, it is said, noticed that a party of excisemen had taken off their wet boots and put them by the fire to dry. The innkeeper moved the boots a little closer to the flames – could the excisemen have been taking a dram at  the time? – the soles burnt through, and the raid by the bootless gaugers on the stills had to be put off, while the distillers dismantled their black pot and moved off to another site. Even the womenfolk of the smugglers played their part, transporting whisky in pig's bladders and tin panniers hidden under their wide skirts.

The Reverend Thomas Guthrie wrote in his memoirs of the late seventeenth century, "When a boy in Brechin, I was quite familiar with the appearance and on-goings of the Highland smugglers. They rode on Highland ponies, carrying on each side of their small, shaggy but brave and hardy steeds a small cask or 'keg' as it was called, of illicit whisky, manufactured amid the wilds of Aberdeenshire or the glens of the Grampians. They took up a position on some commanding eminence during the day, where they could as from a watch tower descry the distant approach of the enemy, the exciseman or gauger: then when night fell every man to a horse, descending the mountains only six miles from Brechin, they scoured the plains, rattled into the villages and

A hidden illicit still. These were seized and destroyed, when found, by the excisemen (left and far left).

Smugglers' tales: casks are hidden in a cave against the day of their sale.

towns, disposing of their whisky to agents they had everywhere ... I have seen a troop of thirty of them riding in Indian file, and in broad day, through the streets of Brechin after they had succeeded in disposing of their whisky, and as they rode leisurely along, they beat time with their formidable cudgels on the empty barrels to the great amusement of the public and the mortification of the excisemen, who had nothing for it but to bite their nails and stand as best they could the raillery of the smugglers and the laughter of the people."

But the smugglers did not have it all their own way. The Board of Excise, though considering it was fighting a losing battle, reported, in 1821, fourteen thousand successful raids on illicit stills, and as late as 1823 there had been three thousand detections of illicit stills in the Elgin area alone. One of the most determined and redoubtable of excisemen was Malcolm Gillespie. He joined the service at twenty years of age. The records show that during his twenty-eight years of service he had impounded a massive 6,535 gallons of whisky, 165 horses, 85 carts, 407 stills, and a massive 62,400 gallons of the wash from which whisky was to be distilled. He had, in his formidable ruffianly band of excisemen, a dog which he had trained to grab horses by the nose to make them fall and tumble their loads of kegs off their backs. When Gillespie was, himself, hauled to the scaffold and hanged for uttering forged bills on 16 November 1827, he could point to forty-two wounds on various parts of his body sustained during his long years of service and bloody battles.

Yet another new system of licensing was set up in 1784. A line was drawn between the Highlands and the Lowlands. Different scales of taxes were set up in favour of the licensed Lowland distillers, to the disadvantage of the small Highland distillers.

The great Lowland houses prospered and started to export huge quantities of spirits to London, some as whisky, some as spirit to be rectified into gin. At the Kilbagie distillery in Clackmannanshire James Stein installed a still capable of producing an amazing 5,000 gallons of spirit a day. Alarmed by this influx of spirit from the north, the gin distillers of London, lobbying parliament vigorously, forced Scottish taxes up.

But, while in these upper spheres there was much arm wrestling, the small illicit stills in the Highlands continued producing their characteristic whisky; for many this was the real stuff, the direct ancestor of our prized Highland malts today.

Whisky Row by James Drummond. Even Edinburgh was not free of illegal distilling. Though more than 200 illicit stills were discovered in the capital, many more must have flourished in the slums of the Old Town.

The triumphal entry of
George IV to Edinburgh in
1822 for the great
reconciliation ceremonies
between the Crown and
Scotland. The Scots were
amazed by the way their
guests got themselves up in
all manner of tartans and
kilts.

Faced with the obduracy of the illicit distillers, various incentives and even more new taxes on old taxes were tried to eliminate the illicit distilling. One such had something of the opposite effect. A premium was offered for reporting an illegal still or bringing it in to the excisemen. The canny Highlanders simply handed in their old broken stills and with the money earned bought new ones. But the system of taxation on whisky had become so complicated that something had to be done.

The Duke of Gordon, whose estates included the famous valley of Glenlivet, appeared first to offer his support for the eradication of illicit distilling. The Illicit Distillation (Scotland) Act was passed in 1822. With the added support of the great landowners, who clearly saw it to be in their own interest to rationalize the system, even more severe penalties were imposed on those detected distilling or possessing illegal spirits. In

that year more than six thousand cases were brought before the courts. As the Duke of Gordon had probably expected, the new law was so severe that real hardship was taking place and there was an alarming dissatisfaction developing among the Highlanders, which even the government in Westminster could not ignore. Clearly, even to them the time was ripe for a fresh start. In near desperation, devoid of ideas, the government allowed Gordon to step in. A Royal Commisssion was set up.

In 1823, after lengthy discussions and wranglings, and with the London gin distillers howling with undisguised alarm, the Excise Act was passed. Duties were slashed. A set licence fee of £10 annually was established and a notional duty per gallon was set up for the now licit stills of over forty gallons.

Not all the former illicit distillers, with their armed bands of cut-throat contraband dealers

George Gordon, 5th Duke of Gordon (1770–1836), by the popular portraitist George Sanders (Goodwood Collection). George Gordon, a leading landowner, was influential in persuading the House of Lords to vote a bill favouring the production of whisky. This much reproduced picture (opposite) has even become the label to a blend of whisky.

and their many satisfied customers, were happy about this turn of events. They obviously wanted things to go on as they had before. True to their old traditions of whisky running in large armed bands, they looked askance at any of their number who fell in with the new rules of the game.

One who decided early to set up as a legal distiller was George Smith of Upper Drumin in Glenlivet. Smith, whose forebears had been distilling as far back as records can show – and it was the contraband The Glenlivet that George IV had asked for in 1822 – built The Glenlivet Distillery whose fine Highland malt gained such a reputation that, by the time of his death in 1871, many other distilleries, with scant regard for true geographical exactitude, appended the suffix "Glenlivet" to their names. After action in the courts, it has been laid down that there is only one Glenlivet, The Glenlivet, though some other distilleries taking their waters from the valley of the Livet still continue to append the mention "Glenlivet" on their labels.

The doughty founder, George Smith, remembered the early days, "When the new Act was heard of in Glenlivet and in the Highlands of Aberdeenshire, they ridiculed the idea that anyone should be found daring enough to start legal distilling in their midst . . . the desperate character of the smugglers and the violence of their threats deterred everyone for some time. At length in 1824, I, George Smith, who was then a robust young fellow, and not given to be easily 'fleggit', determined to chance it. I was already a tenant of the Duke, and received every encouragement from His Grace and his factor Mr. Skinner. The outlook was an ugly one, though. I was warned by my civil neighbours that they meant to burn the new distillery to the ground and me in the heart of it. The Laird

James and John Grant, heirs to a long line of clandestine distillers, surrounded by their employees at the Glen Grant distillery which was founded in 1840 (left). Their label with its two Highlanders (below) has become a byword.

Brass plate from the first Coffey still built by John Miller for the North British Distillery (below centre).

of Aberlour had presented me with a pair of hair-trigger pistols worth ten guineas, and they were never out of my belt for ten years. I got together two or three stout fellows for servants, armed them with pistols and let it be known everywhere that I would fight for my place to the last shot. I had a good character as a man of my word and, through watching by turns every night for years, we saved the distillery from the fate so freely predicted for it." Smith adds laconically, "But I often, both at kirk and market, had rough times among the glen people."

But the new Act worked. Larger legal distilleries in the Highlands were established, the influence of the smugglers broken – though not completely – and export to England, where there were different rates of duty, was opened to all without the need to register. From 1827 to 1837 malt-whisky production increased from 2.7 million proof gallons to 6 million proof gallons. Scotch whisky was on the up.

The great houses were established. Blended whisky, first in cask then, after 1865, more safe in terms of guaranteed quality for the buyer, in bottles, ensured that the Sassenach whisky-lovers could be assured of getting the real thing and the same real thing every time. Despite hiccups of further tax changes and increases, wars

George Smith (opposite), with Gordon's support, was one of the first formerly illicit distillers to take advantage of the new laws, setting up his celebrated The Glenlivet distillery. His former companions in arms looked askance at his newly legal activities.

From its early humble origins (below centre) whisky rose to have a privileged position in the London clubs of high society. Right: Dewar's exploit the aristocratic connection.

disturbing trade, barley harvests lost to bad weather, Scotch whisky continued its ascent up through the beneficial days of the phylloxera brandy drought.

But then the Boer War broke out. Trade and sales were disrupted. The whisky boom came to an end. Moreover, Edward VII, whose merry-making trips to Paris were curtailed by his accession in 1901, led a Gallic fashion for wine and brandy. Under pressure from this change in tastes, with home sales in decline, and smaller blenders going into bankruptcy, the scene was set for the bitter argumen.. that broke out between those still selling single or malt whiskies and the famous blenders.

The old vexed question. What was true Scotch whisky? The single malts . . . or the blends? On the side of the producers of single malts from the Highlands, it is true that there had been abuses by unscrupulous publicans selling adulterated spirits as blends.

Two former dairymen, Robert and Walter Pattison, discovered that they could make better profits from selling cheap grain whisky with a small amount of colouring and a minute dash of malt whiskies than from selling milk. In this way they had produced a so-called "Finest Glenlivet" and had produced blends "for all occasions" including, a nadir in bad taste (in both senses of the word), one to commemorate the heroic death of General Gordon at Khartoum in 1885. Before their bankruptcy for the high sum (in those days) of £85,000, they had set up a publicity campaign, bizarre even by modern-day advertising standards, in which they installed, in retailers' shops and bars, five hundred parrots supposedly trained to squawk idiotically and incessantly: "Drink Pattisons' Whisky."

Matters came to a head in 1905. Islington Borough Council brought a case, under the Food and Drinks Act, against a publican plying his trade within the borough boundaries for selling blended whisky. The claim, upheld by the council, and later in the courts, was that blended whisky was not genuine whisky but an adulteration of the malt, which was thereby the true whisky, the real thing.

The Distillers Company hit back by marketing a seven-year-old grain whisky from their Cambus patent still to demonstrate that grain whisky was truly Scotch. "Not a headache in a gallon," they proclaimed.

The argument reached crisis point. Indeed, neither the single-malt producers nor the blenders, were entirely happy with the decision of the courts. The malt producers quickly realized that their production could not meet the continuing demand for whisky, and they were well aware that Londoners liked, indeed preferred, the blended as opposed to some of the more characteristic single-malt whiskies. More important, it was obvious that the enormously wealthy Lowland malt distillers could simply produce

masses of cheap bland malts in their vast pot stills to replace the grain for their blends.

Yet again, a Royal Commission was set up in 1908 to determine what, in truth, could be called whisky. Experts were brought forward, discussions were heated, pros and cons were weighed, both financial and gustatory. The debate raged on until a true British compromise was reached. It was decided – to the relief above all of lovers of both single-malt whiskies and blends – that whisky was "a spirit obtained by the distil-

lation of a mash of cereal grains saccharified by the diastase of the malt: that Scotch whisky is, as above defined, distilled in Scotland".

Both camps were, quite obviously, in the right. With usual parliamentary zeal and promptness, this ruling was finally incorporated in statute law in 1952.

If all producers of all whiskies had breathed a sigh of relief at the findings of the Commission, this was to be shortlived. In 1909 the teetotal Welshman Lloyd George, disloyal to his Celtic tradition, long an avowed enemy of the whisky trade and Chancellor of the Exchequer, introduced his reforming "People's Budget".

To pay for the social services that he proposed, he increased duty on whisky by a swingeing draconian 33 per cent. Peter Mackie, purveyor of White Horse, with the true wisdom of a man who had seen the way governments for

Not all blends were entirely palatable. The Pattisons were notorious, but taste told – they went bankrupt. The headaches occasioned by their doubtful blends could justly be termed the "Big Boom".

ages past had attacked the Scotch whisky industry by at once decrying its supposed evils and then using it as a milchcow for taxation, remarked that the 33 per cent increase was the work of "a faddist and a crank, not a statesman. But what can one expect of a Welsh country solicitor being placed, without any commercial training, as Chancellor of the Exchequer in a large country like this? I might as well bring into my business and place at the head of it a boot-maker or shoemaker or country solicitor, and any man will know how incompetent he would be for the job."

An economic recovery in 1911 meant that the effects of this ridiculous, crippling tax were not as severe as feared and blenders began to lay down more stocks. At the outbreak of war, sales rose yet again when more and more workers had extra money to spare because of increased employment in the munitions factories. Flags flew, drums beat, columns of young men in khaki marched off to France, medals were handed out, but by 1915 Britain had still not won the war.

Lloyd George quite barmily decided that this failure to win through was due to drink. An obvious solution was an increase in taxation – and stricter licensing laws for the pubs were needed. "Drink", Lloyd George ranted, in full oratorical flow, "is doing more damage in the war than all the German submarines put together." Fighting back, the whisky distillers agreed to sell only, as now, whisky that had been matured for at least three years in the wood. The Distillers Company, under its doughty managing director William Ross, bought up failing distilleries and blending houses, and hoped, and planned, for better days.

The Whisky Association was set up to defend the interests of the distillers and their customers against the more and more extravagant measures of the government. And extravagant measures there were. By 1920, when Prohibition was in force in America, taxes on whisky had gone up fivefold in three years. It is paradoxical to note that the DCL had to take over John Haig, the family firm of Field Marshal Lord Haig, the victorious British Commander-in-Chief at the end of the war. During this period of

helping hand

Whisky during the Second World War became synonymous with comfort (opposite). Dewar's was set up by two brothers, of whom one, "Whisky Tom", was a colourful popular character, owning the third automobile in England after the Prince of Wales and Sir Thomas Lipton of tea fame.

Prohibition, only DCL with its amalgamation of Haig, Dewar, Buchanan and Johnnie Walker, with White Horse making up the "Big Five" in 1927, was strong enough not only to keep its head above water but also to expand.

When the United States had finally come back to its senses and Prohibition was repealed in 1932, the whisky industry began slowly to recover, despite the inroads made by its great rival gin, which had figured in many of the cocktail recipes of the roaring 1920s and 1930s. Then the Second World War broke out. The government responded by slapping on an extra ten-shilling tax per proof gallon, bringing the tax up to £4 2s 6d.

During the post-war austerity years in Britain under a Socialist government, much of the whisky production went to the United States to earn much needed dollars. Despite this, the Socialist chancellors Dalton and his successor Cripps, in what was almost a frenzy of repression, raised tax to £10 10s 6d per gallon. Still the need for good true whisky fought through. By the end of the 1950s, times did seem to be getting brighter, but once more mainly under Socialist governments taxes were raised again and again in 1961, 1964, 1965, 1966, 1968, by which time the tax was at the then staggering £18.85 per gallon. Taking no account of the tastes of many good, true, honest, toiling Scotsmen, simple men of taste, the Socialist government's attitude has always been: save the workers' beer and tax the toffs' spirits.

In 1973 with the advent of Britain's entry into the Common Market and the imposition of VAT, tax on whisky actually went down for the first time since 1896. But, ready to grasp at any straw, successive governments raised the tax on whisky every year from 1973 to 1977.

To protect itself, the Scotch whisky industry has seen further and further mergers, amalgama-tions and takeovers. Today, as ever, the industry in Scotland is at a crossroads. From selling simple blends, then going into luxury, older blends, and then educating the taste for finer single malts, it remains a captive of world recessions, ephemeral changes in tastes such as the idea that white wines are superior or less fattening (which they are not) or travellers coming back with strange perverse desires for tequilla, grappa, or other barbarities . . . All this is compounded with the difficulties of knowing when and how to market a product that has to be produced at the very least three years before it is to be sold . . . though, of course, the maturing process of whisky is often much longer than this.

However, what is clear throughout the history of Scotch whisky is that whatever fate, wars,

FOR THE CLUBS of Pall Mall, Piccadilly and St. James' Street, the thoughtless and the unprivileged have a standard epithet . . . dull. They forget that pleasure has more forms than one. A gentleman's club is correct and urbane as a gentleman's glass of White Horse.

In the older clubs of London, tradition prints the pattern of life and the honoured past is present. A man likes to know that his White Horse Whisky is identical in bouquet and flavour with the White Horse Whisky his father drank, and before that his grandfather and great-grandfather. He likes the mere fact that it comes to him on the very same Georgian salver. He believes it the business of clubs, friends and drinks to be what they always were. White Horse believes so, too.

86.8 Proof. Browne-Vintners Co. Inc., New York, N. Y. Sole Distributors.

WHITE HORSE
BLENDED SCOTCH WHISKY

Advertisement for White Horse in the USA during the Second World War; the unchanging qualities of the blend are linked to the timelessness of the London Club.

George Grant of the Glenfarclas distillery. Five generations have distilled in the Spey valley.

"The worst is at four o'clock in the afternoon (the moment when the work really starts to flow) to start asking oneself: 'What am I going to do with myself until seven o'clock (the time for the first whisky)?'" (Roger Vaillant, *Ecrits Intimes*). Opposite: Harry's Bar, Paris.

governments may produce, the idea of a dram of Scotch remains ever bright for the man of taste.

Proud of its heritage, the Scotch Whisky Association may be excused this slightly effusive statement: "Scotch whisky . . . is of the land and of time . . . Scotch whisky has been the drink of success, of fashion and prestige, drunk and appreciated by people of taste and discrimination all over the world. From its humble origins on the hills and in the glens of Scotland, it has become the best-known international drink of all time. A bottle of Scotch is drunk every tenth of a second in the United States of America, a bottle a second in Venezuela, a bottle every seven seconds in Norway, a bottle every twenty seconds in the Philippines. Each year Scotch whisky earns nearly £2 billion in the export markets of the world. And yet it remains true to its origins

in the remote mountains and glens of Scotland, true to the traditions of patient skill and craftsmanship handed down through the centuries, true to its name . . . *uisce beatha* . . . the water of life."

The British ambassador, Sir Anthony Acland, speaking in Washington at the Grand Banquet of the United States Keepers of the Quaich, adds pithily, "Americans create a pile of empty Scotch whisky bottles as tall as the Empire State Building every three minutes."

Ah! Scotch whisky . . . a drink to toast with. A shining glass of friendship. As an old Scottish lady said with a glass in her hand: "Here's to a' your fouk an' a' oor fouk, an' a' the fouk that's been kind to your fouk, an' a' the fouk that's been kind to your fouk an' our fouk; an' if a' fouk had aye been as kind to fouk as your fouk's been

The piper's dram. The pipers of the Duke of Atholl's Highlanders, the only private army in Britain, warm the cockles of their hearts after parade.

Opposite: a dram echoes the colours of a Scottish gentleman's kilt.

to our, there wad aye been guid fouk i' the warld, sin' fouk's been fouk."

. . . and the devil take the taxman. *Slainte mhor!*

NEW WORLDS, NEW WHISKIES

The *Quaich* – the Gaelic cup – much esteemed by collectors of antiques (centre).

"They call it that good ole
    mountain dew,
And them that refuse it are
    few,
I'll shut up my mug if you'll
    fill up my jug
With   that   good   ole
    mountain dew . . ."

Given the amazing thirst of the Americans in their consumer society it is no surprise that they have embraced Irish and Scotch whiskies whole-heartedly.

But they themselves were not slow in developing their own "whiskey-types", perhaps not true whiskies in themselves but something that comes very close indeed.

All evidence points to the fact that the first distillery in North America was set up in 1640 on Staten Island but even before this, hard-pressed, thirsty settlers had been experimenting with distillations of cherries, plums, apples, blackberries,

wortleberries, carrots, potatoes and even pumpkins.

The Pilgrim Fathers, who came over on the *Mayflower* in 1620, arrived with liquor aboard, and the *Arbella*, which brought over the first governor of Massachusetts Bay Colony, was charged not only with forty-two tuns of beer but also with stronger liquor.

The governor in his journals was compelled to report of his fellow passengers, "They give themselves to drink *hot waters* very immoderately."

Puritan settlers? It must be remembered here that the original settlers, far from being the grim-mouthed Puritans so often depicted in history books, revised no doubt by prohibitionist moralists, were simply men and women who wanted to worship and live in their own way without interference from central governments . . . not an approach to life so vastly different from the men of the Highlands or of Ireland.

To set up home in this inhospitable land they needed to build strong log cabin forts, places to live, places to pray, and places to play; and, when the long day's labour was over – hard days, straining to clear the land, to pull out with straining sinews the deeply rooted tree stumps, to till the unbroken rocky virgin land with rough ploughshares – there would be strange gamebirds bubbling in the pot, and a merry well-known song on the fiddle and something warming in the jug; while beyond the flickering light of their homestead fires, in the darkness, uncouth animal howls came from the almost endless rustling forests.

The Dutch and the Germans had brought over their own gin . . . crude rum was being distilled from molasses from the Caribbean, a pirate's brew born of the sweat of the sugar-plantation slaves, and a pounding of the head with a belaying pin every morning after; but clearly there was the need for something rather clearer, cleaner, something of a true natural nobility . . . a water of life . . . a whisky.

The first recognizable whiskey-type using grain was distilled in Pennsylvania in 1683. Strange experiments perhaps were undertaken, strange after-effects were endured; but then, after perseverence, expertise was brought on the scene by the strong-minded, hard-singing Scots-Irish immigrating to the country after the Ulster Potato Blight in 1716. They brought their pot stills and their coils, looked at the grain, mashed it with the water sparkling in the streams, and heated their stills over the fires in hollowed tree stumps.

But they were not alone. Not only simple men on their small sharecroppers' farms but also the highest in the land felt the need for and the pleasures of whiskey.

George Washington himself was a distiller well known for his Mount Vernon distillery. Thomas Jefferson, also to become President of the United States, was a distiller too, at his estate of Monticello. Spirits . . . whiskey . . . became commonplace.

As always, economic and transport factors were such that it was quickly seen by the early settlers, moving into Pennsylvania and further beyond, that the cost of transporting the grain, the raw material, was higher, and the product less desirable, than the cost of transporting liquor. A horse could carry up to six times the equivalent amount of grain in whiskey form. Very soon Kentucky and Virginia were making corn (maize) whiskey and Pennsylvania and Maryland set about producing rye whiskeys. As in the mother countries of Scotland and Ireland almost every well-set-up farmer, establishing his spread,

Rip Van Winkle, the hero of Washington Irving's novel (1861), symbol of a newly born nation, gives his name to a make of Bourbon (centre).

Opposite: the untamed Tennessee landscape. Scottish and Irish settlers first set up their stills and gave the world Bourbon and the great Tennessee Sour Mash Whiskey.

building his barns, had a still next to his buggy and his ploughshare.

Long cold evenings were enlivened with a jig from the old country, tales filled with Celtic mystery were told by the light of the fireside and a jug of the water of life was raised gently to the parched lips. Tired men broke into slow moving smiles. All was well.

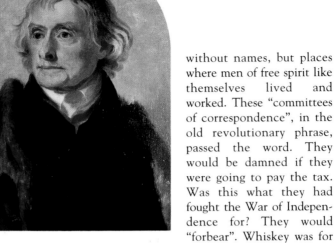

Then we have the old, old story. On 3 March 1791, nemesis struck. The government of the fledgling states, under Washington, slapped a tax of 54 cents per gallon on the capacity of stills and 7 cents on every gallon produced. The tax was to take effect on 1 July.

Not surprisingly the reaction from the farmer distillers was a resounding "No!" to such an impetuous interference in their way of life, exactly what they had left the Old Country to avoid: a direct interference in their way of life.

In Washington, Westmorland, Fayette and Alegheny counties on the borders of Pennsylvania, there were some five thousand log cabin distilleries sending up their plumes of woodsmoke to the crisp blue skies. Distilled whiskey cooled in the coils laid down in the icy streams. Farmers, drinkers of the nectar, strong-armed men of toil, devout men, bearded and without pretence, men of simple and true pleasures elegantly savoured, slapped their Bibles: "Give strong drink unto him who is ready to perish, and wine unto those that be of heavy hearts," they sang in lusty defiance.

The farmers jumped into their saddles and rode from hamlet to hamlet, places perhaps without names, but places where men of free spirit like themselves lived and worked. These "committees of correspondence", in the old revolutionary phrase, passed the word. They would be damned if they were going to pay the tax. Was this what they had fought the War of Independence for? They would "forbear". Whiskey was for them what it was in the Old Country . . . a drink for kissing . . . a drink for fighting . . . a drink for good times and bad. A drink for welcoming . . . a drink for funerals, a drink for saying goodbye.

True liberty was at stake. Once again rebellion was in the air. One would-be tax collector was waylaid by a group of stalwarts, curiously disguised in women's clothes. They cut off his hair, covered him in tar and feathers, and stole his horse. Others suffered similar fates for their interference with that right to be free and live life according to an older tradition.

The old King George had wanted to put a tax on tea and was damned, the new George could hardly expect to impose a tax on their whiskey without similar sanction. The tax collectors retired in a rout of tar and feathers and broken

Rebellion against the imposition of taxes in 1794: George Washington was not slow in taxing the newly independent states. Nor were the farmers backward in their reaction.

skulls. Stronger methods were needed by government; harsh counsel prevailed. In 1794 an army was sent to quell the rising. Gerald Carson in his seminal *The Social History of Bourbon* records, "When one recalls that the President of

the United States, the Secretary of the Treasury and the governors of four states once mobilized against the farmers of western Pennsylvania almost as large an army as ever took the field in the Revolutionary War, it appears . . . as one of the more improbable episodes in the annals of this country. Thirteen thousand grenadiers, dragoons, foot soldiers and pioneers, a train of artillery with six-pounders, mortars and several 'grasshoppers' equipped with mountains of ammunition, forage, baggage and a bountiful stock of *tax*-paid whiskey paraded over the mountains of Pittsburgh against a gaggle of homespun rebels who had already dispersed."

In truth, the Whiskey War simply caused the farmers to up sticks from Pennsylvania and move across the rushing Ohio river with all their goods and baggage in their wagons and buggies to Kentucky where they hoped to set up their stills and evade the tax.

This was a stroke of luck for connoisseurs of the Bourbon whiskey type. Here not only is the land more suitable for growing corn (maize) but there is also a huge limestone shelf running under the blue grasses of Northern Kentucky extending to the golden cornlands of Indiana and Tennessee. Along this shelf runs icy spring

George Washington (1732–1799), the first President of the United States (below left), was a distiller of one of the most famous ryes of Virginia – the Mount Vernon Whiskey distilled on his estate (opposite below right). The name still exists but this whiskey is now distilled in Ohio.

The workers at this old-time Bourbon distillery pass jugs from hand to hand (right). Whiskey, whisky or Bourbon – such as the famous Iris Tullamore Dew – is still sometimes presented in stoneware jugs.

trail with his long-horned herd . . . and whiskey for the buffalo-hunter, hair matted with grease, hands burnt by the heat of his guns, who wanted only his hot bath and his glass of something true and clean.

The American Indians, though they had discovered the soothing effects of tobacco, had not hitherto known whiskey. Whiskey became a currency: there is the familiar image of the drunken Indian, in rough blanket, broken-feathered, exchanging furs, rich trinkets or even lands for a jug of the water of life, but a water of life too poorly distilled, too deeply drunk . . .

This image is burnt into the folk memories of the States. The Indians embraced such sad

water which is free of such minerals as iron that could harm the taste and flavours of Bourbon.

A Reverend Elijah Craig, with a full stone jug propped up on his battered much-thumbed Bible, is regarded as the man who first developed an ideal mix of cereals – corn, barley, malt – for producing a "perfect whiskey" and he it was who set up his stills in Bourbon County (so named in honour of Lafayette and the French who had brought their aid to the American rebels). (Bourbon is a whiskey-type and is not restricted particularly to the Bourbon county.) The Jim Beam company was not slow in perfecting old Elijah's brew.

As the United States spread their empire across the country westward, whiskey followed in the creaking wagons . . . whiskey, a taste of life moving across the long prairies to the shanty settlements where neighbours stretched their hands in traditional welcome . . . whiskey, a pillar of strength and warmth, where ground was broken by the plough for the first time . . . whiskey moving west through the swinging doors of the saloons with their jangling pianos, their faded actresses, hands on hips in red dresses, singing songs and bringing comfort and whiskey to the parched cowboy long on the

The convoys of whiskey were often attacked by Indians (left). Though whiskey was forbidden them, their image was often used to extol the traditional qualities of Bourbon (below centre).

replicas of the amber nectar with such effect that laws were passed – already shades of the deathly Prohibition – to prevent their consumption of it.

That there was a taste for whisky in its purest form is one thing, that they could get only a poor imitation of it is another; and that, seeing only baser images in this harsh distillate, they drank even deeper in order to see more clearly, is yet another.

Moonshining or illicit distilling was rife. (Indeed, as late as

The Old Crow distillery in Kentucky's capital Frankfort, set up in 1835 by the Scotsman James Crow. The buildings are typical of the Victorian industrial epoch and would not look out of place in Lancashire.

1980 Alexis Lichine suggested that, on average, of the 6 million hectolitres of whiskies drunk in the States every year, between 1,350,000 to 3,650,000 are distilled illegally . . . the "good old mountain dew".)

An oldtimer from Atlanta tells me the story of a school marm dismissing her class and saying that they would have no school the next day, adding, "Now, chillun, tomorrer we is goin' to take up mixin' in the mash."

Like poteen, moonshine is hard stuff.

Davy Crockett, king of the wild frontier, tossed off a mug of green moonshine at one pull. Later he admitted that it was so hot that he "didn't need to have

Right centre: a portrait by Naagle of Davy Crockett, the legendary native of Kentucky, the home of Bourbon, shown here without his celebrated coonskin hat.

his food cooked for two months", as the "grub was cooked afore it settled in my innards".

Then there is the old story of "squirrel" whiskey. A moonshiner was up before the judge.

"Now what kind of whiskey do you make?" the judge asked the defendant on a bootlegging charge.

"Well, I'm a'selling squirrel whiskey."

"What kind is that?"

"Well, old man Mose down the crick he makes whiskey in his still that if a rabbit takes a couple of drops of it he will stand up on his hinder legs and spit right in the face of a hound dog."

"Strong stuff, son, but why do you call it 'squirrel' whiskey?"

"Waal, when I goes out on a

The National Congress of Teetotallers at Indianapolis in 1892 (right) – already demanding the imposition of Prohibition.

Mrs "Lemonade Lucy" Hayes (below), wife of President Rutherford Hayes, was a prohibitionist and forbade hard liquor in the White House.

Before Prohibition, Uncle Sam sings the praises of American whiskey (below centre). this is a "straight" that is a whiskey from a single distillery run. It is bottled in bond – a "straight" whiskey matured for at least four years under state control – a guarantee of quality for the consumer.

cool morning a squirrel shooting with ma gun I takes a jug of licker with me and I takes a snort or two, and then some more. And, by and by, when I sees the little ole squirrel on the tree, I forgets all about my gun and I jest runs and climbs up the tree and grabs the danged squirrel in ma mouth."

In the rough old days, the law was bent to accommodate over-enthusiasm. A man somewhat under the influence fell down a hole in the pavement. In an action for damages, the first court held that he was guilty of contributary negligence because he had been drunk. On appeal, the Supreme Court of California demurred. It held, "If the defendants were at fault in leaving an uncovered hole in the sidewalk of a public street, the intoxication of the plaintiff cannot excuse such gross negligence. A drunken man is as much entitled to a safe street as a sober one, and much more in need of it."

Mark Twain, the English-born American humorist, liked his whiskey. He refused to autograph a book honouring the President's wife, "Lemonade Lucy", Mrs Rutherford Hayes, for her stand on banning alcoholic beverages from the White House. When Mark Twain visited the country of his birth he was stopped by customs officers. What had he in his luggage? Only clothing . . . The officer opened his bags and pulled out a bottle of whiskey. Clothing? "Officer," Twain drawled, "for me whiskey *is* clothing."

Then, in 1919, Nebraska, perhaps not a state particularly known for its social evolution, became the 36th state to vote for the 18th amendment. Prohibition hit the States and the mawkish ill-advised Volstead Act was passed. The American lyricist, Vaughan Miller, mockingly penned the theme tune of the thirteen dry(ish) years that were to follow:

The moulded bottles of Old Taylor Whiskey (left) bear the legend "General Taylor will never surrender." The distiller's uncle became the twelfth President of the United States.

"There ain't gonna be no more whiskey;
There ain't gonna be no gin;
There ain't gonna be no highballs to put the whiskey in;
There ain't gonna be no cigarettes to make folks pale and thin;
But you can't take away that tendency to sin, sin, sin."

And indeed whisky was not slow in getting through to the suffering States. The Volstead Act came into force at midnight on 16 January 1920. It is said that the first illegal drink was served within one minute.

The Scots, well versed in their "heritage and freedom gang the gither" and their running battles with excisemen, quickly found ways of supplying their thirsty cousins. The great Scotch-

Cartoon (left) lambasting higher and higher whiskey taxes. A moonshiner drives his buggy to the land of freedom through the mountainous terrain of fiscal repression.

whisky barons set up agencies in Cuba, Bermuda, British Honduras, the Bahamas and the very convenient Canada. These agents quite legally imported whisky which was then shipped to international waters off the American coast. Small ships sailed out to these floating warehouses to collect the cases of whisky for the bootleggers.

The scale was immense. Imports of whisky to the Bahamas soared: 944 gallons in 1918. In 1922, only two years after Prohibition, the figure

Following the example of her Scottish forebears who hid pannikins of whisky in their skirts, this gangster's moll prepares to go out and supply the speakeasies.

14 January 1926: Miss Agnes O'Laughlin (right) sports a new whiskey flask with her initials, a fashion that did little to help the observance of the Prohibition regulations.

The latest fashion in men's waistcoats, specially designed to transport a few bottles of whisky. This smuggler (opposite), arrested in 1923, was betrayed by his unlikely corpulence. He was carrying a dozen bottles of Johnnie Walker.

stood at a massive 386,000 gallons. St Pierre and Miquelon, the tiny French islands off Canada, were at the same time importing 116,000 gallons . . . theoretically enough to provide every man, woman and child living there with 20 gallons per head per year.

It is estimated that at one time more than one hundred floating warehouses lay off the 150-mile coastline from Atlantic City to New York. Some coastguards were not slow in getting into the act, helping (for a consideration), the unloading of the schooners lying at anchor on "rum row". New York policemen were paid so much per bottle to look the other way.

The speakeasy was born. A knock on a bolted door, a muttered password, and the tuxedoed gentleman with his lady in a short, beaded, evening frock would be ushered into the smoke-filled bar, where hoodlum drank side by side with district attorney to the sound of raging ragtime music. Bootleggers set up some thirty-two

During Prohibition illicit distilling took on a new lease of life. There were over 30,000 illegal distilleries in 1930 – this one (right) in Tennessee.

A cask of 4,000 litres of bootleg whiskey found in a private garage in the State of Washington (opposite).

thousand speakeasies in New York to replace the fifteen thousand bars which had been forced out of business. And the supplies kept on coming through. One Scottish distiller packed his whisky, in tough square bottles designed to withstand any shock, into torpedoes to be fired on to the Long Island beaches, whence it would be delivered through the early-morning streets of New York in laundry baskets, to be sipped in teacups by the parched clientele.

America had its own Malcolm Gillespie. US Coastguard Commander, Thomas Baker, an embittered teetotaller, waged some of the greatest unrecorded sea battles of the 1920s and 1930s, not hesitating to blow recalcitrant suspect craft out of the water. The bootleggers were

quick to riposte. One major customer for Scotch whisky controlled his pirate fleet by radio link from the top of a skyscraper in Lexington Avenue, thus, some say, even outclassing the fanatic Baker.

The whisky-runners did not give in easily. Once Baker in his Coastguard destroyer came alongside a whisky boat and gave orders to heave to. A figure in a fedora next to the skipper replied with a most unnautical arm signal, reminiscent of downtown Naples. Before Baker could give the order to sink the boat, a seaplane passed between them trailing a smokescreen. When the smoke cleared the whisky-runners were to his stern. Coming round to give his guns a better shot, Baker was amazed to see a rather shabby

In Raoul Walsh's 1939 film *Roaring Twenties* James Cagney and Humphrey Bogart (right) team up as bootleggers.

The Incorruptibles (right), the famous series of the 1960s in which Eliot Ness (Robert Stack), a special Treasury agent, works the Chicago Eastside in the 1930s. The real-life Ness helped pin down Al Capone (below), the gangland leader, whose story is told in Howard Hawkes's *Scarface* (1931) with a script by Ben Hecht.

submarine surface . . . and blow off his twin screws.

But the runners did not have it all their own way. The British schooner, the *Rosie B*, was captured off Long Island with $300,000-worth of premium whisky on board ready packed in torpedoes. A rotting garbage scow was found in New York harbour. It was packed to the waterline with $90,000-worth of high-grade whisky apparently ordered by bootlegger Frank Costello.

Though the British government had signed a Liquor Treaty with the Americans in 1924, it claimed that it could do very little to stop the traffic as it also, as it said, had to respect the International Maritime Law. In 1925 the American admiral F. C. Billard assembled a fleet of more than four hundred

Navy and Coastguard vessels together with squadrons of aircraft in an attempt to halt the whisky-runners. The British sailing ship *Eastwood* was chased fifty miles out to sea and machine-gunned to smithereens. Another British ship, the *I'm Alone*, was sunk by gunfire from the *Dexter*. But still the water of life continued to get through. Forged certificates for medical requirements took out whiskies long stored in bonded warehouses.

The long, long border between Canada and the USA not only allowed whisky to come through easily to be cut with other spirits and rebottled but also gave a healthy fillip to the Canadian rye whisky industry. The gangster Lucky Luciano said of Samuel Bronfman who acquired Seagram's in 1928 that he was "bootlegging enough whisky across the the Canadian border to double the size of Lake Erie".

Back in London, Sir Alexander Walker of Johnnie Walker, when asked at a Royal Commission in 1931 whether the whisky barons of Scotland would cease running whisky out to America, simply replied with a resounding "Certainly not!"

Treasury agents pour away confiscated bottles of contraband whiskey (left).

A New York speakeasy during Prohibition. There were more than 30,000 such establishments in the city, supplied with whisky by many and devious means.

New York, 1933: the Roosevelt Hotel (below) celebrates the end of Prohibition.

And hoodlums and gangsters such as Al Capone grew rich in Chicago. The repeal of Prohibition, in 1933, finally allowed the American whiskey industry to set itself up on a sound basis, while at the same time the taste for the golden, nobler cousin Scotch was established and continued to develop.

American whiskey is defined as "an alcohol distillate from a fermented mash of grain, produced at less than 190 US proof (95° alcohol) in such a manner that the distillate possesses a taste, aroma and character-istics generally attributed to whiskey stored in oak con-tainers (except corn whiskey which need not be so stored) and bottled at not less than 80 US proof, and also includes the mixtures of such dis-tillates for which no specific standards of identity are prescribed. Bourbon, rye, wheat malt or rye malt whiskey are whiskeys produced at not exceeding 160 US proof, fermented mash are 51% corn (maize), rye, wheat or malted barley, or malted rye and stored at no more than 124 US proof in charred new oak containers and also include mixtures of such whiskeys of the same type." Hm, quite a mouthful.

In fact, the Americans distinguish between four main categories of whiskey, independent of region of origin. Lovers of Scotch or Irish whiskies will throw up their hands at this – and I

New Year 1938: whiskey, a cigar and the sporting news – the best companions of the solitary man.

The first (legal) bottle of Vat 69 is opened after years of Prohibition (opposite).

must allow a certain partisanship here – it does seem to suggest that they have not really sorted out what the real thing is. They have.

Rye whiskey contains at least 51% rye as well as other grains, corn and malted barley. This must be matured in new charred oak casks for at least four years. It cannot be distilled at over 80°.

Bourbon whiskey contains at least 51% corn and must be aged for at least four years in new charred oak casks.

Corn whiskey must have at least 80% corn but can be stored in old casks.

American light whiskey (this whiskey type was developed to combat the sales of Scotch whisky) was legalized in July 1972. This newcomer, which represents 11% of US sales, is a blended whiskey which contains no neutral spirit.

Moreover, straight whiskey (rye, Bourbon, or corn) is a whiskey to which only water has been added to reduce it to the correct strength.

However, the United States continues to be the prime market for Scotch whisky. Beyond the Great Lakes, across the border, Canada, for so long under the shadow of the United States, produces a fine rye whisky. In the first settlements of Scots in Canada set up from 1629 to 1632, the lilting skirl of the bagpipes was heard – much to the amazement and fear of the American Indians. Whisky distilling soon became one of the requirements of life in that brutally cold and utterly unwelcoming climate.

By the middle of the nineteenth century there were some two hundred distilleries along the banks of the St Lawrence and on the shores of the Great Lakes. In this vast empty land of echoing

Experienced Traveler

PEOPLE WHO TRAVEL on the country's de luxe trains will tell you this, if you haven't already discovered it for yourself . . .

It's a mighty cheery thing, on a trip, to meet up with that experienced traveler, that aristocratic friend, Four Roses.

For Four Roses is a whiskey with a most distinctive and different flavor . . . endowed with a rich,

mellow and satisfying smoothness all its own.

We sincerely believe that the Four Roses you are buying today is the finest we've ever bottled. And, to us, that means it is the finest whiskey on the market.

Fine Blended Whiskey—98.8 proof. 40% straight whiskies 5 years or more old, 60% grain neutral spirits.

FOUR ROSES

AMERICA'S MOST FAMOUS BOUQUET

Frankfort Distillery Corporation
New York City

prairies and clashing ice one name stands out like a glorious burning beacon: Hiram Walker. Hiram Walker was born in the United States in 1816. Progressing from vinegar-brewing, milling and other activities he finally rolled up his sleeves and determinedly set up in 1858 as a rye-whisky distiller in Canada.

He was a great entrepreneur, larger than life and without any possible inklings of modesty. His company town and the centre of his barony is called Walkerville. He sold his first whiskies in branded barrels marked with his name, at a time when the idea of "brands" as such was almost unknown. Then he used earthenware jugs stamped with his mark, finally progressing to bottles. Such was the reputation that he gained for his whisky in the clubs, and among the

Opposite: the Marlborough Club, New York, in 1933: happy days are here again . . .

The great transcontinental trains of the United States all had their panoramic bars where the connoisseur could sample his favourite Bourbon.

Corn whiskey (left) contains at least 80% corn. It is generally considered a country drink drunk locally.

United States-born Hiram Walker (above centre) crossed the Great Lakes to found the modern Canadian whisky industry. He created a more distinguished whisky than his American counterparts, using a lengthier distillation. Canadian Club was born – to enjoy a continuing success.

patrons of the better hotels, that he then sold his rye whisky in bottles and the name on the label was "Club". In 1882, with amazing vigour and verve, he started to sell it in his mother country. The success of his whisky was so great that the American distillers pressed for a law obliging him to add the word "Canadian" on the bottle. Surely all true Americans would buy the domestic whisky rather than some foreign brand from across the border? Not only from across the border, but actually distilled at the spot where the rough-spun American armies in 1812 had invaded in their failed and misplaced attempt to free the inhabitants from the English yoke.

This labelling stricture dismayed Hiram Walker not one bit. He had learnt early the importance of a strong brand name in promoting his products. "Canadian Club" as a mark was born, and it continued to be much sought after, despite all the Kentucky distillers' efforts. Indeed "Canadian Club" more and more became a byword for those who felt that their native efforts were far from being up to the mark.

And then, of course, imitations abounded. In 1900 more than forty fake versions of Canadian Club were detected. Unresting, unrelenting, the doughty Hiram Walker would advertise on billboards that such and such an establishment was selling other ordinary Canadian rye whisky-types

with the label "Canadian Club". Angry clients broke mirrors in the bars, shots were fired at rickety pianos, punches were thrown. Sparks flew. Where the guilty parties sued . . . Walker won. Worse, one retailer, Charles Klyman of 232 East Kinzie Street, Chicago, was indicted for an even more heinous offence. He sold American whiskey as Canadian Club. He was bound over to take out grovelling advertisements in the newspapers, headed "A Confession", admitting that he had duped his public by selling inferior goods and not the real Canadian Club. The US Food and Drug Act of 1906 led hard-pressed American competitors to point out the possible, and to them quite probable, dangers of importing spirits that had not been produced under American control and, indeed, by American methods. Six thousand cases of Canadian Club were seized at the frontier. The representative of the Hiram Walker company reacted with vigour; lovers of Canadian Club rye raged with anger. The government wavered, hesitated and then, as is the way with governments at a loss, set up a committee to ponder on the problem. After a long commission hearing it was finally agreed that the term "whisk(e)y" should include "all potable liquor distilled from grain". Canadian Club was deemed to be true whisky. The spirit of Hiram Walker had won again.

With three or four more men of Walker's grit,

The longest consignment of whisky in history – more than five hundred metres of cars charged with some 200,000 litres of rye made up the Corby Special down from Montreal to the border to supply the speakeasies (below left).

THE WORLDS' GREATEST SHIPMENT OF RYE WHISKY
THE "CORBY SPECIAL" WHISKY TRAIN, CARRYING A RECORD SHIPMENT OF RYE WHISKY
NEARLY HALF A MILE OF CARS, containing over 50,000 GALLONS of Corby's Famous Rye Whisky, equivalent to 300,000 QUART BOTTLES.
To get the best Rye Whisky, insist on getting CORBY'S SPECIAL SELECTED."

Canadian whisky could have been a world leader. Prohibition allowed the Canadian whiskies to develop further but it was not until 1929 when the vast Seagram's empire was founded, and the Hiram Walker concern expanded, that this mild and characterful whisky became better known worldwide. Perhaps not well enough known. Its Scotch-like qualities have a true timbre of their own. But alas . . . these Canadian whiskies occupy the same modest place on the world stage as their country of origin.

The maturing sheds of the two Canadian whisky greats: Seagram's at Montreal (left) and Hiram Walker's at Windsor (below).

THE CELTIC COUSINS

The Isle of Man, midway between Scotland and Ireland, used to have its own distilleries. Of

Seagram appeals to the well-organized businessman – the man "who plans beyond tomorrow".

Celtic tradition and with a similar climate to that of Ireland and the Campbeltown region, they produced their whisky – but with very little staying power and with very little success. They are now closed.

In Wales a claim is put forward that whisky distillation was started there early, in the year AD 356 by a certain Reauilt Hir on Bardsey Island off the tip of North Wales. No doubt high up in the remote hills of Wales, in season, Welsh farmers (just like their cousins in Ireland and the Highlands) were distilling spirits from their excess barley for their own use.

Dafydd Gittins of Y Cwmn i Chwigi Cymreig, the Welsh Whisky Company, smilingly points out that a member of the Evan Williams family set up a commercial distillery in Wales at the beginning of the eighteenth century to be fol-

The early Scottish immigrants felt a touch of nostalgia in the countryside of the Great Lakes, where the first stills were set up on the shores of Lakes Erie and Ontario and along the St Lawrence (left).

Canadian whisky, matured in Bourbon or sherry casks for a minimum of three years, has already taken on the sparkle of liquid gold (opposite).

lowed by the Daniels family some years later, and that both these families emigrated to the United States to become leading members of the Kentucky distilling industry.

In 1887 Robert Willis built a major distillery at Frangoch to provide whisky for the industrial towns of Wales, but it closed in 1906 in the wake of a fierce temperance movement which left Wales almost completely dry.

True to their Celtic traditions, Dafydd Gittins and Mal Morgan started blending whiskies from Scotland in 1974, filtering the blend through herbs in the old traditional Welsh way. Dafydd Gittins prefers to keep the full secret of these herbs, but suggests there is marjoram and safrifach, a local herb, among them. In its Welsh idiom, I found this blend very fine.

In 1990 the first distillery to be established for over a hundred years was set up in Ffrwdgrech, and, in August 1991, it moved to Brecon where reputedly the clearest and finest water in the whole of the British Isles is to be found. The men of Wales are on the move again . . . They have the traditions; time will tell whether the distillation is just right, the maturing process and the climate kindly to the spirit . . .

In Brittany, too, whisky is being distilled in small charentais-type stills, and is being enjoyed by the Bretons who seem to prefer to sell it locally.

OTHER WHISKIES

Evelyn Waugh writes in his novel *Scoop*, "The steward placed on his table a syphon and a bottle of whisky which carried the label *Edouard VIII: very old Genuine Scotch Whisky: André Bloc and Cie, Saigon,* and the coloured picture of a Regency buck, gazing sceptically at the consumer through a quizzing glass.

"'Alphonse,' said Corker, 'I'm surprised at you.'

"'No like?'

"'Bloody well no like.'

"'Whisky soda,' the man explained patiently, almost tenderly, as though in a nursery, 'Nice.'

"Corker filled his glass, tasted, grimaced."

The glories of whisky being such, it is inevitable that other countries have tried to produce whisky.

At best most of these remain undrinkable curiosities.

There is a mystery in the making of whisky that cannot be easily grasped by the Brazilian or the Spaniard . . . it is not of their culture nor of their climate.

Scotch whisky as the world market leader is clearly the most often imitated. The Scotch Whisky Association carefully analyses samples of whisky sent to it from the airports of the world, from the Gulf States to Georgia, to eliminate imposters. In some cases, alien producers of blends imagine that by buying Scotch malts in bulk and adding to them locally distilled grain spirits they can indeed produce a "Scotch whisky blend". This is to be blind not only to the true qualities of Scotch but also to the law: Scotch whisky is whisky (both grain and malt) distilled and matured in Scotland.

In the most flagrant cases the whole distillation has taken place outside Scotland and no amount of sticking on of spurious tartan labels proclaiming that it is the whisky of the GlenMacDiana can change the vile contents. The Scotch Whisky Association is most vigilant, but casual consumers travelling on the other side

of the world, faced with some weird and mysterious blend of which they have never heard but which proclaims its high Celtic origins with a vivid exuberance of Scottish regalia, should stick to their regular tried and trusted blends.

Rumours of sherry casks being bought up by Korea and Taiwan and Indonesia have caused irritated eyebrows to be raised by Irish and Scottish distillery purchasing managers – more one suspects because of their own imminent shortfall in supplies of casks for their own use rather than because of fears of serious competition from outlandish imitators. There is in the making of whisky a mystery that is difficult, almost impossible to export.

In Australia and New Zealand, Scots and Irish descendants have tried, without receiving much acclaim even from their own very nationalistic countrymen, to produce a distillation of their own.

India, which produced a kind of paint stripper for the less discriminating British serviceman during the great days of the Raj, has had even less luck – unless the production of paint stripper was indeed what they had in mind, in which case there is some confusion over the labelling.

JAPAN . . . THE GREAT EXPECTATION

The Japanese being a logical race, knowing a very good thing indeed when they see it, have always been ready to adapt, refine and develop it for their own uses and tastes.

The unthinking purist, always ready to sneer at such early whiskies produced and labelled as "Queen George VIII Famous Scottish" and "King Victoria's Sporran" might do well to reflect on the early approbation heaped on the fledgeling Japanese motor car and electronic industries.

In 1918 a young man, Masataka Taketsuro, went to Glasgow University to study applied

Suntory's distillery towers at Hakushu (right) combine the traditional and the contemporary, the Scottish and the Japanese style. The distillery houses a museum and is surrounded by a huge bird sanctuary.

chemistry. Whether he had heard the skirl of the pipes beside the lily pads before he arrived in that grey watery city, or whether the cold winter nights of the Lowlands had induced him to take up some extramural studies in the rough pubs of Glasgow, he became fascinated with whisky, as

many have been before and since. He abandoned pure science to pursue what for the man of taste is the study of pure art. Taking up his pilgrim's staff he went, surely a curious figure, from distillery to distillery, knocking at the doors in search of a job. Finally, he was taken on. Some say at Rothes, by the Glen Grant distillery, some say by The Glenlivet. The records seem vague. Perhaps the Scots are not too willing to own up? Recent Japanese visitors to the Lowlands distillery of Auchentoshan suggest that it was here that Masataka Taketsuro first learnt the art. But perhaps this is just a form of Japanese politeness . . . Auchentoshan's own records were destroyed in a fire. However, one way or another, the father of Japanese whisky returned to Japan in 1921 with a good working knowledge of Scotch whisky-distilling and production and with a

A master blender at Suntory examines the vast range of malts from Scotland. He can test up to a hundred malts during an average working day.

Scottish wife (the first ad hoc quality control manager for Japanese whisky?). In 1923 he and Shinjiro Torii, an entrepreneur who sold imported Spanish wines, established the first Japanese distillery in Yamazaki.

On the outskirts of Kyoto the setting is strangely evocative of Scotland with a steady gentle climate. Here, they started producing the first Suntory whiskies, and later set up another distillery at Hakushu near the Japanese Alps. In 1934 Taketsuru set up independently in the north on the Island of Hokkaido – Japan's Islay. Not only did it have a climate suitable for maturing the Nikka whisky but it also had its own peat. When the Second World War broke out both companies were ready with an aged single-malt whisky. But, during the long American occupation, the GIs brought the taste back to the more traditional blends.

Again the purists may scoff: both Nikka and Suntory produce

a light whisky, a whisky ideal for the Japanese "salariman", or office-worker, to drink in the way he prefers in the dimly lit, late-night, after-work sessions in restaurants or Karaoke bars . . . drunk 20 per cent whisky, 80 per cent ice and water . . . his way, the way he likes it. This light whisky is made also by such foreign firms as Seagram's distilling in Japan. And Scotch blends take this taste into consideration. Whatever our feelings about such whisky, a great deal of it seems to be drunk on the way home to the patient mama-san. Faces glow red, but next morning the look is one of the man who has sat by the lily pool all night listening to the soft plucking of a one-stringed guitar. The Japanese say that they clear their heads in the morning by eating a pickled cherry. Perhaps they simply get by with all the water they drink with their whisky.

Lovingly and very seriously the Japanese are developing their young art, which is hardly seventy

Shinjiro Torii (centre), founder with Masataka Taketsuru of the celebrated firm of Suntory, is the father of Japanese whisky. He started out as an importer of Spanish wines and thus had a good stock of sherry casks ready before starting up his distillery.

Sammy Davis Junior (far right) promotes a famous brand of Japanese whisky. Others have followed his example, including the Scot Sean Connery, causing cries of scandal in the streets of Glasgow.

One of the earliest advertisements declaring the virtues of Japanese whisky (right).

years old. They are already marketing their interesting old malts at home. Will they later want to market abroad? As whisky, it may lack the long traditions of the Celtic north but of all the non-Scottish whiskies it is the closest to the real thing, the water of life of the Scots. It will develop. Meanwhile we raise our golden glasses to the memory cherished of Masataka Taketsuru-san,

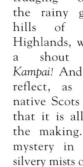

trudging over the rainy grey hills of the Highlands, with a shout of *Kampai!* And we reflect, as the native Scots do, that it is all in the making. A mystery in the silvery mists of the glens.

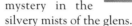

Up the road from the pagodas of Kyoto, I visited the Yamazaki distillery. The young manager who was showing me round pointed to the rooftops of the distillery. "Look," he said, "pagodas . . . just like in Scotland."

Eccentric Japanese whisky bottles (left). The connoisseur is not deceived. He knows that it is the contents and not the shape of the bottle that count.

In the nosing room, and in the greatest of secrecy, the choice of whiskies, malt and grain, that makes up the perfect blend is decided (page 104).

The Art of Distilling

eyond the simplicities of the basic principles . . . fine barley grown in the fertile fields of the north-east of Scotland and in the green valleys of Ireland . . .

. . . clear shining water sparkling in the burns under the subdued sun of the north, water infused with the subtle caress of the essences of peat and heather . . .

. . . the happy fact that alcohol evaporates at a lower temperature than water . . .

. . . the slow maturing in oak casks, slumbering in cool cellars . . .

. . . beyond these simplicities lie the mysteries of chance and experience, skill and invention developed over a period of loving elaboration of more than a thousand years.

Whisky is in the age-old Celtic tradition . . . the sheaves of ripe barley cut with the shining sickle, the reaper under a changing lowering sky of heavy clouds which break to pour down the rain, trickling first through the thick heather of the hillside, then through deep peat, faster and faster, in a shining stream down the brooks and burns and on to a loch tinged red, then purple, set ablaze by the setting sun . . . the dying of the light . . . the gloaming lit by a single fire.

It is that Celtic tradition of barley cakes roasted on stones by that fire of peat . . . the fermented porridge of this same barley giving, first, a beer, and then, by a distillation, strange and mysterious, that water more than water . . . the water of life . . . *uisce baugh* . . . whisky.

Michael Burkham, Heritage Controller at the great house of United Distillers, gives a terse definition, "Today, Scotch whisky is defined as a distillate made, in Scotland, from the elements of cereals, water and yeast." But he adds, happily, "That's rather like describing the *Mona Lisa* as a painting . . . accurate but inadequate." Jean

Biolatto of Bar le Forum, grand connoisseur of whisky, is wont to state shortly, "Whisky is an element born from earth, water, fire . . . and mystery."

The pragmatist, the man of science, is chagrined. He will ask the question "Why?" And so often the answer will be "We don't know." And he will be sent away with the impression that it is all a mystery, a mystery tinged with a great deal of magic, a mystery that is in the golden glow in the shining glass.

We can take him by the hand to lead him through the process step by step. We can see a little of the secrets of what makes that golden product, that comforter of hearts, that merry maker.

THE MALTING

The barley, giving off the aroma of sunny autumn harvest days, the smell of long childhood holidays in the sun when all was innocence, is cleaned. Then, traditionally, the cleaned barley is steeped in water . . . the same magical water that is used for making the whisky itself. This takes on average two days. Drained in a couch,

The long rows of barley in the malting sheds of Laphroaig distillery on Islay, the only distillery to be run by a woman – Bessie Williamson – from 1954 to 1972.

Barley in the lofts, the light filtered through the motes dancing in the air. The wooden shiels prevent the bruising of the barley when turning it (opposite).

the softened barley is then spread out thirty centimetres deep on the malting floor where the barley wakes.

A solitary sparrow flies overhead. Soft rays of sun pierce the dusty windows of the malting floor. Rootlets begin to form. This takes another seven to ten days.

Three times a day the germinating barley is turned – to stop heat developing and mould forming, and to control the germination. The men in the maltings, using wooden ploughs and rakes, turn the barley, then, with shiels – shovels of wood to prevent the barley being bruised – the barley is tossed in a dazzling shower. This tossing prevents the delicate germinating rootlets from knotting.

Then, only when the maltster feels the moment is ripe – depending on his own exper-ience, handed down to him by his forebears according to the secret unwritten tradition of his distillery – the germination process is halted. At this point the rootlet is twice as long as the grain itself. This modification, this malting, is tested not by complicated chemical analysis but the maltster rubbing and smelling the grain and by biting the kernels: there is a clear taste of sweet malt.

Tradition holds that the barley is ready when the maltster can take a kernel and write his name on the rough wall with it. The names stand there: Jamie, Ian, Angus, Rory . . .

The chief effect of germination on the physical structure of the barley is the breakdown of the cell walls. This process will greatly ease the conversion of starch to sugar when the crushed barley is combined with hot water.

To halt the malting process, the barley is dried in kilns heated by peat fires (centre right).

The "green barley" is then dried to prevent further germination, which would involve a later loss of sugars. This is done in kilns. The barley is spread out over permeable floors, made either of wire mesh or perforated tiles, set over a slow smouldering fire, with each flooring adding just a little more to the quality of the end product. How? It is not known. The speed of infusion of the peat? Perhaps.

The smell of burning peat is elemental, something basic, a harsh acrid smoke, a smoke that takes us back to the rough bothies of that first Celtic distiller. Originally in the Highlands all malt was dried over slow-burning peat fires, and this aroma drawn from the fire gives to many malt whiskies the first element of their distinctive flavour. And again, here the peat may be rich with leaves from ancient forests; there the peat may have seaweed in it thrown up by long-forgotten storms, and there, further beyond, it may reflect flowers from summers at the dawning of long lost days.

Peat is, most often, the accumulated decayed matter of moss. On Islay where the peat is such an important element in the making of whisky, it is said that a depth of 30 centimetres of peat takes a thousand years to build up.

The key to this drying of the germinated barley is that the temperature of the fire must be raised slowly, gradually . . . and on no account should the heat of the kiln exceed 65°C. Above this the enzyme starts to be destroyed, giving a lower yield in the mashing and fermentation processes.

To stand in a drying kiln, ankle deep in the sweet-smelling barley, and watch the first hints of smoke come up through the grain is to know that the process of whisky making is not just some humdrum industrial process. Yes, we are visiting a factory for producing spirit, but what a factory! Look up at the smoke-cured rafters to the pagodas, the dark beams of ancient bothies . . . this is no ordinary place.

The original kilns were made of stone and were bowl-shaped with an arched furnace beneath. These thatched kilns were also used by farmers to dry other crops, such as wheat and oats. Often they also served as bakeries for the barley bread of those Highlanders of long ago. Then, from the mid-1700s onwards, more elaborate kilns were built, with tapering roofs capped with horizontal ventilators, to allow the smoke to circulate. Many distilleries which no longer do their own malting maintain these pagoda-like structures – indeed, often, they are classified monuments. The pagodas, seen from afar, give an unexpected golden crown to the simple granite or whitewashed buildings beneath. They shine out like church steeples . . . they seem to say: this is a very special place . . . sacred, too, to old traditions.

After drying and cooling, the rootlets, "culms", are cleaned off the malted barley in a dressing machine.

There is a soft, sweet, comforting smell of

The peat fire perfumes and dries the malted barley. This countryman (opposite) has no need to worry: the reserves of peat on Islay should last some 5,000 years, both for domestic and distillery use.

The degree of germination in the barley is tested by the colour and the taste of the grain: one of the first elements to contribute to the quality of the end product, whisky.

Harsh black scars cut across the green landscape where man has dug for peat. Fresh cuttings shine brightly in the sun.

malt in the air. The distillery cat waits. The malt is a comfort to mice too. Cats grow fat, but not too fat, because other professional rodent exterminators get there first. Nothing must be allowed to pollute the final whisky.

The Irish, true to their own tradition, dry their barley in closed kilns, where the reek of the peat, or other fuel, does not flavour the malt. For the Irish, with their triple distillation, this peaty flavour hides the true tastes and flavours of whisky. No one knows when the Irish started closed kilning. When asked they will shrug and say simply, "This is how it has always been done since I can remember." The implication

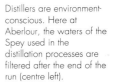

is that the Scots can do what they like; but theirs is the real thing.

How did the early distillers realize that malted barley would give a greater yield than the unmalted? In Ireland the story goes that a farmer stumbled and dropped a sack of barley in the stream. Bringing it back home, he spread it out on the floor of his cottage to dry. It started to sprout . . . or possibly to smell musty. To stop this happening, he dried it out over his fire. When he came to mash, ferment and distil he discovered with happy amazement that he had a higher yield of spirit. He asked no questions. The next day, smiling gently, a

Distillers are environment-conscious. Here at Aberlour, the waters of the Spey used in the distillation processes are filtered after the end of the run (centre left).

Malt distilleries with their distinctive pagoda-like roofs for the kilns where the malted barley is dried. These buildings (left) can be found in the Spey valley, where there is a great concentration of distilleries.

merry song about his lips, he went back to the bubbling stream and dropped into it another sack of barley, or maybe it was two . . .

Wine-makers watch the weather during grape-growing, and during the picking. Their slopes, their vineyards, their plants are an integral part of the high reputation of their precious product. More basic, barley, or the sugar it produces, does not affect the final whisky. The final whisky is the product of the pure skill of the distillerymen.

Chemists will quibble with this, and do – what goes in, as barley strains, they say in their prosaic, plodding way, must affect what comes out. Well, this has yet fully to be proved. What is known is that certain barleys can give higher yields, but the rest of the secret lies in the magical process of whisky making itself.

Many distilleries take their malted barley now from central maltings. Here the barley, during the 1950s and 1960s, was laid out in concrete troughs, called Saladin boxes, named after their French inventor. Controlled warmed air is passed through the sprouting grain which is turned continously by Archimedean screws. Today, revolving drums are used.

It can be argued that using malted barley from central maltings destroys something of the character of the whisky produced. Distillers are always more than quick to point out that the loads of barley delivered to their gates have been produced to their own specifications with, in the case of Scotch malts, exactly their own prescribed and desired peatiness.

Cynics may sniff but, in the end, the test is always in the finished product . . . and its noble

Drying peat on Islay. It takes some 3,000 years to produce one cubic metre of peat, which is an accumulation of decayed vegetable matter: mosses, heather, gorse, flowers, all of which add their special aroma to the matured whisky.

reputation, jealously maintained by the men who make it. Tradition is one thing, but only a fool would not use modern advances to improve on tradition.

The malted barley is then ground into a rough flour, grist.

In the traditional way of things, we have passed from the grainy harvest smell of the raw barley, the chiaroscuro of the malting floors with the soft rhythmic shuffle of the rakes or shiels as the men gently work their way along in unhurried orchestrated lines like their forebears scything those fields of ripe gold barley. We have smelt the sweet tang of the malt. Our eyes have smarted and we have smelt the elemental reek of the fire, that peaty reek that still rises from the bright fires of the cottages of the Highlands and of the pubs of Dublin. We have heard the floury

grinding of the grain in old tried mechanical mills built, very often, in the 1920s, and built to last. And already a golden light is filtering through the motes in the air.

THE MASHING

Mashing completes the conversion of the starches into sugars. The grist is added to water. Not just any water . . . the distillery's own water, that water which is so essential to each part of the process. Some take their water from deep wells, some from springs gushing from the ground since before the age of the monasteries, springs dating

Peat is often used to feed the fires of the kilns (below).

back to some more mystical Celtic age. Some take their water from fast-flowing burns and rivers. Whatever they may be, these sources are tenaciously guarded. The title deeds of the distilleries make mention of them – without them the distillery would be nothing. In the past, battles were fought over water where two or more distilleries used the same source. Today, lawyers grow rich.

Water is at the very heart of the distinctive quality of the whisky. New distilleries are set up where a goodly supply of the right kind of water is available. The Irish set up their vast new distillery complex at Midleton where they could draw on more than 150 years of water records. Chivas built their newest distillery at Allt à Bhainne in the Highlands, "the place of the creamy streams", where eagles fly and where there is, indeed, a bountiful source of sparkling water from the high grey hills behind.

In very simple terms, soft peaty water is best for the heavier whiskies such as the Islays and the Campbeltowns. Harder waters such as those of the Speyside are deemed best for the lighter whiskies.

The water for mashing is heated to about 65°C and the grist mixed in through a copper tube with a revolving screw. This porridgey substance, the mash, is run into the mash tuns which are usually some four metres in diameter and made of steel panels, but they can also be made of wood, traditionally larch. Here the action of the warm water releases the sugars. These mash tuns can hold anything from 9,000 to 36,000 litres.

The mashing takes about eight hours. The malting action of the diastase begins again, converting the remaining starch or maltose into sugars. The mash is continuously stirred by revolving rakes or paddles to help extract the remaining starches from the grist into the liquor. This warm sweet liquid, now called wort, is then run off into a receptacle called the underback. The wort may be recycled three or four times. Hot water is again added to the grains and husks in the tun to extract remaining sugars and, finally, some of the liquor left over is kept to be added to start the process in the next mashing.

In the United States, the de-alcoholized fermentation from the next step is added to the mash to produce their "sour mash whiskey", as opposed to sweet mash. This is thought by the American distillers to provide for a continuity of character and a reinforcement of bouquet and flavours.

The spent grains, or draff, are processed to produce feed for cattle. Nothing is wasted. John Ryan of Ireland adds, with a wink, that some-

Laphroaig distillery in Islay, famous for its very characteristic malts (centre left).

Once the kiln fire is lit, it must burn evenly without producing overmuch heat but producing enough smoke to infuse the barley (right).

A raging stream on the Isle of Jura – an island of deer and seals, whose solitary distillery produces an amber red malt.

tionally, they are made of Oregon pine, Douglas fir or larch, but stainless steel is also often used. It is argued that the wooden washbacks contribute a little to the flavour of the finished whisky and this may well be so. Again, nothing can be proved . . . except that the stainless steel can add nothing. The case proclaimed for stainless steel – often I suspect by efficiency experts from south of the border sent up with their calculators to gauge man-hours – is that it is easier to clean. A dirty or insufficiently cleaned washback with lingering bacteria is the primary cause for off-notes later found in the whisky. However, meticulously cleaned with steam under pressure, wooden washbacks are seen by many – most of the men who work with them – as being the real thing. Bowmore's recent decision to go back to wooden washbacks has been hailed by its distillerymen, the producers of their excellent Islay malt, as entirely for the best. Jokingly, at Knockando, I asked the distillery manager, the gentle giant Innes Shaw, whether he would not prefer to go over to stainless steel. The look of horror and amazement at my question was answer enough. Not an answer about what wooden washbacks give to the whisky, but proof that the men using them know, or quite simply feel, that they are better.

Yeast is added to the wort. Fermentation begins.

The sign above the door of the Old Fitzgerald Bourbon distillery in Louisville, Kentucky, reads: "No chemists allowed. This is a distillery not a whiskey factory."

In cold terms, by the action of the yeast, the sugars are converted into ethanol (alcohol) and carbon dioxide. In practice, when this happens the wash froths violently and the washtub shakes. Suddenly, we are in the realms of alchemy. Something very special is happening. It is a benevolent version of the *Macbeth* witches' brew: Bubble, bubble . . . The brewers' tales of

times, depending on barley harvests and prices, a higher price can be got for these "brewers' dark grains" than for the original barley itself.

The mash tuns are scrupulously cleaned . . . any wayward microbe will affect the distilled spirit. Steam under pressure is used, steam from that same water so special to the distillery.

We have moved on from the heavy sodden barley porridge in the mash tuns and we now have a liquid from which there already wafts a promising sweet, sugary smell. The wort is pumped from the underback to coolers which reduce the temperature to between 22° and 24°C.

THE FERMENTATION

Fermentation converts the sugar into alcohol.

The cooled wort is pumped to the tun room and then into washbacks. Set into the floor of the tun room these are usually some 4.5 metres deep, sometimes deeper in modern distilleries. Usually a distillery has a battery of six or eight washbacks, each holding 40,000+ litres. Tradi-

The Strathisla malt is dry with hints of sherry. It is at the heart of Chivas Regal deluxe blend. The distillery buildings (opposite) recall the architecture of the surrounding farms; formerly distilling was part of the farmer's yearly round.

The fermentation of the wash at Jack Daniel's distillery in Tennessee. The sour mash is produced by reserving a little of the de-alcoholized fermentation from previous distillations in order to maintain character and quality.

young apprentices peering into the lidded washback and falling in, asphyxiated, are legion. Today, visitors to a distillery may be jestingly invited to sniff at this frothing brew. Try it, but beware: the lack of oxygen can give you a punch that will make you kick back like a mule. Or ghostly hands will pull at you and drag you toppling into the seething ferment . . . Old distillerymen feel that all is not well in the process unless the very floors shake beneath them. Modern yeasts do produce a more controlled ferment; however the fermentation process can still sometimes be so violent that electrically controlled paddles are set near the top of the surface and are used to beat the surface to control the boiling froth. In the old days young boys were employed to beat the wash with heather switches.

After some forty-eight hours the frenzied liquid settles; the turmoil dies down. The washbacks become still. What we now have is a wash, a clear liquid, which consists of water and yeast and stands at about 7–8° alcohol per volume. In short, what we have been making up to now is a beer, and indeed, in the United States the wash is called "beer". Innes Shaw let me taste some at Knockando. I sniff. A yeasty smell, a smell of beer, still warm. I taste. Not a very good beer as beer goes, but one that has a yet nobler end. The brewer has done his job.

Is the fermentation a vital point? "There are so many factors that affect the final taste and bouquet," says Stewart McBain of The Glenlivet, thoughtfully, but not helping us overmuch. "You start to create the character at the malting stage and it continues right through fermentation,

The washbacks at the Glenfiddich distillery (left) are traditionally of Oregon pine, Douglas fir, or larch. Elsewhere stainless steel has been tried, with little support from the traditionalists. Whisky making remains relatively mysterious, and if the traditionalists cannot tell us exactly what wooden washbacks bring to the taste of the final whisky, they are unanimous that stainless steel can contribute nothing.

distillation and maturation. My experience suggests that the fermentation stage is indeed very important in its effect on the quantity and quality of a malt whisky's character . . . Ah, but then so is the long period of maturation and the quality of the casks."

The turbulent seething liquid calms before passing on to the distillation process.

Up to now we have seen tubs and tuns, in whitewashed sheds whose ceilings are crisscrossed with pipes painted in various colours denoting wash or wort or steam. The machinery is carefully polished, everything that can be painted is painted, fresh and bright. The vast copper or stainless steel lids of the washbacks shine; iron gleams black. We could almost be in the bowels of a ship. Perhaps this sea-going ambience should cause us little surprise. Though many of the younger generation of distillerymen come with degrees in biology, many brewery managers, such as the genial Iain Henderson of Laphroaig, have followed, at some time, that other traditional Scots calling of marine engineer.

Looking through the thick mesh metal flooring at the depths of the washbacks below, still singing softly after the ferment, we move out of the cool into the heat and glow, and the savours, of the still room.

THE DISTILLATION

Distillation is the boiling of the fermented wort, now called the "wash". This is done in order to leave the water behind and to extract the alcohol. Alcohol, more volatile than steam, is driven off first and is collected by condensation.

Generally, in Scotland, distillation takes place in two copper stills, in two separate stages. The shiny copper stills, basically swan-necked kettles, are individual to each distillery. In one distillery, the stills, pear-shaped, may be squat and wide; at another neighbouring distillery, tradition will opt for tall elegant stills. But whatever shape or form the stills have, the men of the distillery will take pains to maintain exactly that shape. When sections wear out and must be replaced, they are replaced exactly as they were before. Where there might have been a dent, this will be reproduced. Where the particular angle of the lyne pipe leading out of the still is at such a degree, often originally to take into consideration some defect in the still-house construction

Modern stainless-steel washbacks at Cambus grain distillery, between Glasgow and Edinburgh (left). Here the washbacks add nothing to the taste of the whisky.

Cleaning at Frankfort, the capital of Kentucky (opposite). Ill-cleaned washbacks are often the cause of off-notes in the whiskey, which neither maturing, nor blending, nor redistillation can completely eliminate. They are scrupulously cleaned with water and steam under pressure.

that has subsequently been rectified, this angle of the pipe will be maintained.

This is part superstition, part traditional Scots conservatism. Scientists can not gainsay it. The stillman is after all the man who is applying his art and his skill to the finished whisky.

However, it can be said – but again this is not necessarily the case – that tall stills produce a lighter, more vivacious whisky and that low squat stills produce a heavy, deeper and even oily whisky. Again, some distilleries maintain that polishing the outside of the copper still affects the spirit. Strathisla maintains rugged unpolished stills for its sparkling dram.

The wash is pumped into the first, larger, still which is slowly heated. As the wash boils, it froths – there is still yeast in the liquid. Here is the first risk that the stillman runs. If it boils over the whisky will be ruined. And then there is the danger that the particles of malt or yeast in the wash might catch the sides of the still and burn, thus again risking spoiling the whisky. This problem can be solved by having rummagers of chain mail which mechanically scour the inside of the still during distillation. With steam-heating the difficulties are reduced, but again many distilleries continue to heat, because they always have done so, by peat, coke or anthracite or a mixture of these. Today's computer-assisted systems can control the heat in the stills, but

Traditional wooden washbacks at Suntory's Yamazaki distillery, not far from Kyoto (below); a region of pines and mists and silver streams between the trees, reminiscent of Scotland.

The Caol Ila distillery, near Port Askaig on Islay. The distillery has six long-necked stills and produces a vigorous and peaty whisky (pages 124–5).

The five stills at John Power's distillery in Dublin in 1910 (right). To combat the success of the Scottish blends, which used grain whisky, the Irish distillers began to use larger and larger stills in order to produce more and more, which led, some say, to impurities being allowed to pass through the lyne arms, and which necessitated a third distillation to eliminate them.

even so it is the distiller who must make the decision, the distiller who controls the heat.

The wash finally boils. It is cooking on a grand scale. The vapour given off rises to the neck of the still and, from there, it is condensed. Though many distilleries use modern shell condensers, others still use the traditional worm, a spiral copper tube of decreasing diameter, an intricate example of the coppersmith's art, in a tub of constantly renewed cold water.

At Tomatin distillery, one of the largest in Scotland, the warm water produced was once used to breed eels. Other distilleries, such as Glenallachie, pump the water into ponds where sybaritic ducks paddle in the misty waters, steaming in the sharp winter air. At Morrison's Glen Garioch, the excess heat from the still houses is used to grow tomatoes and exotic vegetables in greenhouses. At Bowmore, there is a heated enclosed swimming-pool donated to the town, beside the long white distillery along the shores of the cold sea loch. Along the coast, at Laphroaig, warm waters are pumped out to the sea. Interfering conservationists came from the mainland to complain. It was politely explained to them that the distillery had been doing this for over a hundred years. They could stop doing it but what

would happen to all the fish that came to breed in the warm waters?

From the resulting boiled wash, the condensation we get is called "low wines", a crude "whisky" from which the yeast and other unfermentable matter has been eliminated. Is it whisky? No. To be called "whisky" it must be distilled again and then matured for at least three years. After condensation, the low wines, sparkling clear, pass through the "spirit safe". Whatever the tradition for the stills, these spirit safes are always highly polished.

With the reforms of 1823, which laid the foundations of modern whisky production, the device of the spirit safe was introduced. Essentially a long glass box bound in brass, it is secured by Customs and Excise locks – the Queen's locks. Traditionally, one key was kept by the distillery manager and the other by the resident exciseman. Both were needed to open the lock, which was further protected by a numbered paper which would be defaced by a device of needles if illicitly opened. Despite all precautions there were always distillery men keen to get at a taste of the first distillation, this echo of those first early fiery liquids of the Celtic distillers high up in the heather.

The low wines spirit safe allows the stillman to control the spirit being produced, without having direct access to it. In the safe there are two glass receptacles with a tube down which the distillate flows. This can be directed by the stillman with a lever. He can discard or keep the distillate without being able to touch it. He can also control hydrometers from outside to test the specific gravity of the colourless liquid to see if the low wines are still running or if they are now

Each distillery has its own traditions about the care and upkeep of the stills. Some polish them; others leave them as they are, the dents and scratches carefully left in place lest the taste of the whisky be affected (opposite).

Stills are usually heated with peat (centre left) but in certain areas coal is used. Modern installations equally often use steam heat. Traditionalists again deem that this takes something away from the final taste of the malt.

The Caol Ila distillery, one of Islay's seven distilleries, whose modern buildings date back to the 1970s.

Close-up of the inspection hatch of a still (centre right). This allows distillery men to go in and carefully clean the still between runs.

simply producing distilled water. In this way, he knows when the process should be stopped.

The cooled low wines, which still contain impurities, with an alcohol content of some 25°, are then pumped into a charger above the smaller spirit still. Something like 11,000 litres of wash give 2,500 litres of low wines, this conversion process taking some six hours. The low wines are then distilled for a second time. Here the stillman comes into his own.

For Iain Henderson of the marvellously complex Laphroaig, with its hints of the sea and its peaty timbre, the late-night dram in front of a dying fire, this is the make or break moment for the future whisky.

Looking out from his wood-panelled board-room, with its comfortable leather armchairs, at the chilly sea where a vagrant heron hunches its ruffled feathers, he tells us, "If the stillman does not get things right here, however much care has been taken with the mashing and the fermentation, however much time may be spent in maturing the spirit, it will not be of the highest quality . . ." – the quality that they, the men of Laphroaig, desire.

What the stillman is looking for is the "middle cut", or heart of the run. The first vapours that come off, called "foreshots", contain alcohols which have an unpleasant taste. Again, via the spirit safe, the stillman can add

The size and shape of the still has its effect on the taste of the whisky. A squat still does not give the same whisky as a graceful swan-necked still.

Lawns, culverts, a dam for the distillery waters, where ducks splash; this is in general what the visitor first sees when he comes to a distillery.

water to the distilled spirit. If it turns cloudy, he is still producing foreshots and they will be diverted back to the low wines receiver still to be added to the next low wine distillation from the wash still, for further distillation. When the foreshots have passed through, and the spirit is running clear and bright, crystal clear, the middle cut is drawn off to the spirit receiver. Then again, towards the end of the run, various oily elements start to vaporize which would equally damage the taste of the whisky. These, the "feints", are also detectable in the spirit safe by cloudiness formed with the addition of water. They too are separated off and returned to the low wines receiver for another distillation. With the foreshots and the feints eliminated, what we have left is the middle cut – the heart – or, now, the "new make" which, condensed, is piped to the spirit receiver.

Again praise should be given to the stillman. He it is who, working with the spirit hermetically confined in the spirit safe, with very little in the way of testing equipment, using a pot still essentially unchanged for over three hundred years,

The distilling process is one of the secrets of the quality of the whiskey produced: the distillery at Michter in Pennsylvania (right), a classified monument, continues to distil over traditional open fires.

The distiller's art is shown at every step of the process. The heart of the run in the second distillation calls on the stillman's great experience. Bottom right: Highland Park distillery in the Orkneys.

knows when to cut out the foreshots and feints. It is he who, relying on intuition, long experience and traditionally handed-down skills and a great deal of love for his own product, manages to get his distillation just right day after day, as he and his predecessors have done for many, many years.

Automation and computers can help – a little – but it is the stillman who can pierce the mysteries and who knows just when the middle run, the heart of the run, that true heart, is flowing clear and pure. Scientists have analysed the process and have understood a little, but the stillman reigns supreme.

Before legislation in 1916 when compulsory bonding and maturing of three years was imposed, "new make" was regularly drunk by some connoisseurs. Some old retired distillery workers accustomed to receive a dram of it at the beginning or end of each day claimed, and perhaps still claim, actually to prefer it. Indeed, simple tests on this colourless spirit, at about 75° alcohol, show clearly that it has many of the qualities of the matured whisky. A few drops, rubbed in the hands and smelt, sing in childish treble with the promise of the matured whisky. At Knockando up in the wild Highlands, the smell was of pears; at Rosebank down in the Lowlands appropriately the smell was of roses; at Bowmore much to the surprise of the manager,

Jim McEwan, I thought I smelt heather blossoms and honey, and the sea. Tasting the new spirit wherever I could, I found it not unpleasant. But the experiments showed that it also gave a harsh headache and deep desire to close my eyes and lie down in a quiet cool place.

In Tennessee whiskey country, at Jack Daniel's, the distilled spirit is passed through a thick filter of finely milled sugar maple charcoal. This process is deemed to leach out any impurities in the whiskey, and takes up to ten days. The Scot would politely suggest that if the distiller has done his job properly there would be no im-

purities in the whisky left that could not be eliminated in the slow mellow maturing processes. But this was not an American invention: the grand new Welsh distillery at Brecon still filters its spirit through seven native herbs. The Scot ponders on . . . would not this filtering also leach out not only what so churlishly are considered impurities but also those elements which are part of the essential flavour of the finished whisky? This process at Jack Daniel's does add a certain jejune smokiness to the taste of the whiskey.

The new spirit that comes from the stills after the distillation process (left) cannot yet be called whisky. Its scent is often that of pear juice.

Strict controls are made at Jack Daniel's distillery in Tennessee in the United States (opposite); the whiskey is distilled from a mix of maize, rye and barley.

The spirit safe, a strange safe that can be opened only by the exciseman and the distillery manager jointly, allows control and testing of the new spirit without direct hands-on contact (pages 132–3).

Jim Beam's master distiller at Clermont in Kentucky checks that the spirit has all the qualities necessary for a Bourbon of the highest traditional order.

In Scotland in general they distil twice. In Ireland at Midleton and Old Bushmills, as they have always done, they use a triple distillation for their mixtures of unpeated barleys and grain. Proudly, and why indeed not, the Irish claim that their true art is the distiller's art and that the Scots depend too much on the blender who, they say, by artifice, can cover up a vast range of mistakes.

Ah, half-jest the Scots in reply, how typical of the Irish to have to distil a third time because they cannot get their distillation of low wines right the first time. The well-tempered Irishman, as fiercely patriotic about his fine whiskeys as the men from Islay and the Highlands about theirs, will now shrug and remind them that it was, after all, the Irish who first exported three things to Scotland: the bagpipes, the kilt, and whiskey . . . and the first two of these were only meant as jokes.

However, whisky pundit Gordon Brown reminds us that in the early sixteenth century – when theoretically the barber surgeons had the monopoly of whisky making – there were three qualities of spirit according to the number of distillations used: *uiscebaugh* (*simplex* – twice distilled as now; *treastarraig* (or *composita*) – triple distilled, and *uiscebaugh-baul* (or *perfectissima* – a distillate run four times. The argument now, in Scotland, is that, with the distillation techniques

of today built on long experience and skill, quite clearly, two runs are enough.

However, both Auchentoshan and Rosebank (the latter "mothballed" in 1993) in the Lowlands have always run their whisky three times, and very good drams they are, too. Perhaps here, as in Ireland, where they built bigger and bigger pot stills to keep up production in the face of the highly efficient Coffey or Column stills producing grain spirit, the size of the still and dimensions of the lyne arm allowed some negative elements to pass through the second distillation, which had then to be eliminated by a third run. Springbank, the great survivor of the Campbeltowns, also has an adapted form of triple distillation: one distillation of the wash, one of the low wines, and another linked distillation of the foreshots and feints.

The gleaming copper pot stills were the traditional and only form of distillation of spirits for whisky acceptable to the Scots . . . until, that is, the former Irish exciseman Aeneas Coffey developed his patent still, the still that was to play such an important part in the development of blends in the 1840s and which allowed the great Scottish whisky houses to overtake the Irish, who were to continue to use pot stills only, building them larger and larger in an attempt to keep up with the Caledonian competition.

Jack Daniel's unique filtering system gives his whiskey its very special flavour. The new spirit passes through a filter of maple charcoal ten metres deep (centre left).

THE CONTINUOUS PATENT OR COFFEY STILL

The spirit produced by the patent still is grain whisky. The pot still process in Scotland uses only malted barley. The continous still uses mixed grains. It is true

Legend has it that if the ducks no longer peck up the maize spilt around the Jack Daniel's distillery then the maize is not good enough for use in the whiskey (centre right).

that in the late nineteenth century the larger Lowland pot stills also produced spirits, and whiskies, using other grains or a mixture of malted barley and other grains as today in Ireland at Midleton. Cheekily, the Lowland distillers of the pot grain whisky sold it under the generic name of "Irish whiskey". Much of it too was rectified into gin.

What Aeneas Coffey invented and developed was a system of continuous distillation, in which different grains are used. Maize is most commonly used, though wheat and even unmalted barley may be used, depending on prevailing price fluctuations. In all cases, malted barley is also used. As in the preparation of all the North American styles of whiskey, the grain is cooked. This breaks down the cellulose in the walls of the grain and the starch absorbs the water and gelatinizes. In some cases a kind of pressure cooker is used; others use open-to-the-air systems with the introduction of steam. This is not quite as efficient in extracting sugars for fermentation. So some 10 per cent of malted barley is added to this mash to provide the diastase which converts the starch to maltose, sugars, for fermentation. The cooled wort is pumped to washbacks; yeast is added and fermentation begins. A wash is produced. So far, the system is much the same as it would be for the production of malt whisky.

The Coffey still

consists of two copper columns, the analyser and the rectifier, which are divided into chambers by a series of perforated plates. These huge columns are some eleven metres high. Briefly, the process is this. Steam is pumped through the bottom of the analyser and the hot wash is pumped through the top. When steam and wash meet on the perforated plates of the analyser, the wash begins to boil. A mixture of steam and alcohol rises to the top of the column. This mixture of steam and alcohol vapours is run down to the base of the rectifier and then rises up through the chambers of the rectifier. The mixture condenses at different points on the tube through which cold wash is being pumped. (The cold wash is thus heated by the mixture of hot vapours being cooled on the tube through which they, in turn, are being pumped to the analyser: a simple heat-exchange system.) Lower in the rectifier the water condenses and is allowed to fall to the bottom of the rectifier where it is then drained off. The alcohol condenses near the top of the rectifier and is then cooled and taken off to the spirit safe. There is a system for redeploying the first and last parts of the distillate which are redistilled. The alcohol which is produced is between 94° and 94.8° by volume. It is bland and almost tasteless.

But the great advantage of the Coffey still is that it is continuous as long as wash and steam are pumped through. The process does not need to be stopped, as it does in pot still distillation, for the meticulous cleaning between each run. Tradition also plays a small part in the Coffey still. Originally, the armatures binding the columns were of wood. Thus, for easy construction, they were of rectangular section. Today, with the use of metal, this rectangular section is maintained even

though a circular section would be more practical.

Locally, near the grain distilleries, grain whisky would be sold in the pubs, where it was drunk and enjoyed and was by no means considered an inferior product. Scotch grain whisky is a Scotch whisky in its own right, either served as grain whisky or, more normally, used in making blended whisky. Today, Invergordon markets a matured grain whisky.

But a grain distillery has nothing of the romance of the old pot still distilleries. Here we are very much in something of a laboratory, but even if the spirit does gush up under a glass inspection dome in one continuous unending flood, one should not be misled into thinking that the men of the great grain distilleries, such as Cambus, take any less care of their product than the men of Talisker or of Oban. And the spirit is matured with just as much care and attention as any malt whisky.

The time taken to produce the youthful spirit, the infant whisky, according to traditional methods, is: malting – seven to ten days; mashing – eight hours; fermentation – two to three days; distillation – twelve hours. From the cool lofts, with their bags of unmalted barley, and motes dancing in the air, to the heat and fine rosewater or peardrop aromas of the still house with its gleaming copper cauldrons, the making process has taken on average some twelve days. This is just a small beginning – now the long process of maturation begins.

THE MATURING OF WHISKY

What has come out of the still, the pot still or the Coffey still, is spirit: alcohol, but not whisky.

Truly, one of the great glories

The column still invented in 1830 (centre right) allows for a continuous and cheaper distillation, as opposed to that of the pot stills which have to be cleaned after each run. It is used for the production of grain whisky, that essential element in the make-up of blends.

Like wine, whisky is brought to maturity in casks, casks that have already been used either in the United States or Spain. Opposite: casks are rolled out to the former maturing sheds at the Jameson distillery, which was in the heart of Dublin.

The cooperage of Jameson's distillery; the casks are assembled without glue or nails, only the wood itself should be in contact with the young spirit. A good cask should last some thirty-five years and be used three or four times for the maturing of whisky. These days few distilleries keep their own cooperages.

of whisky is that it has spent such a long time in oaken casks in the dark, breathing the surrounding air, maturing, developing flavours, expelling impurities . . . growing up. The legal expert, rubbing his papery hands and blinking behind his bottle-glass spectacles, will tell us quite simply that by law all Irish and Scotch whiskies are matured in casks for a minimum of three years. This is the very minimum. A very minimum – and only a simple legal requirement. The reality is very much more complicated, and longer.

The distiller, proud of his reputation, will keep the whisky longer, or as long as he feels necessary, until it is just right, right and true enough to bear the label of his distillery.

The story goes that an illicit distiller under pressure from the excisemen put his whisky in barrels and hid them in the ground or in some cool cave. Coming to retrieve this whisky some years later when the heat was off him, he dug up the casks and was agreeably surprised to discover

that the whisky tasted smoother, sweeter and gentler.

This most important stage in the manufacture of whisky is seen to be the best way of eliminating those undesirable elements which still remain in the whisky after its distillations. In the cask, the whisky is in contact with air and wood. Chemical and physical changes take place. Fusel

Over the long years of maturation the progress of the whisky is regularly checked. Below left: at Lochnagar near Balmoral Castle. All the art of the distiller is brought to bear to decide when the whisky is at its peak and can be sent for bottling.

oils (*fusel* means "rotgut" in German), aldehydes and other sharply flavoured products, congeners, are modified. Oxidization takes place. Elements are absorbed by the wood; others interact through the catalytic effect of tannins and other compounds. Colour is given to the whisky.

Stewart McBain again: "We really know so little of what actually happens in the cask when whisky matures. Fresh young spirit gathers character, smoothness and subtlety from wood, from the Highland air, from the natural elements – barley, peat, water . . . that gave it birth."

To the men of the sixteenth and seventeenth centuries, barrels were what amphora were to the Romans, or what the tin can was to the housewife of the mid-twentieth century. Quite simply the easiest way of storing things. Barrels were used for transporting grain, eggs, pickled vegetables, fish, salt beef or pork . . . and liquids. By a happy chance, when the canny Scots and Irish wine- and spirit-merchants received sherry from Spain in oak casks, instead of breaking them up, they quite simply re-used the empty casks for their own products. Fino sherries are said to be best for the lighter whiskies and an Oloroso will help mature the deeper, heavier whiskies.

The American whiskeys are aged for a minimum (again a minimum) of four years. Again, by a happy chance, the American oak timber industry together with pressure from trade unions have seen to it that their casks should be used only once. Over there, an early distiller is said to have recovered some casks damaged in a fire and found them to have a special magic in the maturing process. Another tale has it that a

The role of the cask in the ageing process is primordial. It is in the cask that the whisky takes its colour and some of its bouquet. The casks at the Maker's Mark distillery (left) can, by law, be used only once.

cooper came across some casks which had been used for storing fish. He charred them to rid them of their pungent rotting odour. Today Bourbon casks are still charred, giving their product its rich reddish gold colour. Being used only once they provide an excellent source of casks for the the heavier, peaty whiskies of Scotland as well as for the Irish whiskeys.

Scientists have tried to analyse the maturing process. And they have experimented. Faced, often, by a shortage of casks from Spain and the United States, they have tried rejuvenating casks. The insides of sherry casks have been shaved and refilled with sherry. Bourbon casks have been shaved and recharred and treated. All with differing results. Again, in the face of shortages, companies have approached the Bourbon producers, offering them a premium for their casks ensuring that no short cuts are taken such as the manufacture of barrels with thinner staves, which would change the maturing process for Scotch. Sherry casks are bought at source in Spain and rented to the *bodegas* before being sent to Scotland or Ireland. Whisky distillers have even set up their own *bodegas*. Casks are a valuable element in whisky production which the producers do not fully control, though it must be said that with up to three fillings and good handling a good cask can have a working life of as much as forty or fifty years.

Other weird experiments have been undertaken to overcome the dependence on casks from external sources. These include the use of metal casks with inserted oak rods. Logically it sounds as though it could work but, admittedly after a few glasses of Suntory Old, I did ask my Japanese guide whether this experiment was any good. He smiled and I am quite sure there was the slight lilting trace of a Scottish accent in his polite English reply: "No, not at all."

A malt whisky can bear on its label the mention of its age: five years, eight years . . .

fifteen . . . twenty-one and more. *Pace* the producers and the marketing men, this does not mean as much as the buyer may suspect. Age is not necessarily and absolutely a sign of quality. Malt whiskies mature at different stages depending on many factors. A malt may peak twice: at an early point and then later, in a quieter old age.

In Ireland, an Old Comber whiskey, from the now silent distillery, was marketed, when its warehouses were cleared, at the advanced age of thirty years. It had a very distinct musty taste to it – no good at all to anyone. On the other hand, at Laphroaig there is some whisky laid down at the request of an unknown client, most untypically for this very characteristic peaty elixir, in

In the very modern distillery complex at Midleton in Ireland, the casks are untraditionally stacked upright.

140

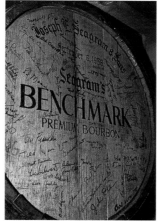

sherry casks, which is over forty years old. Tasting it, I found it astonishing and very fine: a smooth Laphroaig with none of its whisky quality lost. The great house of William Grant & Sons recently opened some fifty-year-old casks of Glenfiddich to the market. It was very, very exceptional, though it must be said that some of its whisky qualities had been lost, albeit becoming a very fine matured old alcohol, much akin to something like a very old rum, cognac or armagnac . . . an excellent mature digestif but with, alas, for me little of the true whisky taste.

Some single malts no longer bear a mention of their age. The great William Grant's Glenfiddich from Dufftown is one such. Its many admirers know that the Glenfiddich label itself is a guarantee of the highest quality whatever the age in the wood. Others such as Justerini & Brooks' marvellous Knockando ("the little black hillock", *Cnoc-an-dhu* in Gaelic) – a smooth, nutty whisky – gives the year of the season of distillation, as well as mentioning the year of bottling on the label. The excellence of the product again speaks for itself, without the need to emblazon an age on its label. The local taste of the buyer may also decide when a malt should be bottled. Though the seaweedish Bowmore malt whiskies are usually bottled at eight, twelve or fifteen years, the Italian youth market prefers a malt of five years with a macho bite at the back of the throat to it. And it is the largest Scotch malt whisky market in the world.

Factors that decide the length of maturation and the taste of the final amber product often result simply from those ever-recurrent "sublime accidents" in the story of making whisky, but two factors are seen as clearly important: the climate and the casks.

On Islay with its fairly constant temperature, nurtured by the Gulf Stream, the casks expand less than they do with the variations of temperature elsewhere. The siting of distillery warehouses near the sea – a boon to early smugglers' ships – indeed helps give these whiskies their "phenolic" flavours. The maturing sheds of Bowmore, some below sea level, form part of the seawall. Laphroaig is lashed by the winter spray. Up in the Highlands the cool damp air aids the maturing process of the whiskies. The somewhat drier climate of Speyside allows the malts to reduce in volume more rapidly.

It is not fanciful, but equally not measurable, to suggest that the ambient atmosphere and air gives to some their seaweedy flavour and to others their hints of honey or heather. As an experiment – and *only* as an experiment it must be clearly stressed – Stewart McBain sent some casks of new spirit from The Glenlivet to be matured in the United States. The end result was quite different from The Glenlivet, naturally matured up in its home glen. Stewart McBain notes, "Only casks matured here ended up as The Glenlivet. In America it began well but in three years the change was quite clear."

Casks of Bourbon ready for bottling at the Ancient Age distillery at Frankfort, Kentucky.

And it must be remembered that Scotch whisky is defined by law – and here it wins over all base imitations concocted near steamy jungles or the Argentinian pampas as "whisky that has been distilled *and* matured (for at least three years) in *Scotland*".

It can be no surprise that casks of strange and unworthy "whisky" types matured in countries with vast swings of climate, such as Taiwan, Bulgaria or even Spain itself, can never have those qualities we expect from the real thing from the north. So, the weather of Scotland, whose intemperate chills and rains gave rise to the need for that little dram to keep off the chill, in turn, plays its part in the final product. The casks themselves are Spanish casks made from Spanish oak. This is more resinous than the American. This, with the sherry effect, creates a quite different whisky from those using Bourbon casks, as do Spanish sherry casks using American oak.

The late Ian Mitchell, when manager of Aberlour, smilingly remarked of his absences in Spain, "People may wonder what a whisky distiller is doing tasting up to forty different sherries but there is a very logical reason behind it all. In purchasing empty casks to mature our spirit, I am looking for certain sherries that will impart a slightly sweet flavour and also help to give the malt whisky its light golden colour."

Whiskies from the same distillery matured in different types of casks can underline this influence. At Knockando I examined whisky from different casks: sherry, Bourbon, new, second fillings, third fillings. The bouquet and the flavours of the whiskies they contained were markedly different. The Scotch Malt Whisky Association will provide whiskies matured in different casks for comparison. The evidence in the tasting is quite clear.

And again tradition plays its part in the maturing process. Conservative as ever, distillery managers will not take off that harsh black fungus – the *champignon ivrogne* – that grows, living off the evaporating alcohol, on warehouse walls. Surely, they hint smiling slowly, it has grown there for a purpose? Another distiller will not clean away the cobwebs from the barrels lest

Rural scene on the banks of the Spey; a partridge perches on a whisky cask (below left). Certain distilleries, like the Glendronach, age their malt in either a mixture of Bourbon and sherry casks or sherry casks alone. The connoisseur can thus compare the effect of the wood on the matured whiskies.

somehow the whisky will be affected. At Aberlour, assistant manager Kenny Fraser plays his bagpipes to the whisky as it slumbers deeply in the half-light, and the great Aberlour malt does have qualities of smoothness in it that cannot be explained away in the laboratory.

As time goes by, as it gently matures, some 18–25% of the whisky is lost every ten years to evaporation into the air as the barrels contract and expand slightly, as the essence of the whisky develops and permeates the wood. This is "the angels' share". It has been estimated that some 90 million litres of whisky evaporate in Scotland every year – in other words some 160 million bottles go up to the angels.

Finally, the size of cask used has an influence on the end product. This is caused by contact with the wood. The most commonly used cask is the hogshead of 250–305 litres. Tom Thompson, manager at United Distillers, reminded me of the days when distillerymen were given a dram a day to encourage them and hearten them in their work, and an old worker would be known as a hoggieman – one who had received up to the equivalent of one full hogshead over a lifetime of devoted service. In some cases, there were gnarled oldtimers who were two-hoggiemen! Today this has ceased and, more prosaically, distillery workers receive a bottle of their own whisky at the end of the month.

Other casks in use are the butt – 500 litres; the American barrel – 173–91 litres; the quarter – 127–59 litres, and the octave – 45–68 litres . . . each with its role to play in creating the final glorious matured water of life.

Sometimes strange things happen which

should never happen. The Campbeltown Distillery of Springbank, for example, finds itself with one thousand bottles of an eighteen-year-old malt. Nothing very surprising, except that the contents of the bottles are green. Not quite what one usually expects. The manager, John Macdougall, explains, "Eighteen years ago someone put the spirit in casks that had been used to store rum. When we opened them we didn't know quite what to expect . . . certainly not that the whisky would be green." Orders are being taken from all over the world for this palatable curiosity, especially from Japan. Neil Clapperton of the malt whisky sellers Caldenhead's in Edinburgh notes, "The whisky is slightly sweeter than most malts . . . but it's a good dram and traditionalists should not be put off by the colour." It is being sold at £55 a bottle.

But then, regardless of the factors and influences on it, the distillery manager will regularly test the progress of the whisky and, whatever its age, when it is just right it will go to be bottled. Nevertheless, it must be remembered that the age on the label will be that of the youngest whisky in the bottle. Neil Gunn says, "To listen to the silence of five thousand casks of whisky in the twilight of the warehouse while the barley seed is being scattered on surrounding fields might make even a poet laureate dumb."

The mysteries remain but the scientists make their tests.

The very learned Dr Lalli Nykanen, head of a Finnish research team, weightily reports his mystification: "It is very difficult to say what the main components of the flavour are. We have found that there are six hundred or eight hundred compounds in whisky but how they are related and affect the flavour is not clear. You smell and taste whisky using your nose and mouth, but combining sensory tests with chemical analysis is very difficult." He adds bravely, "I think that it will be five or ten years before we can say what makes the flavour." A pleasant programme if they stick just to the sensory tests.

Dr John Conner has also been at it at the University of Strathclyde: "You can follow the changes that take place in aroma over time, but pinning down the particular components is very difficult because they all change at the same time." Perhaps some things should, indeed, be left unspoken. But then, perhaps the piper Kenny Fraser has it just right. He raises the glass of his own Aberlour, gives it a long welcoming sniff, smiles, drinks, smiles again and sighs, "A very nice wee dram . . ."

The matured whisky is then taken out for bottling. The malts are used for singles or, combined with the matured grain whisky from the Coffey stills – just as lovingly matured and cared for as the pot still whiskies – taken for the careful, lovingly delicate process of blending.

BLENDING

"Love makes the world go round."

"Rubbish," he cried, "whisky makes it go round but twice as fast."

Compton Mackenzie, *Whisky Galore*.

When Andrew Usher, originally agent for The Glenlivet, first produced his blended whisky using a sharp Highland malt (which was thought to be too heavily characteristic for the London market) together with grain whisky from a Coffey still, he was doing nothing particularly

THE HIGHLAND DISTILLERS

T
150
1963
TAMDHU
GLENLIVET
5 G

new. Malt whiskies which had off-notes, or which had been too long in the cask, had in the past been treated with heather, honey or herbs to make them more acceptable. Such whisky liqueurs as Drambuie are a direct, though very much sweeter, descendant of this process.

Even before this, malt whiskies, and indeed grain whiskies, from pot stills using a mixture of grains, had been "vatted" to create a more regular product – as indeed is the case in Ireland today.

Vatted malts are malts married and recasked. They may come either from one, or from three or four (and in some cases more) distilleries.

With the advent of better transport to England during the Industrial Revolution, with the development of the taste for whisky in the south, and with the increased demand for it after the brandy drought caused by the phylloxera (rightly named) *vastatrix*, the need grew for a constant supply of an unvarying whisky with a standard recognizable taste.

The great Lowland distillers had tried to meet the demand by producing more and more mixed grain whiskies from their huge pot stills but they were still unable to provide the quantities and the regular quality that the southern drinker

demanded. The blenders were able to meet this demand.

There are those who take the cynical view that blending allowed the Scots to sell more by mixing old and new. This may to some extent be true. But again, the test is in the end product. In the end, it is the connoisseur, the drinker of the blend, who gives the final verdict. Lesser blenders have always gone to the wall when their product was deemed to be unsatisfactory and not of a consistent quality. The Pattisons with their squawking parrots were one such. On the other hand it is interesting to note that among the original pioneers of blended whisky, the products of John Dewar, the elegant James Buchanan of Black & White, James Mackay's White Horse, Johnnie Walker and John Haig are not just still on sale today; they are the market leaders. Today, blended whiskies represent some 95% of the whisky market.

There are those – and the number is increasing, as malt is more commonly marketed – who, either from educated taste or from local tradition, or simply from purely élitist snobbery, try to open up the old debate and suggest that only malt is the true whisky, turning up their

The casks at The Glenlivet were once hauled by steam engine (right). Three kinds of cask are generally used: the barrel (180 litres), the hogshead (250 litres) and the butt (500 litres).

With age comes wisdom; the fifteen-year-old Laphroaig, aged in the pure sea air of Islay, is known the world over.

noses at the blended whiskies. However, this attitude does not take into consideration the vast range and glory of the finely blended whiskies. It is not only an error of judgement, but also an error of taste to suggest that blends are an inferior product.

The poet Hugh MacDiarmid writes (perhaps paradoxically for him): "I have little patience with the pseudo-poetical attempts to describe the differences of flavour of the various malts. It was once explained to me by a lover of Laphroaig, an Islay malt that rolls on you like a sea haar: 'Scottish whiskies are like an orchestra. The Islay malts are heavy and sombre as cellos. Highland malts are like violas. Lowland the discursive violin, and grains are like pianos – sometimes *fortissimo*, sometimes *pianissimo*. But such clichés are futile. You can only know any of them by actually drinking them." True . . . and by drinking the blends as well.

And the blends are not one single instrument but whole full concert orchestras, with each instrument playing in harmony with the others. There are lovers of the peaty Islay malt who will drink it at all times, but who would doubt that the heavy cello notes would destroy the savour of a meal were it to be drunk as an aperitif, just as the gentle light Glenmorangie or the Glenfiddich would surely lose something taken after a dinner that was accompanied by a heavy wine?

Briefly, blending is the assembling of thirty or forty or more malt whiskies together with fully matured grain whisky to produce a characteristic product of constant and unvarying quality. Blending is a complex and finely calculated business.

The master blender, using the bouquet recipes for the blend, will test the whiskies and, from this experienced deliberation, will assemble his selection of whiskies, based on the product that he has to provide. The nose of the blender is primordial here.

Patrick Ricard, President of the important Pernod Ricard Group, compares the role of the master blender with that of "the Maître Parfumier . . . but with one great difference, the 'perfume' that the master blender is producing must also be drunk and savoured, and be appreciated as being exactly what the man of taste was expecting".

The White Horse, for example, must be exactly the same as the White Horse produced in the past, with exactly the same undertone of Lagavulin, that neighbour of Laphroaig. The Famous Grouse, as well as preserving other elements which may vary according to availability of supply and maturation, must not let its Orcadian Highland Park flavours become too dominant. It must be the same as previous

Modern blends were developed in the middle of the nineteenth century to encourage exports of Scotch to England; the English found some of the more distinctive malts rather difficult on their palates. Balmoral Castle, where Queen Victoria spent the summer months, symbolizes the region.

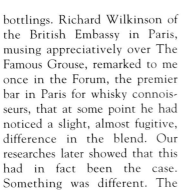

John Walker was not yet called "Johnnie" when the firm was first set up by a former grocer (centre right). In this blend we find the hearty notes of the Cardhu malt, a distillery acquired by the firm in 1893.

bottlings. Richard Wilkinson of the British Embassy in Paris, musing appreciatively over The Famous Grouse, remarked to me once in the Forum, the premier bar in Paris for whisky connoisseurs, that at some point he had noticed a slight, almost fugitive, difference in the blend. Our researches later showed that this had in fact been the case. Something was different. The group ownership of the merry Grouse had changed and the blender had been asked to include malts under the new ownership which he had not hitherto used. The many enthusiasts of this great blend should now hasten to assure the sadly casual drinker of the Grouse that the slight wobble in blending has been rectified and that it is very much a bird that will fly.

As Jim Milne, master blender of Justerini & Brooks, probably the most distinguished and knowledgeable of all master blenders – though his modesty would shy away from such a description, told me earnestly, "Character drift [a change in qualities] strikes true fear in every blender's heart."

The master blender tests the samples from his suppliers, by nose, in charentais-type glasses. The whiskies will, depending on the blender's nose, be reduced with about 50 per cent water. Jim Milne again: "What we are establishing here are the taste and blending qualities of the whisky; we are not at this stage interested in colour." The blender will rarely taste the whisky. Once you have tasted a whisky the flavours linger on in the mouth, and will, of course, react with another whisky tasted subsequently. The nose is the thing.

Very pretentious whisky-tastings, with the "experts" rolling great swigs of whisky in their mouths before spitting it out and then exclaiming fulsomely on the bouquets, aromas and tastes they have encountered, underline the fact that there is in some quarters a great deal of pretentiousness in whisky writing. Besides, my Celtic heart shivers at the thought of actually spitting out whisky!

Samples of whisky will differ with age, availability and market forecasts or fluctuations. I likened blending to making a jigsaw puzzle with the pieces constantly changing shape. "Yes," said Jim Milne, "except that we do know what the final picture should be." The blender will follow whiskies from his own and other distilleries as they age and develop.

When the choice has been made according to the blend's secret recipe, based on a general, and then more specific, description of it, the casks of whiskies chosen will be taken to the blending hall.

Here the casks are emptied into vast troughs

James Buchanan created several blends: the House of Lords blend (left) and the blend in the black bottle with the white label, the world-famous Black & White.

before being pumped into vats where the different whiskies are stirred or agitated with compressed air, to "rouse" the blend. Some blenders, such as Richard Paterson at Whyte & Mackay, prefer to allow the single malts to lie in casks for up to eight months to "marry" the blend . . . in fact, creating a vatted malt. Then they repeat the process, and mix the grain whiskies and the vatted malts before marrying the resulting mixture again in casks for about another year. Some blenders do not opt for this double marriage and perform only one blending process. But either way, at the very least, the blended whisky has now been aged in casks for a further year.

The most sophisticated and pleasing blending process is that of the J. & B. master blender. Jim Milne explains, "If I need to produce a blend for one year hence, I start right now. In December I will marry the Speysides, then I will marry in the Islay and other Highland malts in the following June, in the October I will marry in the grain whiskies, and the blended whisky should be ready for the next New Year celebrations."

De luxe blends, such as Chivas Regal and Johnnie Walker Black Label, are produced using the same processes but with older whiskies. Again where an age is given on the label, this will be the age of the youngest whisky in the blend.

Other attempts towards a more elaborate marrying of whisky have been tried. William Whiteley, the so-called "Dean of Distillers", whose relations with Frank Costello the prohibition bootlegger should be glossed over, remembering the round-the-world East Indies sherry shippers, loaded casks of his King's Ransom blend into sailing ships as ballast, believing that the rolling motion of the ships and the humid sea climate would produce a more perfect marriage. Whether this did indeed produce a smoother whisky blend is open to some serious speculation, but at least he saved a fortune in warehousing costs, as well, no doubt, as providing some surreptitious pleasure to pilfering seamen. Bottles of King's Ransom whisky are today said to contain a drop of the whiskies married in the sailing ships. The marketing boys must really have been burning the midnight oil to work that one out.

In early days the proportion of grain and malt was about fifty–fifty. Today, opinions vary but in a reputable blend the mix will be something like 60 per cent grain to 40 per cent malt, though the great whisky connoisseur and undisputed expert Wallace Milroy suggests that the proportion of grain is slightly higher – two-thirds to one-third. Ill-informed would-be purists, dangerous in their ignorance, try to decry this use of grain whisky from the Coffey still. Again here it must be firmly stated that grain whisky is a whisky in its own right, using malted barley and matured in exactly the same way as spirit from the pot still.

Ageing in casks does not necessarily produce the same colour in the whiskies. Variants in the age, the provenance, the number of times the casks are used, the ambient temperature from year to year, produce whiskies of differing colour. To maintain colour – and again the drinker of a blended whisky will demand that his favourite personal choice not only tastes the same but also looks the same – caramelized sugar, which is tasteless, may be used in infinitesimal quantities in some cases. The would-be purist will yet again cry out in horror,

Black & White, a prestigious collector's item sold at auction by Christie's in Glasgow (centre). A sixty-year-old bottle of The Macallan went for £5,500 to a Japanese buyer.

Whiskies are constantly analysed and tested with the most advanced techniques. At the Glen Ochil laboratory in the Highlands, United Distillers test the effects of casks on the maturing process.

but almost certainly he will not be able to tell which of his chosen blend has had a little harmless colouring added to it and which has not.

However, on being asked why Cutty Sark had such a light colour, Hugh Rudd of Berry Bros and Rudd smilingly retorted, "Why are the other whiskies so dark?" Jim Milne with his own very pale J. & B. Rare strikes the nail solidly on the head, "Colour is not a determinant indication of quality, age or strength . . . only an indication of the amount of caramel used." But we, the drinkers of the blend, like it always to look the same. Inescapably, we cannot get away from the idea that darkness implies age or sweetness in whisky and that a pale whisky implies dryness or youth in a blend. Though chemical analysis of whiskies plays a minor role in the blender's art, what is amazing is that, by his knowledge of the palette of whiskies available to him and his skill in getting the "formula" just right, the master blender is able to arrive at a product that is consistent over the drinking lifetime of aficionados and even further back in time.

On my grandfather's death, going through his

cellar, I came across not only a marvellous selection of, alas, unlabelled single malts – he went on a mini-Barnard's tour of distilleries in the mid-1920s – but also some curiously overlooked wooden cases of Black & White dating from the same period. I made a comparison. Perhaps I detected a slightly higher degree of smoothness in the 1920s Black & White. Whisky does not, of course, mature or change once bottled, and this could have been my romantic imagination playing tricks on me – but the 1920s Black & White was, on detailed and loving comparison with its 1970s descendant, quite unmistakably the same thing . . . the golden nectar of the blender's art, handed down, in this case for over fifty years. And there is no reason to believe that even older forebears had been less diligent in the practice of their skills.

The cases of Black & White have long since been emptied. My imbibing of those single malts, however anonymous, has laid down a taste that goes on still. There should be no war between single malts and blends. In the words of the great whisky connoisseur, Michael Jackson, "There are

Bottling Old Times at the turn of the century in Kentucky (opposite). The bottles shown here are 50 cl but there is a wide range of capacities between the traditional, 65 cl, bottles and 5 cl miniatures.

Bourbon bottling line at the
Old Taylor distillery in
1909 (right). In years gone
by whisky was sold by the
cask; it was only with the
advent of blends that
whisky started to be sold in
bottles.

dullards who will consort exclusively with one or
the other but a palate treated to such monogamy
will eventually be driven to drink. The joy is in
the encounters and the exploration."

BOTTLING

Before bottling, whiskies (blended or single
malts) are reduced to 40° for the home market or
43° for export, by adding water. Only the noble,
light, delicate Glenfiddich in the Highlands, and
the triple distilled Springbank with its slight
sweetness from Campbeltown, are bottled at the
distillery site. All other producers rely on the
vast clanking bottling plants and thus, possibly,
they use ordinary water from the tap – after it has
been filtered and purified – very much as does

the enlightened drinker of whisky at home. Such
is the quality of the end product that this can in
no way spoil it. Again purists and fanatics, who
clamour and debate over what water should be
used to put in their favourite whisky, will pull
faces. Theoretically for them the Islays should
have only peaty water from Islay added; The
Glenlivet water from the Livet – a thought that
when I mentioned it sent a serious Glasgow
school of connoisseurs and drinkers into gales of
laughter, and calls for more drams.

It is to be noted, however, that the Scotch
Malt Whisky Society do sell malts at cask
strength, at about 60°+ per volume. At this point
it is significant to mention that true connoisseurs
of whisky reduce their malts to about 33°. This
allows them greater enjoyment of the bouquet
and flavours. To drink a whisky at 60° per

volume is, to my mind, not only to lose much of the enjoyment of the qualities of the whisky, but also to burn the mouth with the alcohol, so deadening the taste buds. To my amazement, I did once see a very eminent lady publisher in Paris sip at a cask-strength malt in Harry's Bar and declare it perfectly excellent. Perhaps she was confusing pure brute strength with taste?

The blended whisky then is chill-filtered to prevent a slight cloudiness occurring when additional water is added; or it is filtered by passing it through cardboard-type baffles.

In the old days distillerymen would pour boiling water into old casks which had held whisky in them for up to fifty or sixty years, "grogging the cask" to extract the last of the whisky for their own use. In one bottling plant near Glasgow it was discovered that some thirsty workers had evolved a modern equivalent of this. The used-cardboard filtering baffles were disappearing. These had been taken home and put in the spin-driers of their washing machines in the hope of extracting the very last drops of the golden nectar.

Finally, the blended whisky is labelled.

I reach out for a bottle. On the label I read, "J. & B. Rare Blended Scotch Whisky". Over this inscription there is the royal coat-of-arms. Spinning out the pleasure, I read that Justerini and Brooks have enjoyed the happy patronage of George III, George IV, William IV, Victoria, Edward VII (despite his curious fantasies about light French wines), George V and George VI, and also Prince Bernhard of the Netherlands.

I take the green bottle and unscrew the cap. I pour a decent measure into a tumbler. It glows a gentle pale gold, the way whisky should look, the way J. & B., my J. & B., has always looked. I pour in some clear cool water. Swirling the glass a little in my hand, I smell the blend. What orchestra is here? The fine elegant Speysides, singing strings, the more robust Highlands . . . a mellow clarinet perhaps? . . . the hint of the cello in Islays, but just a hint so as not to overwhelm the whole. A complex fragrance. When had I first met it? In a high building overlooking New York on that first visit to the United States. I had been offered a dry Martini. I had made a better choice. I sip.

The fine, soft-tasting whisky warms my mouth, its sweet flavour gently singing a song for all seasons. I swallow and feel the warmth spread down, the long finish echoing away in slow diminuendo. I sip again . . . the same sweet warmth, the same as in Santa Monica, sitting on a balcony watching a humming-bird pierce an exotic flower with its beak, the same as in Cape Town with the rollers dashing against the bright sand, in Stockholm against the fast-fading light, in a slow train passing in the night through the sweltering heat of Rajastan . . . a bar in Berlin, a café terrace in Paris, a noisy private view in London, a bleak hotel room in Moscow, a rain-washed afternoon in Venice overlooking the lagoon . . . a warm book-lined room at home. I raise my glass, "Thank you, Jim Milne."

The bottles of Maker's Mark are sealed with ruby wax (opposite); an old tradition for this Kentucky "whisky", as it styles itself – not "whiskey".

The mahogany Harry's Bar (page 158) sports more than fifty whiskies from the world over for the delight of its clients, who have included Ernest Hemingway, Marlene Dietrich, the young Prince of Wales (Edward VIII) and Brendan Behan.

The bottling line at Maker's Mark (below). This precious liquor is worthy of its nickname, "the Rolls-Royce of Whiskey".

Pure Malt
or Blend?

John Haig stakes its claim to be the oldest distiller in the world (page 159). This family of Norman stock was indeed in the business in the seventeenth century.

To hold a glass of whisky in the hands is to dream. To dream of the long summer's sun on the barley . . . of the fire, the earth and the water. . . of the stills where it was made, conjured up out of the vapours and held . . . in the distilleries high up in the Highlands where the winter winds blow sharp . . . on the isles where the sea beats the whitewashed walls of the maturing sheds in uncontrolled fury . . . in the long green fields of the Lowlands wrapped in gentle morning mists . . . the distilleries where it was made, lovingly, kindly, not to a chemist's formula, but according to the traditions stretching back in time.

To inhale the whisky is to breathe in something of the magic of the place, fugitive hints of meadow grass and herbs, tangs of the sea and the heather, lost echoes of far away honey – again and again all the strange fundamental evocations of earth, fire and water are held in the golden glow of the gentle spirit.

To let the first sip linger on the tongue, in that first tentative kiss of pleasure, is to let all those scents and aromas, hints and subtleties, loose in the mouth and then to let them sing, to echo and expand within . . . to be truly whisky, the genial spirit released from the bottle, released into life.

To swallow the glow is to feel a warmth more than warmth in that water more than water, a warmth to sit back and luxuriate in, marvelling as the flavours ebb, a gently changing will o' the wisp, ebbing to a sweetly fading song falling softly into a night where all is calm and contentment.

To dream of whisky is to dream of pleasure . . . the glow of its gold, its shades and its fire, its smile and its promise, its textures and its quirks.

It is pleasure, it is sensual. There is nothing tightlipped, nothing of the puritan here; it is pure joy.

It is not a pleasure to be rushed at. The bottle

This whisky buff on Islay (left) drinks one of his seven local malts neat but with a glass of water served on the side.

stands there with its promise of warmth, friendship, hospitality. There is a white napkin on the table; the man of taste feels the woven grain of the linen under his finger and places his glass upon it.

THE GLASS FIT FOR THE GLOW

He takes his glass.

Blenders use tulip-shaped or charentais-type glasses for their whisky. They know from long professional experience that these will best form and channel the aromas and flavours. This is what the connoisseur might well use on first meeting a new and rare malt.

Probably best for everyday use, for whiskies that are old friends, is the crystal tumbler-shaped glass. It fits well to the hand, its wide base stands firm and the meditative drinker can take pleasure in the broad generous swirl of the whisky in it. It is a glass for drinking from, and if the more fastidious drinkers of malts prefer their tulip glasses, the tumbler is the undisputed ideal for taking pleasure from the blended whiskies that the man of taste knows so well. The tumbler itself will be of the best crystal, cut with possibly a thistle design – usually a full-lead crystal, which can be recognized by a faintly blackish glow along the pattern. For the timorous who are worried about

There are forty-two whiskies in this glass of their blend served à l'américaine, say J. & B. (opposite). The soft crackling of the ice tells us just why the tag "Scotch on the Rocks" has such a mellifluous sound. As for the British, they prefer to drink their Scotch with a dash of cool, clear water.

Kentucky delights – and pure serenity. An aficionado (opposite) tastes his favourite Bourbon.

the effects of the lead in the glass, there is nothing to suggest that it would not take at least hundred and fifty years of drinking out of good crystal before any noxious effects would be apparent. This, of course, does not take into account the compensatory beneficial effects of whisky, when taken in moderation.

Those who really insist on taking their whisky without water (though I would gently disapprove of this way of missing out on so much of the pleasure of, in particular, malts), might use a small dram glass. (Originally a dram was one-eighth of a fluid ounce before, towards the end of the sixteenth century, coming to mean simply a small measure of spirits.) *In extremis*, wine glasses can be used. The old Highlanders used horn beakers apparently without suffering any ill effects.

WATER AND ICE

For the truly reflective enjoyment and appreciation of whisky, a measure of Scotch should never be the measly London pub single measure – simply enough to cover the bottom of the glass with an all-too-ephemeral hint of the real thing – but rather a whisky tumbler, poured to at least a depth of the width of two fingers. The poet anthropologist James Holden Taylor suggests that three fingers' depth is neither greedy nor necessarily a simple labour-saving device.

The true lover of whiskies will, of course, drink his whiskies as the professionals do – with a little clear water. He wants to taste and enjoy all the flavours and depths of the whisky. Enough clear water to bring the alcohol content down from 40° or 43° to about 35° allows for a releasing of the aromas and volatiles, thus giving a greater pleasure and appreciation of the full whisky experience.

The redoubtable Wallace Milroy does not go

as far as this and suggests that the admixture of water should be, at the most, no more than "the early morning dew on the rose". Jean Biolatto, the reigning expert at Bar le Forum in Paris, opts, in his blends – he is a great aficionado of The Famous Grouse – for a single cube of ice melted in a good measure. When it comes to blends, perhaps their robust orchestras of malts and grain whiskies can support this. In a malt never; this is a pure product of nature and should be drunk at natural room temperature.

Kenny Fraser, the piper of Aberlour distillery, deems that the glass should just be slightly wet before pouring the malt.

The cartoonist Gilles Nicoulaud, no mean connoisseur of fine spirits, follows the old Scottish proverb, "There are two things that a Scotsman likes naked and one of these is malt

The barman is the acknowledged specialist of the water of life; adviser and teacher, he knows how to lead the beginner through the vast choice of blends and malts at his disposal. The Bar le Forum, Paris, is a port of call on many men's personal whisky trail.

whisky." This does, to my mind, smack of a rather macho approach and many of the delicate lingering qualities of the whisky are lost by such uncompromising treatment.

However the whisky is drunk, it will, and should, be sipped and nosed gently.

The great Harry's Bar in Paris serves malt in stemmed funnel-shaped glasses with a glass of water on the side; indeed, as a compromise to the Nicoulaud approach, some Scots do drink their whisky neat with a glass of water to hand. After a sip of the whisky they then take a little water and "shuggle" the resulting mixture in their mouths. Inelegant though it may seem, this certainly does have the effect of releasing the flavours in the mouth and leaving nothing to the air. To drink

malts, and indeed blends, at 40° or 45° or even at cask strength (65°) is simply to run the risk of numbing the mouth and rendering the drinker incapable of tasting what he has in his hand, as well as precipitating intoxication, which is not what we are about at all.

Again, it is a question of taste. But let the would-be connoisseur take note. Pour a little of a newly discovered malt in a tulip glass, swirl it around a little and sniff it deeply. Pause a moment and mull over the scents playing their music in your nostrils, then add some water to the malt and repeat the process, and marvel at the growing bonus of aromas that comes to you. You will be surprised. Knowledgeable Bourbon-drinkers drink their favourite liquor fifty–fifty with water.

The serious whiskey-drinker in Ireland will know that when he calls for a ball of Jameson's or Power's, the barman will place a jug of cooled water next to his order. The jocular John Ryan reminds us of the old Irish saying: "There are two things that a man should not do; borrow a man's wife or water another man's whiskey."

Yet again, as I say, it is a question of taste.

The use of soda water with whisky seems to me an aberration – except in some less-developed countries where it is safer than the fresh water. Perhaps the practice dates back to the time when most bottled waters, concocted in spas claiming a special purity, were fizzy. A little cool clear water in your whisky should be all that is needed.

However, such rules, as all rules, are made to be broken. The head of a distinguished whisky house has been seen slipping a slice of orange into his whisky . . . perhaps he was drinking a blend from a competitor. Many Scots themselves, and here I cannot suppress a slight shudder, drink their whisky with lemonade. These seem to be quite serious adult connoisseurs of the water of

life and, having tried it myself, I must admit that it was not quite as brutal a treatment as it sounds – if you really like the lemonade and are willing to forgo the taste of your blend. Of course, no true connoisseur of sound mind could possibly do this to a single malt.

Opinions are divided among the ill-informed as to the use of decanters for whiskies. Perhaps some of these are a just a little wary of drinking something without the benefit of a label. Moreover, dreary would-be perfectionists claim stridently that the light will harm the precious liquor within. This does not take into consideration two facts. First, that many distilleries have their malts, and their blends, bottled in clear glass. Secondly, that to spurn decanters is to

deprive the connoisseur of that rare sensual pleasure of sitting back and admiring the diverse shades of gold of the malts as they gleam from the myriad facets of the cut-crystal glass.

Perhaps I am biased because my malts never stand long enough in the decanter to be spoilt by bright light. I always have ten or so of my favourite malts in decanters in my library. On the silver tray, their colours smile out to me against the books along the walls . . . the Highland Park, solemn, dark, almost red; the delicate Glenfiddich tossing its blondish locks; the Knockando, pale gold from the hills; the flowery Aberlour with its amber tones; the elegant Auchentoshan pale – almost colourless – coy about its deep flavours; the Balvenie, mellow deep gold with hints of red; The Glenlivet, the pale gold of an old and cherished ring; the Laphroaig, like a cello,

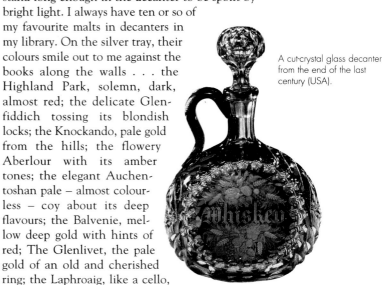

A cut-crystal glass decanter from the end of the last century (USA).

Michael Jackson, the great connoisseur, affirms: "There are always timid souls who simply fix on one whisky, and leave aside the joys of chance meetings and discovery." The different tones of a Glenfiddich, an Auchentoshan, a Macallan, a Talisker and a Laphroaig shine out, hinting at the bouquet and tastes to come.

dark wood brown; the bronze of Glenfarclas, shining pagoda bright; the Edradour with its muted gold born in the ice and snows; the Bunnahabhain, the colour of melted toffee in autumn sun; the Laphroaig pale amber from the sea; the Linkwood, an old and rare friend, dark and sherry red warm. They make my choice difficult but I know that they will wait for me.

A jug of water at hand, glasses at the ready, the connoisseur reaches out to the whiskies before him.

THE SHINING SINGLE MALTS OF SCOTLAND

The connoisseur of single malt has seven glasses set before him. In one he puts a little of his regular blend with a little water to bring out the flavours. Gently he inhales the familiar aroma. He does not proceed scientifically, but in a logical well-measured order, an order imposed to enhance and bring out the pleasures before him. In one watered glass he puts a little Auchentoshan from the long rolling farmlands of the Lowlands. In another he pours some Glenfiddich from the Upper Spey. In yet another the Edradour from high up in the Grampian Mountains,

on the harsh pass between Perth and Inverness, a desolate place with a heart-warming welcome. Into the fifth glass he pours some Oban, Oban with its tiny harbour high up on the west coast. Then, in the sixth, some Talisker from the Isle of Skye, Skye dominated by Dunvegan Castle and the songs of Bonnie Prince Charlie. In the last glass, he pours the Laphroaig, Laphroaig and Islay, home of the smoky waters of life.

The man of taste looks at the subtly different colours, each teasingly hinting at further pleasures: the Auchentoshan, pale gold, almost yellow; the Glenfiddich, pale with a gleam of a deeper gold; the Edradour, slightly different, a paler gold; the Oban, alive with a gold tinged with red, an amber from the sea; the Talisker, amber itself; and the Laphroaig, of all the Islays the deepest cello brown. They are jewels and the connoisseur lets his eyes play on the shades and brightness with all the loving attention of a jeweller peering into the mellowness of an opal or at the fire struck from a diamond.

He inhales a little of his favourite blend again and then takes up the pale dry Auchentoshan. Swirling the glass slightly and warming it, he takes in the light delicate nose, the slight grassy sweetness, a clean aroma. He pauses and then

"Being moderately taken, it [whisky] lighteneth the mynd, it cureth the hydropsie, it puffeth away ventosite. . . and truly it is a sovereign liquor. . . if it be orderlie taken. . . " wrote Holinshed in the sixteenth century. Bars, high places of true conviviality, are the ideal place to put his delectable theory to the test.

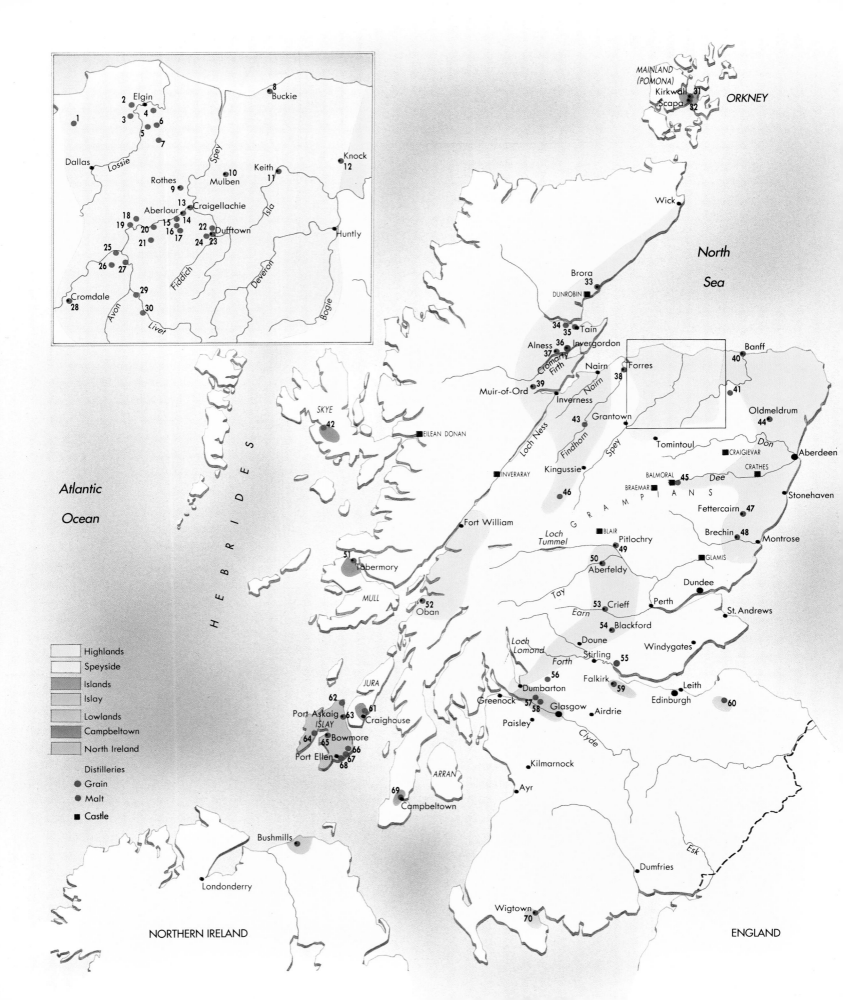

Inset map (top left):

Buckie 8
Elgin 2
4
3 5 6
1 7
Dallas
Lossie
Spey
Knock 12
Rothes 9
Keith 11
Mulben 10
Aberlour 13 Craigellachie
18 15 14
19 20 16 22 Dufftown
21 17 24 23
25
26 27
Cromdale 29
28 30
Avon
Livet
Fiddich
Deveron
Bogie
Isla
Huntly

Main map:

MAINLAND (POMONA)
Kirkwall 31
Scapa 32
ORKNEY

North Sea

Wick

Brora 33
DUNROBIN

Banff 40
41

34 35 Tain
Alness 36 Invergordon
37
Cromarty Firth
Nairn
Forres 38
Oldmeldrum 44

Muir-of-Ord 39
Inverness
Nairn
Grantown
CRAIGIEVAR
Aberdeen

SKYE
42
EILEAN DONAN

Loch Ness
43
Findhorn
Spey
Tomintoul
BALMORAL 45
Dee
CRATHES
Stonehaven

Atlantic
Ocean

HEBRIDES

INVERARAY
Kingussie
46
BRAEMAR
Fettercairn 47

GRAMPIANS

Fort William
Loch Tummel
BLAIR
Pitlochry 49
GLAMIS
Brechin 48
Montrose

51
Tabermory
MULL

50
Aberfeldy
Tay
Dundee

52
Oban

Earn
53 Crieff
Perth
St. Andrews

54 Blackford
Doune
Windygates

Loch Lomond
Stirling
Forth
55
Falkirk
Leith
59
Edinburgh
60

JURA
62
61
Port Askaig 63
ISLAY Craighouse
64 65 Bowmore
66
Port Ellen 67
68

56
Dumbarton
57 58 Glasgow
Greenock
Paisley
Airdrie
Clyde

Kilmarnock
ARRAN
69
Campbeltown
Ayr

Esk

Dumfries

Wigtown
70

Bushmills
Londonderry
NORTHERN IRELAND

ENGLAND

Legend:

Highlands
Speyside
Islands
Islay
Lowlands
Campbeltown
North Ireland

Distilleries
● Grain
● Malt
■ Castle

takes the Glenfiddich, fragrant with flowery hints from the grasses. Is that an elusive hint of smoke?

Perhaps refreshing the nose with his blend, he gently holds the glass of the Edradour in his cupped hands and breathes in deeply . . . a hint of the peat again, light not overpowering, a touch of the heather as if brought by the breeze. Then the Oban, betraying its seaside home, giving him, too, a whiff of the malt, a touch of the smoke. Then the Talisker, with the sea coming through more strongly. And then the malt with the peat and the smoke suddenly easing through. Then the last, the dark Laphroaig, dominating, blasting through with all those Islay qualities . . . robust, dry, peaty, the sea roaring, throwing the seaweed high on the craggy rocks, belying the sweetness.

Then he will want to taste and sip, to feel the texture of the body on his tongue, to feel and taste the flavours developing in his mouth and to linger on the follow-through, that rising note, the widening ripples of sensation spreading out further and further. An echo of the song. But then the tastes and aromas will become too

complex, mingling, adding to one another, finally blasted out by the richness and power of the Laphroaig.

He will take them up again another day, one at a time. He will start with the Auchentoshan from the Lowlands and learn to know its balanced, rounded body, its fresh taste giving out hints of herbs, and its long finish full of gingery tangs and spices.

The next day it may be the Edradour with its the heather-honeyed start, soft and gentle, leading to notes of malt and summer grasses fading, long and sweet. The last, late at night, will be the Laphroaig, before a dying fire, with a rough-haired dog slumbering at his knee; Laphroaig, the long bass trumpet call of the peat, the smoke, the sea and, under it all, a fine round sweetness fading long in the flickering embers.

The single malts . . . a positive palette of whiskies, diverse, changing and different. The pragmatist will know that the malt whiskies are divided into four regions, which have much to do with old regulations and taxation systems. The connoisseur will know that each of these regions has malts whose qualities and savours are proper

The whisky-producing regions of Scotland: The Highlands, Lowlands, Islay and Cambeltown. Part of the Highlands, the Speyside, with its many distilleries is featured in the insert, as are the islands: Jura, Mull, Skye, and the Mainland Orkneys. A red dot indicates a distillery mentioned in the text. Glenburgie-Glenlivet (1), Glen Moray-Glenlivet (2), Miltonduff-Glenlivet (3), Linkwood (4), Glenlossie (5), Benriach, Longmorn (6), Glen Elgin (7), Inchgower (8), Caperdonich, Glen Grant, Glen Spey, Speyburn (9),

Auchroisk, Aultmore (10), Glen Keith, Strathisla (11), Knockdhu (12), Craigellachie (13), The Macallan (14), Aberlour-Glenlivet (15), Glenallachie (16), Benrinnes (17), Cardhu (18), Knockando, Tamdhu (19), Dailuaine (20), Glenfarclas (21), Balvenie, Glenfiddich (22), Convalmore, Glendullan, Mortlach (23), Dufftown-Glenlivet, Pittyvaich-Glenlivet (24), Cragganmore (25), Tormore (26), Tomintoul-Glenlivet (27), Balmenach (28),

The Glenlivet (29), Tamnavulin-Glenlivet (30), Highland Park (31), Scapa (32), Clynelish (33), Balblair (34), Glenmorangie (35), Invergordon (36), Dalmore (37), Dallas Dhu (38), Ord (39), Macduff (40), Glendronach (41), Talisker (42), Tomatin (43), Glen Garioch (44), Lochnagar (45), Dalwhinnie (46), Fettercairn (47), Glencadam (48), Blair Athol, Edradour (49),

Aberfeldy (50), Tobermory (51), Oban (52), The Glenturret (53), Tullibardine (54), Cambus (55), Glengoyne (56), Little Mill (57), Auchentoshan (58), Rosebank (59), Glenkinchie (60), Isle of Jura (61), Bunnahabhain)62), Caol Ila (63), Bruichladdich (64), Bowmore (65), Ardbeg (66), Lagavulin (67), Laphroaig (68), Glen Scotia, Springbank, (69), Bladnoch (70).

Highland cattle, renowned for their meat, are fed on the draff from the wort (below).

The Isle of Skye dominated by the Cuillin Hills; hints of the sea are caught up and married in the gingery malt from the island's only distillery, Talisker, buffeted by the west winds. This malt forms a part of two interesting local whiskies, Te Bheag, a blend, and Poit Dhu, a vatted malt.

to it and to the climate that nurtured them.

The Lowlands: south of a line drawn from Dundee in the east to Greenock in the west. These malts reflect the rolling farmlands they come from. Some find them bland, many find them elusive and elegant, slow to open up their secrets.

The Highlands: rugged country with soft sparkling streams, a warm-hearted robust people, and a warm-hearted robust malt, giving a varied range of sensations from the coy to the hearty; perhaps spicy to the north; in the south, with a fruitiness and, at the heart of the Highlands, that truly golden triangle of the **Speyside**, an accepted subdivision of the region with its deliciously elegant and delicately complex malts. The Highlands include all the isles except for Islay. The words "and Islands" are sometimes added to the appellation "Highlands" without this being an accepted subdivision – more simply a geographical annotation.

The Campbeltown: on the Mull of Kintyre, the peninsula to the south-west of Scotland. An area in decline with many distilleries closed. The

remaining malts – Glen Scotia and Springbank – are fine, smoky, and full-bodied with a hint of the sea in their sweetnesss.

And then **the Islays**, from that island which is peat, the peat of the maltings, the iodine tang hiding their sweet nakedness nurtured in the mists coming off the sea.

In preparing this book I tasted some four hundred different whiskies: blends – standards and de luxe; vatted malts – that is to say assemblages of malts without the addition of grain whisky; grain whiskies; single malts from Scot-

Strathisla distillery (below left) was formerly a brewery set up by the monks in the thirteenth century. This malt is at the heart of Chivas Regal.

land and Japan – some hundred and twenty of these; Bourbons, Tennessee sour mash whiskeys and Canadian and American ryes – as well as whisky, or shadowy "whisky-types", from origins as diverse as Spain, New Zealand, the Argentine, Taiwan, Bulgaria, and – the only ones of this last group that should concern the true whisky-lover – Japan.

I first began drinking whisky some thirty years ago, allowing myself to enjoy and to contemplate and to compare the blends and their de-luxe brothers, learning something of their secrets and the malts that go into these blends. Travels abroad allowed me to note the qualities maintained by their careful blending, and introduced me to a few not uncreditable local makes. And I quickly learnt, as the connoisseur will have, the pleasures of, say, a Famous Grouse on a northern cold winter's day and the cool calm pleasure of J. & B. Rare in the southern summer, this followed by the equally happy realization that the one is just as kindly in the south as the other is in north.

The glorious development of the availability and sales of malts, single and vatted, opened a yet wider spectrum of sensations to me. When asked, as whisky buffs are, "What is your favourite malt?" I was soon in the happy position saying, "It depends when. After a brisk cold walk in the country? Lingering at home in front of the fire on an autumn afternoon? Before, during or after dinner? As the last mellow malt when the ashes slip in the fire towards dawn?" And, as I pondered this, I was happy when friends brought out their favourite malts to comment, compare and, above all, enjoy in laughing good fellowship.

Malts are many. They are complex, different, fine. Among a selection of the most readily available of my favourite single malts, the connoisseur will find his own favourites as well as discover new friends, to be drunk as aperitifs, good all-rounders or meditative after-dinner drams.

ABERLOUR (Highlands – Speyside). Amber-coloured with hints of red, from sherry casks. A rich nose with hints of mint and sweetness, a fullish body, a taste to match, with notes of the sherry, spices and an underlying sweetness, with a lingering smooth follow-through. An after-dinner dram, or even a strongish-tasting aperitif before well-seasoned food.

AUCHENTOSHAN (Lowlands). Pale, pale colour, coyly belying its later taste sensations. A delicate, sweetish nose, with a faint note of

Fine copper water jugs at Rosebank distillery in the Lowlands (left). Before bottling, water is used to reduce alcohol content. Whisky is rarely sold, or drunk, at cask strength.

citrus, which is reinforced in the taste. Rather soft body; the taste develops in sweetness, and the follow-through is well defined and fresh. A really excellent aperitif.

BALVENIE (Highlands – Speyside). Mellow deep gold from sherry wood. Deep pronounced aroma, rich with honey notes and some orange peel. The flavour is sweetish but twisting into a certain dryness, giving way to a long sweetish aftertaste. Almost certainly among the best after-dinner drams. Impossible to beat. Pure delight.

BLADNOCH (Lowlands). Pale, pale primrose. Elegantly light nose with some grass at the start. Lightish body. The taste is delicate at first and then expands to a surprising fullness, verging on the voluptuous. The follow-through twists back to the grassiness with some hints of lemon, and lingers on quietly. A premium aperitif.

BOWMORE and BOWMORE Distillery. 1849.   Ralph Steadman ¹⁄₁

BOWMORE (Islay). Golden. The nose is not so peaty for an Islay with underlying fresh herbs and grasses, together with some sweetness and smoke. The body is lightish; the taste brings out some heatheriness, vague hints of the salt, which develop, giving way to sweetness. The follow-through is warming, and drops away rather quickly. A very good after-dinner dram.

BRUICHLADDICH (Islay). Palish gold. Sea-weed, mild peat and smoke on the nose. The peatiness in the taste is elegant and almost refined and there is a crispness to it that develops into a rounded sweetness. The follow-through is full without heaviness. For an Islay it is a good aperitif but could be used after dinner, by those who find *all* Islays too heavy.

BUNNAHABHAIN (Islay). Gold. The nose is delicate and not overpowering in its notes of smoke and peat and seaweed. Rather fresh. The lightish body yields to a round sweetness with almost a walnutty edge. A good after-dinner dram.

CAOL ILA (Islay). Very, very pale. The light nose has the characteristic hints of peat and seaweed, but also pleasant tones of sweetness. The body is firm. The typical Islay flavours are overlaid with a spicy, perhaps even peppery flavour, while remaining light. The pepper develops in the warming follow-through. A fine after-dinner dram beside the fire.

CARDHU (Highlands – Speyside). Pale gold in colour. Nose, slightly smoky with a rich touch of sweetness. The smooth body paves the way to a smooth, mellow malty sweetness of taste, which gives a long well-developed finish. An almost perfect after-dinner dram.

CRAGGANMORE (Highlands – Speyside). Pale to light golden. The lightly aromatic nose is fragrant with notes of sweet grass, and hints of

malt and then herbs. The body is lightish but very smooth. The taste starts sweetly enough with some malty smokiness and then develops elegantly into a dryness overlaid gently by the malt and a flowery grassiness. The finish is long, broad and warm. A very good, top-level, after-dinner dram.

Edradour (near right) is Scotland's smallest distillery, and its still is the smallest legally allowed, for fear that it may be carted away and used for some illicit distilling. The distillery is run by three men and it uses only oloroso sherry casks (below right).

DALMORE (Highlands). Amber gold from the sherry casks. An assertive nose, rich with fruit and a sweetness of malt. A full body. The taste ventures out in a rather restrained way developing heathery smokiness and then the

tang of bitter oranges becoming drier in the follow-through. An excellent after-dinner malt.

DALWHINNIE (Highlands – Speyside: many people would not regard this as a Speyside). Palish gold. The nose is light and aromatic with gentle touches of peat. The body is firm with almost a slight, pleasant oiliness to it. The taste strikes out with heather honey fading into subtle hints of grassland and malt, with a long, long finish, sparkling with hints of sweetness. A very good all-rounder and a truly perfect aperitif.

EDRADOUR (Highlands). Fine gold. The nose is full of the sweetness of fruit and the malt, with hints of mint. The creamy smooth body flirts a little with dryness to give clean-tasting creamy maltiness, with a warm, mellow follow-through. A very good all-rounder and possibly an aperitif.

GLEN DEVERON (Highlands). Full gold. A pleasant bouquet with sherry notes, and hints of appetizing malt. A smooth, lightish body with a full taste of the malt, finishing clean and drily malty. A fine after-dinner drink.

NEW GLENDRONACH TRADITIONAL (Highlands). Gold from the sherry casks. The nose has

a hint of sherry, some dryness, overlaid by malt. The body is fullish. The taste definitely on the sweet side, with almost fugitive touches of caramel, which give way to a long, delicate dryness. A first-class after-dinner dram.

GLENDULLAN (Highlands – Speyside). Deep reddish gold from sherry casks. The nose takes on the sherry and develops hints of fruit and touches of flowers. The body is fairly full. The dry start to the taste, full of malt, moves on with mellow fruitiness and the follow-through is assertive and long. A good robust after-dinner dram.

GLENFARCLAS (Highlands – Speyside). Deep bronze. A straightforward rather sweet nose, strong in sherry. The body is very full. The taste is sweet and without any complexes after a surprisingly dryish start with some smoke. The follow-through is long with slowly fading hints of fruitcake. A really good, rich after-dinner dram.

GLENFIDDICH (Highlands – Speyside). A very, very pale gold. The nose has just a hint of peat, a whisper of smoke, a touch of pearlike sweetness. The body is light. The taste starts drily, and then allows the elegantly balanced fruitiness to come through. This develops aro-

The imposing architecture of the Bowmore distillery (pages 174–5), the oldest distillery on Islay (1779). The maturing process takes place below sea level.

matically with just a little smokiness and a murmur of the malt, leading to a well-measured, gentle sweetness. The absolutely perfect restrained aperitif. The world-beater.

Whisky can, sometimes, be compared to wine, to better understand its complexities. *Cépages, châteaux* and *crus* are not in the vocabulary, but Jean Biolatto of Bar le Forum, Paris (right), knows exactly how to equate wine and whisky, be it a blend, a vatted malt or a single malt.

GLEN GARIOCH (Highlands). Golden colour. Mildly peaty and smoky to the nose, a firm body and sweetish, raisiny flavour with a long, malty finish. A good after-dinner dram.

GLENGOYNE (Highlands). Pale, pale gold. Almost a Lowland malt, some hints of sherry casks, but light and soft in the nose, giving a clean, slightly sweet taste, with a pleasant follow-through that fades into dryness. A neat aperitif.

GLENKINCHIE (Lowlands). Pale gold, almost yellow. A dry, slightly smoky nose with hints of sweetness and grass. A medium body with a fresh taste with accentuated herbal notes giving way to an amazing finish full of spices with hints of ginger dominating. Personally, I enjoy it very much as an aperitif, and as a good all-rounder.

THE GLENLIVET (Highlands – Speyside). Fine pale gold. The bouquet is delicately flowery, the body medium light with a remarkable flavour full of peaches and custard. After the flowery start, a delicate path between dryness and

Speyside's Glenfarclas distillery (left) draws its pure water from the streams of the celebrated Ben Rinnes. Founded in 1836, it has been rebuilt and its stills are among the largest in the region.

sweetness with a long, gentle finish. A really excellent dram among excellent drams and a good all-rounder.

GLENMORANGIE (Highlands). Light gold. A very fine aroma of spices, subtly hinted peat and flowery sweetness. The lightish body gives way to an elegant, spicy, malty taste with a long, rounded finish. An aperitif and good all-rounder.

GLEN MORAY (Highlands – Speyside). Almost colourless, very, very pale gold. The nose is elegantly light and fresh with notes of cut grass and wheat, the body light but firm, a full, malty taste and a clean, grainy finish. An aperitif.

GLENTURRET (Highlands). Pale. Impressive nose of dryish sherry becoming sweeter and flowery on acquaintance, light, malty, sweet taste with a good, long follow-through. A very good all-rounder.

GLENUGIE (Highlands). Shining gold. The nose is heavy with autumnal fruit. After some sweetness in the start the taste becomes drier, almost austere, with a long, dry finish. Aperitif.

HIGHLAND PARK (Highlands – Islands). Dark gold, almost red. A rich, sweetish nose with heather hints, a medium body smoky with dryness giving way to a sweetness of honey and malt that fades in the finish to a long dryness. A really first-class after-dinner dram.

ISLE OF JURA (Highlands – The Islands). Light golden. A light, dryish nose with just a hint of the peat and some slight maltiness. The light body gives an almost pearlike vanilla taste of some dryness with a long follow-through of salty dryness. Aperitif.

KNOCKANDO (Highlands – Speyside). Pale gold. Dry nose with hints of smoke fragrant with touches of ginger. The body is very smooth and light. There are tastes of flowers and nuts and some sweetness with playful touches of mint.

The long, pleasing finish has a clean sweetness with murmurs of smoke. An excellent dram, a great old favourite – I consider it to be a good all-rounder, but perhaps to the newcomer it should be kept as an after-dinner dram.

LAGAVULIN (Islay). Cello golden brown. The nose may knock the head off with its heavy peat, dry seaweediness and, somewhere under all that, some sherry. The robust, round body leads to everything you expect from the nose, but once you settle down to it there is some sweetness. The follow-through is dry and seasidey and blares

The Braes of Glenlivet distillery (left, above) dates from 1973. Its elegant buildings, roofed in blue slate, house a completely automated distilling plant.

The small Glenmorangie ("The valley of tranquillity") distillery (left, below) is run by a reduced but faithful team who have followed on from generation to generation.

The Speyside distillery of Knockando (left) was set up in 1898, but the far-sighted owners secured the water rights eight years earlier.

For the real purist, Fionnar Water from the Highlands (below) is the perfect accompaniment to a lusty malt.

on, gently fading. Unless you become hooked, when you will want to drink it as an all-rounder, this is very much a post-post-after-dinner dram.

LAPHROAIG (Islay). Light amber. Peaty, smoky nose, lighter in intensity than its neighbour Lagavulin, with a touch more sweetness. Medium body. The taste is definitely on the seaweedy side, with hints of sweetness, vanilla-ish and flowery, which fade tantalizingly to give a long, dry finish. Late-night dram.

THE MACALLAN (Highlands – Speyside). Amber from the oloroso casks. Sherry in the light nose and a surprisingly full body. The taste is sherryish and rather elegantly dry and then twists to a malty sweetness. The follow-through passes slowly from the sweet to an almost smoky, gingery dryness. A complex and elegant malt that should be drunk as a first-class all-rounder.

MORTLACH (Highlands – Speyside). Pale reddish gold. A good, well-rounded aroma of malty smokiness. The rich body leads to the development of the malt and smoke with a charmingly sweet fruitiness. The follow-through is long with hints of the sherry wood coming through. A first-class after-dinner dram.

OBAN (Highlands). Reddish gold to amber. Sweet, spicy nose, with hints of peat and a little malt. The smooth body underlies a smooth, smoky maltiness with little touches of sweetness leading to a more predominant smoke flavour and then a pleasing, smooth sweetness in the follow-through. A perfectly first-class all-rounder.

SPRINGBANK (Campbeltown). Medium gold. Nose a touch salty to start with, then developing a slight sweetness. Smooth, light body. The first impression of the taste is of sweetness, which then quickly becomes more and more inclined towards a neat and elegant saltiness reminiscent of the neighbouring Islays. This is continued away into the long, long warming finish. An excellent after-dinner dram.

TALISKER (Highlands – The Islands). Amber. A sweet, heavy nose with island characteristics of peat smoke and sea. Medium-bodied. Very malty and sweetish to start with, then developing an austerity that slips back to some sweetness leading to a long, lingering, warm finish with pepper and sweetness overlaid. Fantastic, an almost perfect digestif.

TAMDHU (Highlands – Speyside). Lightish amber to gold from the sherry casks. Light, sweetish nose. Medium body giving a caramel-ish sweetness with definite notes of malt, developing into some peaty dryness, which becomes sweeter in the follow-through. A good after-dinner dram.

TOBERMORY (sometimes known as LEDAIG) (Highlands – The Islands). Clear gold. A peaty nose, with definite hints of smoke and some sweetness. Medium body. Hints of dryness, peat and then hints of fruit in the taste, the finish is light, full of aroma and with a slight, curling uplift of sweetness at the dying. All-rounder or after-dinner dram.

TOMINTOUL (Highlands – Speyside). Gold. The nose is delicately light with hints of grass. The light body leads to a sweetish taste of the barley with a long and gently vivacious finish. All-rounder, perhaps aperitif.

TORMORE (Highlands – Speyside). Deepish gold. Slightly smoky nose, dry, almost with hints of toast. Medium body with a balanced mix of smoke and sweetness in the taste, with the sweetness slightly taking over, and a long, rippling follow-through. An after-dinner dram.

The great United Distillers Group, with almost thirty distilleries producing malt whisky, markets a pack of miniatures of their very sound selection, Six Classic Malts. This is a quite admirable introduction to single malts – the regions, the bouquets and the flavours.

The malts that have been carefully selected from the many are: Glenkinchie (Lowlands), Cragganmore (Highlands – Speyside), Dalwhinnie (Highlands), Oban (Highlands), Talisker (Highlands – The Islands) and Lagavulin (Islay).

SINGLE GRAIN WHISKY

Perhaps, these days, something of a curiosity. Matured or even unmatured grain whisky used to be sold in the pubs around the great grain distil-

Tobermory's picturesque harbour on the Isle of Mull (left). It is still possible to taste the whisky from the distillery which is, alas, now idle.

leries where it was much appreciated by the habitués. Grain whisky is, of course, normally used for the assembling of blends and is rarely commercialized. Thus, the Invergordon is the only one (at the time of writing) on sale to the general public.

INVERGORDON SINGLE GRAIN WHISKY (Highlands, though this is not truly meaningful – it is a grain whisky). Very light in colour with a ghost of greenish gold to it. Nose sharp, astringent, with a faint hint of oiliness. Body very light with an astringent front of tongue confirmed by the follow-through. Pre-dinner drink or to accompany very strongly smoked fish or rich food. Perhaps could be used in some cocktails to replace gin. Described in an unseen tasting as a "goodish matured vodka" by the Polish cartoonist Wozniak.

THE SCOTCH BLENDS . . .
AMONG THE BEST . . .

For everyday use, at any time of the day, as opposed to some of the more characteristic malts, blended whisky, as many discovered in London towards the end of the nineteenth century, is the means of enjoying a guaranteed unchanging taste and pleasure, drunk either "on the rocks", as a long drink with water, or, if one must, neat. Blended whisky is made from a marriage of matured single malts and matured grain whisky from column stills. The devotee of whisky who has not finally settled on his own favourite, or who would like to dally with new sensations, might well like to try any of the following good old standards. (The majority of blends are prepared in the area between Glasgow and Edinburgh and a note on the region is not appropriate.)

BALLANTINE'S. Despite its high market position, this fine blend has suffered unfairly in that it was the most readily available blend on the Continent in the immediate post-war years. Drinkers of whisky tended rather to abandon it in search of other taste sensations when other blends started to come on the market. Delicately peaty with touches of Islay and some dryness from the Highlands.

BELL'S. Slightly peaty with sweetish hints giving way to a dry finish.

BLACK & WHITE. An elegant blend with a light dry smoothness. One of my great favourites.

CLAN CAMPBELL. A very well-rounded blend with pleasurable hints of the delightfully smooth and well-aroma-ed Aberlour malt. A relative newcomer, it is probably among my most favoured blends. The Clan Campbell is the largest and one of the most renowned clans, under its chief, the Duke of Argyll.

CUTTY SARK. This light-coloured, soft whisky, with its elegant overtones of fruitiness with pleasant hints of the malt, was much exported to the Caribbean during Prohibition, which allowed it to establish an early foothold in the United States after 1933.

DEWAR'S. A fresh and well-balanced, medium-bodied blend.

Reconciliation between England and Scotland? Bell's – a market leader in England – uses *trompe-l'oeil* to symbolize the essence of Scotland (far right).

WHYTE & MACKAY. Married twice, the malts first "vatted" before being married a second time with the grain whiskies, it has a delicately complex taste for a blended whisky and a pleasant, lingering aroma.

THE "DE-LUXE" BLENDS AND MALTS OF GREAT AGE

Although marketing managers and some self-appointed pundits will shake their fists and fall to the floor and gnaw the carpet, I have noticed very little real added pleasure in tasting and drinking the de-luxe blends. Indeed many of the tests carried out by panels of well-experienced tasters tend to under-line the fact that there seems to be not much, if any, discernible difference between the de luxe and the standards. Moreover, what is said to be "de luxe" varies from producer to producer. Clearly the proportion of old whiskies is higher in the de luxe as is the malt content. But is it worth it? Given the current availability of more and more single malts, the amateur would perhaps do better to buy these than to travel along the path of de-luxe blends where the added taste sensation is not necessarily so rewarding in terms of quality and price.

It is true that the very old de-luxe blends may have a much greater roundness, but with very old single malts I feel that this

THE FAMOUS GROUSE. For me the bird that really does fly. In the way of things, many lovers of this well-rounded, soft, velvety blend, which admittedly has a fairly low malt content, seem to have noticed a dropping off in consistency some time ago. Things have got back together, and old friends should definitely try again. A very great favourite.

HAIG. Light and very consistent.

J. & B. Light, it has a good nose and a pleasant, lingering sweetness. The blending process is probably the most elaborate and sophisticated of all and it never disappoints.

JOHNNIE WALKER RED LABEL. With a well-stated aroma, perhaps from its Talisker malt, and its hints of Cardhu, it is a refreshing blend that adapts well for use as a long drink.

LONG JOHN. A standard blend; smooth, dark with strong hints of the Islays.

TEACHER'S. A sweet, malty blend. Best with a little water to appreciate fully its relatively high malt content.

WHITE HORSE. The one you can take anywhere; smooth and quite heavy on the peat for a standard blend. Dark-coloured, it includes Islays from the Lagavulin distillery.

much greater age loses in whisky characteristics what it gains in "brandy-ness" and smoothness. Again, old singles can very often be quite marvellous, if they have not been allowed to go over their peak, but would the casual, albeit educated, taster, faced with a very old cognac, a very old rum or an armagnac, and one of these venerable whiskies, really be able to discern all the flavours and aromas he could in a younger bottling? I would make an exception for the Clan Campbell twelve-year-old de-luxe. Perhaps because I like the standard blend so much, I did find a deliciously deeper smoothness to its elder brother, together with a more rounded kiss of the malt. Partisans of other blends may well find this true of their great favourites. I have not found it so.

The only other exception I would make in de-luxe blends is the Chivas Regal, which pioneered, to some extent, the sale of de-luxe

blends in Europe. Gently sweet with a hint of the wood to it and a touch of mellow smokiness, this malt has at its heart the marvellous, fruity yet rather dry Speyside Strathisla malt. A really elegant after-dinner dram, this malt is almost unobtainable.

At a recent visit to the Strathisla distillery I was suitably drammed with their eight-year-old, their amazing twelve-year-old and their soothing fifteen-year-old, but I found it impossible to buy one of their bottles at the distillery. Most had gone to the Chivas Regal. And here is a dilemma for the producers: whether to sell as a single and please connoisseurs facing a personal Strathisla drought, or to continue to use it for their blends?

Of course, one feature of the de-luxe blends is, after all, that they are often sold in perfume-type bottles at airport duty-free shops. For those who are beguiled by such wrappings, this is clearly a bonus.

My strictures with regard to de-luxe blends apply equally to vatted malts, assemblages of malts from several distilleries, usually from the same region, without, of course, added grain whisky. Originally produced by the devotees of malt whisky, as opposed to the devotees of the blends, in the latter half of the nineteenth century, the result so often for me is that the general timbre of the finished product, though pleasing enough, clearly hinting at the qualities and characteristics of the region, hides the special delights of the single malts themselves. Perhaps an exception could be made for the McClelland's Vatted Islay, and this if only gradually to introduce the often very characteristic peaty, seaweedy, almost phenolic taste of the Islays to the newcomer to the single malts.

Here it should perhaps be noted that the adjective "pure" with respect to malts applies to all whiskies made exclusively from malted barley distilled in pot stills, and which contain no grain whisky from column stills, and the term in essence dates back to the time when blends (i.e. not "pure" malts) were making serious inroads on the pot-still whiskies. Thus "single" malts (malts from one distillery), "single-single" malts (malts from one cask) and vatted malts (marriages of single malts) are all "pure" malts. A request in bars on the Continent for "Glen", meaning a malt whisky, as Jean Biolatto often points out, is a terminological inexactitude, possibly owing much to the great sales thrust of Glenfiddich, Glenmorangie and Glenfarclas. Distributors of whisky often sell specially labelled, dated bottles, often presented in boxes of precious exotic woods – such as the very fine Aberlour 1964. These make excellent presents but are ultimately destined for the collector who leaves them displayed unopened in his bar. I find this difficult to understand. For me, always, the proof is in the tasting not the presentation.

THE GREAT OLDTIMERS OF IRELAND

Irish whiskeys owe many of their characteristic charms to the fact that they are triple distilled, that the malted barley used is dried without the infusion of peat, and that the grain used for the mash is a mixture of malted barley and other grains – maize, wheat and, indeed, unmalted barley. To my mind there are no blended Irish whiskeys as such; rather there are vatted

Jean Castel, connoisseur *extraordinaire* of blends and single malts, presents the newly-born children of the habitués of his club with a bottle of J. & B. Rare, to be kept in a showcase on the stairway until their majority.

whiskeys compounded from casks which can produce the specific quality and characteristics of the whiskey marketed. The undeserved calumny that Midleton is one distillery with several taps, rather than a distillery complex, is easily confounded by actually tasting the whiskeys. And ask your man in an Irish pub whether he has been served, say, Power's rather than the Jameson he called for, and the distinction will be clearly made.

With its two distilleries, Ireland produces only one single malt, distilled in pot stills from a mash and fermentation of malted barley.

BUSHMILLS MALT (Northern Ireland). Medium golden. A pleasant, light, smoky aroma with some sweetness. The sweetness is developed in the smooth body, which lingers on beguilingly in the follow-through. A good all-rounder malt. Possibly aperitif.

The Whiskeys:

JAMESON (Republic of Ireland). Round, slightly oily, with good perfume-like aroma.

JAMESON 1780 (Republic of Ireland). A twelve-year-old de-luxe with the matured warmth and tones of the above.

POWER'S GOLD LABEL (Republic of Ireland). What it may lack in aroma it makes up for with a good, bustling maltiness of taste.

PADDY (Republic of Ireland). A good, well-rounded body with a bright austerity and attractive crispness in the follow-through.

TULLAMORE DEW (Republic of Ireland). Light, light on the nose, it is a gently dry whiskey.

MIDLETON VERY RARE (Republic of Ireland). Produced from a selection of the very best of the casks matured at Midleton, it is very smooth, very round, with a good, sweetish malt song to it.

OLD BUSHMILLS (Northern Ireland). A blend with a

Irish whiskey is still delivered in these charming oldtime cabs (centre right).

Irish whisky production. At the beginning of the century more than 200 distilleries were in production, often in the very centres of towns. Today production is concentrated on two towns, Midleton and Bushmills (red dots).

sweetness echoing the malt with a dry follow-through.

BLACK BUSH (Northern Ireland). A de-luxe blend with naturally more malt than the above, which is reflected in its perfuminess.

THE LIGHT WHISKIES OF JAPAN

The man or woman who has vowed never to buy Japanese cars, transistors and electronic goods, and hates raw fish even to the point of spurning smoked salmon, will probably read no further. His or her sensibilities will be shocked by my saying that of all the non-indigenous whiskies, the Japanese is the closest to Scotch. This is not because the Japanese use much bulk Scotch whisky for their blends, which they do, but because of the attention they pay

to production methods, in malting, fermentation and distilling, and the sites of their maturing sheds are chosen very much on the Scottish model for temperature and climate. It is not Scotch whisky and does not pretend to be. It is Japanese whisky, up to now essentially for the home market, though these whiskies are to be seen more and more in specialist shops. They are lighter because that is the way the Japanese like them, drunk with some 80 per cent water. Were the Japanese to decide that they wanted a more aromatic, heavier whisky, I am quite sure that they would be able to produce it using the trusted methods of the Scots, which they have most assiduously learnt.

Single malts:

KARUIZAWA (Central Honshu). Darkish gold, probably from the sherry casks. A very light nose. Taste is sweet with malt and the follow-through slightly dry and rather abrupt.

When eating Japanese food definitely an after-dinner drink. Otherwise possibly an all-rounder.

YAMAZAKI (Southern Honshu). Gold. Little nose, starts rather drily and then flourishes with hints of malt and a fairly deep warmth. After Japanese dinner and an all-rounder.

The Japanese blended whiskies are produced in the same way as Scotch blends using malts and grain whiskies, both of these either domestic and/or, in some cases, Scotch whiskies.

The **SUNTORY** whiskies tend to be rather lightly peated and have overtones of fruitiness.

The **NIKKA** whiskies have rather more body to them and more characteristic notes of peat, fruit, and elements from Bourbon casks – my personal favourites.

SUNRAKU OCEAN are notable for their malt and sweetness but, like much whisky in Japan, tend towards a quick, sharp, dry finish.

The fine **KIRIN SEAGRAM** whiskies are closest perhaps to the Scotch blends and have a smooth,

slightly smoky, peaty flavour with a little more sweetness than usual to them, but with the rather typically Japanese short finish, designed for use as a long drink with much water.

CANADIAN WHISKIES

Canadian whiskies are blends, in the usual way, with at least 51 per cent rye in the make-up of

Whisky-producing regions of Japan. The first distillery was set up in 1923 near Kyoto; today the largest distilleries are in the centre of Japan, except for the Yoichi distillery on Hokkaïdo and the malt distilleries of Sendaï and Noheji. The red dots indicate distilleries mentioned in the text.

their mixed-grain mash, which is distilled in column stills.

Hiram Walker's **CANADIAN CLUB** is probably the best known of the rye whiskies from Canada and rightly so. It has a dry start, much fruitiness of the rye and a fairly austere finish with vague smoky notes.

Other Canadian whiskies of note are the whiskies from the Corby group of distilleries, of which their hallmark is a rather light style, as in their **ROYAL RESERVE**.

Schenley's have a good, firm, rye character and are well rounded. Particularly notable are their very smooth **GIBSON'S FINEST** and their well-rounded, deeper **SCHENLEY'S AWARD**.

Seagram's, happily, are marketing in Europe more and more of their **CROWN ROYAL** blend, developed it is said for the royal visit of George VI in 1939. This has, under its oaky flavour from the cask, a neat, well-rounded tang of the rye and a fine, delicate follow-through. **CROWN ROYAL** could make serious inroads on Canadian Club but amateurs of the often sadly overlooked Canadian rye whisky should rejoice that they now have at least another blend to enjoy and compare.

AMERICAN WHISKEYS

These close cousins of what I have considered the true "Celtic"-style whiskies all tend to have a cloying, lingering quality which I, like many devotees of Scotch whisky, found not entirely pleasing at first tastings, but with perseverance have come to appreciate more and more. However, because of this lingering quality, I still

prefer, of the American whiskeys, the Tennessee sour mashes. Sour-mash whiskeys are made by adding the de-alcoholized fermentation from the distillation to the mash. This gives a certain reinforcement of the flavours and bouquets. The distilled spirit is filtered through three metres or so of maplewood charcoal for ten days, which gives it a cleaner, neater taste, before maturing in new casks.

JACK DANIEL'S (Tennessee). A dry lightness with good aroma, crisp on the nose, becoming mellower, with slight hints of sweeter grain on the palate, twisting back to a very warming neat finish of some dryness. A very fine introduction to all American whiskeys.

Crown Royal (below), a de-luxe blend, the great rival of Canadian Club, was perfected after testing some 600 samples, for the occasion of the visit to Canada of King George VI and Queen Elizabeth.

Hiram Walker's distillery offices at Windsor on Lake Erie, the headquarters of one of the giants of Canadian whisky (right and above right).

GEORGE DICKEL (Tennessee). Possibly my favourite American whiskey, if I were really pressed. It spells its name "whisky". A very much more rounded and smoother whiskey than most, it starts with a truly dry hint of grain and then drifts through a little sweetness, and ends with very elegant crispness, for its kind, with an echo of warmth.

The Bourbon whiskeys are produced, mainly,

Whisky-producing regions of the USA. The principal distilleries of the United States are marked with a red dot, concentrated principally on Kentucky (Bourbon) and Tennessee (Sour Mash whiskey). Louisville (1), Frankfort (2), Bardstown (3), Clermont (4), Lawrenceburg (5), Loretto (6), Tullahoma (7), Lynchburg (8). In Canada the distilleries are based on the Lakes Ontario and Erie, and along the St Lawrence, from Windsor to Montreal.

in Kentucky. (Bourbon is type of whiskey and no longer comes from Bourbon County as such.) Bourbons are distilled from a fermented mash which contains at least 51 per cent corn (maize). Like all the American whiskeys that are regularly marketed, they are produced in column stills and are matured in new charred casks which give to the whiskey much of their strong vanilla flavour.

Bourbon connoisseurs look for the bubbles or beads that come to the top of the glass of the liquor. The larger the bead and the longer it lasts indicates the relative highness of proof. They deem that the richer the whiskey the more it adheres to the glass, indicating also the developing oiliness in tonguing that Bourbon drinkers like. The aroma is judged by how long it lingers in the glass after use. Scotch whisky enthusiasts tend to find Bourbon not absolutely to their taste. Given the developing taste sensations offered by the more characteristic single malts of Scotland, I feel the time has come for Scotch drinkers to persevere more with this whiskey type. Like me, they could have some very pleasant surprises indeed.

Among the best Bourbons and the most readily available worldwide are:

ANCIENT AGE (Kentucky). Relatively dry, could be drunk before dinner.

EARLY TIMES (Kentucky). A light sweetish Bourbon with a quiet and relatively quick, neat finish. A good choice for those who are not especially drinkers of Bourbon.

Jack Daniel's, like all the distilleries of the United States, was forced to close its doors for the thirteen long years of Prohibition, and then later during the Second World War. The distillery reopened only in 1947 when it was sure of obtaining the very best cereals for its high-quality product (left and below).

The tasting room at George Dickel's distillery in Normandy, Tennessee. The other Tennessee distillery, Jack Daniel's, is in a "dry" county and cannot sell liquor retail.

EVAN WILLIAMS (Kentucky). Straightforward, classic Bourbon with full, lingering flavour.

HEAVEN HILL (Kentucky). Heavy in malt qualities both in nose and body. Rather cloying at first tasting but quickly becomes an echo not without charm.

I. W. HARPER (Kentucky). A lightish-bodied Bourbon with gentle hints of sweetness with a slow warmth in the follow-through.

JIM BEAM (Kentucky). The standard brand (White Label) has all the qualities that the Bourbon-lover delights in but which might not necessarily be to the taste of the hardened Scotch malt-whisky drinker. Big in its aroma, rather sweet flowery tones to it, grand oiliness, with a long, almost unending – to some – finish.

MAKER'S MARK (Kentucky). Full-bodied, full Bourbon with some delicacy in its follow-through. Like George Dickel, it spells its name "whisky".

OLD FITZGERALD (Kentucky). Very full-bodied, very, very smooth, a fine and elegant Bourbon. Compare it with the Dalwhinnie malt.

OLD FORESTER (Kentucky). Lightish, delicate Bourbon but with a full flavour, fruity yet dry.

WILD TURKEY (Kentucky). My eventual preferred Bourbon. Full-bodied but with a neat finish that does not linger overmuch. A king among its kind. Wild Turkey also produces a rye, which is notable for its smoothness, with sweet hints of the grass. It too has a neat, stylish, uncloying finish.

A Wild Turkey presentation jug (below) sets off the high-quality whiskey from Lawrenceburg, Kentucky.

Maker's Mark, a listed monument, the smallest distillery in the United States, has been run by the same family for four generations.

LIQUEURS

Drambuie is perhaps the oldest and best-known liqueur made from whisky and is an important ingredient in the "Rusty Nail" cocktail so popular on the Continent (q.v.). Whisky liqueurs are the direct descendants of the drinks made from blending herbs and honey with whiskies that may have been a little too characteristic to be drunk on their own. Other Scotch whisky liqueurs include Columba Cream, Clanrana, Glayva, Glen Mist, Lochan Ora and Sconie.

In Ireland, there is Irish Mist and Irish Velvet, a kind of bottled version of Irish Coffee, and Bailey's Irish Cream, which does include cream.

In the United States, Southern Comfort is a mix of Bourbon and peaches, oranges and herbs. Wild Turkey do a whiskey liqueur with Bourbon, citrus fruits and honey.

These liqueurs are very much for the sweet tooth, and though I am sure that there are those who must appreciate such potions, the true whisky drinker would be advised to abstain from experimenting with them – though probably he has tasted them as a child – as they will almost certainly dull his palate, rendering him incapable of tasting the niceties of the hints of sweetness in his favourite whiskies.

WHISKY AND FOOD

The true whisky lover will, of course, need no prompting when it is suggested that whiskies can be used, with great success and *élan*, for any recipe that requires alcohol in its make-up or for flambéing. Indeed a few drops of whisky in soup will transform the most humdrum mess of potage into a dish suitable for the man of taste. A crêpe Suzette flamed with cognac is simply an *arriviste*

Drambuie
Prince Charles Edwards
LIQUEUR

The recipe for Drambuie liqueur – the name means "the drink that satisfies" – is said to have been brought from France by Bonnie Prince Charlie and given to his hosts on Skye, when in hiding after the collapse of the '45 Rebellion.

pancake strayed into the realms of expense-account lunches. Flamed with whisky it becomes a dessert of rare delights, of flavours singing in mystical harmony together.

Moreover, it entirely eludes my comprehension that otherwise quite discriminating and fastidious establishments, adhering to the approach of that grand old man of gastronomy, Robert Courtine, continue to serve smoked salmon with a glass of vodka. Vodka is a very charming spirit but what more acceptable accompaniment to an hors d'oeuvre of good smoked Scottish salmon, marinated herrings or smoked haddock could there be than the dry Lowland Glenkinchie, the well-balanced Glenfiddich or, for its touch of sweetness, the creamy smooth Edradour?

Though Robert Courtine – himself President

of the Académie de Pure Malt Scotch Whisky – demurs politely, I would go as far as to take, say, the triple distilled Auchentoshan to accompany caviar, whether the homely Sevruga, the much underestimated Osietra or the noble Beluga – caviar served, it should go without saying, on freshly toasted and buttered white bread.

It would take a great deal for me to renounce my mid-morning ritual of a glass of the flowery aroma-ed Bunnahabhain accompanied by a thick slice of pressed smoked cod's roe on rye bread before starting work – despite the modern fad for a split of champagne – any more than I would give up my afternoon's sweet digestive biscuit and dram of Clan Campbell twelve-year-old – or on high days, and there are many such as the winter days draw in – of the fine lingering Aberlour.

Described by Robert Burns as "Great Chieftain o' the pudding race", the haggis is a delightful dish, despite much mockery from ignorant foreigners who, in the words of the food writer Judith Hirst, take it for "a small furry animal commonly found in the vast purple hue of the heather on the moors". Haggis . . . that merry-making dish, and that companion on cold nights with the wind howling outside, shaking the chimney stacks . . . that dish praised by the bards and accompanied in at great Highland dinners to the brave music of the bagpipes . . .

Haggis: 1 measure Scotch; 1 sheep's pluck: liver, lights and heart; the large stomach bag of a young ewe; 250 gms fresh beef suet; 1 measure stock; 1 cup fine oatmeal; 3 onions; pinch of cayenne; salt and white pepper. Clean stomach bag thoroughly, scraping in cold, running water, and then leave to soak overnight in cold, salted water. Then turn bag rough side out. Wash and clean pluck and put to boil in cold water for

90 minutes, leaving the windpipe hanging over the side of the pot to expel any impurities. Cut away pipes and remove any gristle. Mince the heart and lights and *half* the liver. Chop suet and onions finely. Toast oatmeal slowly in a warm oven. Mix all ingredients and salt and pepper, and add cayenne. Pour the whisky over this mixture and mix in well. Fill the bag two-thirds full. The mixture will swell on cooking. Press out all the air from the bag and sew up. Put in a pot of fast-boiling salted water and prick with sharp skewer when it begins to swell. Reduce heat and allow to cook for up to 3 hours. Serve with Gadney neeps (a purée of 50 per cent turnips and 50 per cent salted butter) and baked potatoes *à la Faudry* (baked in rock salt, which is knocked off before serving). This . . . together with a glass of whisky and a little water. *Bon appétit!*

Those who are unable to procure the ingredients for this most traditional Scottish dish should take heart that ready-prepared haggises are to be found at the fine food shops at most Scottish airports.

The debate continues to rage among gastronomes as to what to drink with that most subtle and exciting element, chocolate. It is as subtle and exciting as whisky and most wines have been tried with it. All the regions of France have been scoured. In vain. You will be able to predict my solution with some accuracy. With a Black Forest gateau, the Dalwhinnie malt was spot on. I tried it again with Jack Daniel's Tennessee Sour Mash and was not disappointed in the least. A deliciously thick, marvellously bitter chocolate mousse had quite clearly been waiting for a glass of Balvenie Founder's Reserve for some time, and it was no less enthusiastic about a nip of Karuizaka Malt from Japan, and Lafayette would have been proud of its charming, lingering marriage with Early Times Bourbon.

Smoked fish (opposite) – salmon, eel, or herring – as well as caviar, is perfectly set off by a glass of Glenkinchie or Glenfiddich.

Leaders of gastronomic fashion take an interest in whisky. The Troisgros at Roanne offers a ten-year-old Auchentoshan (below) as a light aperitif.

A Manhattan and an Irish coffee (page 192) – two famous cocktails invented in the bars of the USA and Ireland – proof (if proof were needed) that, pure or blended, whisky is a suitable companion at any hour and on any occasion.

Connoisseur's Guide

The man of taste would not and could not use a single malt for cocktails. The complex characters of single malts must be drunk alone to be fully appreciated and savoured. Blends marry well in cocktails. Such is the flexibility of whisky that it can be said to develop truly and enhance the other tastes of the cocktail. Blended whiskies give life, as always, and verve, to ingredients whose qualities have been lying dormant. Purists and faddists will raise fastidious eyebrows at the water of life being used in cocktails. Perhaps the better argument is that if one likes something well enough one should not hesitate to drink it in other ways. Moreover, what better way of introducing the magical elixir to those whose tastes have not yet developed enough to enjoy it on its own? True devotees of whisky, at whatever stage in their search for perfection, might do well to experiment with the following cocktails, remembering, of course, to use only the finest blends. Bad cheap whiskies will produce only a bad and nasty cocktail.

Here are some cocktails I have tested and retested and have enjoyed:

SCOTCH WHISKY

ATHOLL BROSE: 250 gms heather honey; 250 gms fine oatmeal; 1½ litres Scotch. Mix the oatmeal and honey with a little cold water until smooth. Gradually add the whisky, while beating vigorously until the mixture froths. Rebottle the mixture and allow to settle for two days before serving.

The most traditional Scottish "cocktail" is Atholl Brose. Naturally it is some two thousand light years away from the more modern cocktails sipped ice cold in dimly lit bars with a piano playing softly in the background. Drinking it, one will notice, after a very short time, the definite drone of the pipes in the reddened ears. Tradition has it that, in 1475, the Duke of Atholl captured his mortal enemy, the Earl of Ross, by filling the well where the Earl was used to drink with this glorious mixture. Overcome by such a variant of Highland hospitality, or possibly believing that this was just another munificent example of God's mysterious ways, Lord Ross drank deeply, only to fall asleep, and thus into the hands of the brave men of Atholl.

SCOTCH TOM COLLINS: 5–6 dashes lemon juice; 1 large measure Scotch; 2–3 lumps of ice. Pour into a large glass and fill with soda.

SCOTCH HORSE'S NECK: 5–6 dashes lemon; 1 large measure Scotch; dash of Angostura Bitters; 2–3 lumps of ice. Fill the glass, to taste, with ginger ale.

WHISPER: 2 measures Scotch; 2 measures French vermouth; 2 measures Italian vermouth. Mix and add cracked ice.

ROB ROY (named after Sir Walter Scott's roistering hero): ½ measure Scotch; ½ measure dry Italian vermouth; dash of Angostura Bitters.

HIGHLAND SPECIAL: 3 measures Scotch; 2 measures French vermouth; ½ glass orange juice; a grating of nutmeg after mixing.

SUMMER SCOTCH: 1 measure Scotch; 3 dashes crème de menthe; 1 lump of ice. Fill glass with soda.

SCOTCH RICKEY: 1 lump of ice; juice of half a lime; juice of a quarter of a lemon; 1 measure Scotch. Fill glass, to taste, with soda.

DERBY FIZZ: 5 dashes lemon juice; 1 teaspoonful powdered sugar; 1 egg; 3 dashes curaçao; 1 good measure Scotch. Mix well and add soda water.

Bonnie Prince Charlie, who raised the '45 Rebellion, reached as far as Derby on his march south. The London banks panicked and closed. Prince Charles hesitated at Derby. Some of his Highland supporters faded away with the cattle and other booty pilfered along the march. Charles retreated. London banks reopened. Charles was defeated at the bloody battle of Culloden and sailed off to France, after wandering as a fugitive in the Highlands, to spend an unhappy retirement. Supporters of Charles continued to make toasts holding their glasses over a bowl of water "to the king over the water".

HIGHLAND COOLER: 1 teaspoonful powdered sugar; juice of half a lemon; 2 dashes Angostura Bitters; 1 measure Scotch; 1 lump of ice. Mix and add ginger ale according to taste.

EARTHQUAKE: 1 measure gin; 1 measure Scotch; 1 measure Ricard or Pernod.

Yes, well, possibly very well named indeed. Certainly I found that the inclusion of the gin induced a considerable amount of liverish testiness after absorption, preceded by a curious sensation of undue euphoria.

FLYING SCOTSMAN (named after the celebrated train that brought sportsmen to the north for the grouse-shooting season): 2½ measures Italian vermouth; 3 measures Scotch; 1 tablespoonful Angostura Bitters; 1 tablespoonful sugar syrup.

WHISKY SOUR (the great classic whisky cocktail): 2 measures Scotch; juice of half a lemon; ½ teaspoonful sugar. Shake with ice and add soda.

PURPLE HEATHER: 1 measure Scotch; 1 measure cassis; ice to taste. Top up with soda.

BANNOCKBURN: 1 good measure Scotch. (Scottish spirit); 1 dash Worcester sauce; 1 measure tomato juice (English blood); 1 slice lemon; 1 lump ice.

A commemoration of the battle of Bannockburn, 24 June 1314. The troops of Edward II of England, 20,000 strong, were marching north to relieve Stirling Castle, which was under siege by the Scots. Robert Bruce, King of Scotland and ancestor of Lord Elgin, Patron of the Keepers of the Quaich, with 7,000 men, took cunning advantage of the boggy vileness of the terrain and succeeded in defeating the English forces.

Despite its rather unfortunate historical connotations, this cocktail is surely a preferable alternative to that truly ghastly, stomach-churning Bloody Mary.

Experimental variants on these can be made using rye whisky or Bourbon. No doubt, in the case of Bourbon, the "Bannockburn" would become the "Yorktown".

WHISKY COBBLER: 1 measure Scotch; 1 measure water; 1 teaspoonful sugar; 1 teaspoonful orange juice; 1 measure curaçao. Add ice and decorate with fruit and slices of orange. Serve with a straw.

WHISKY COCKTAIL: 1 measure Scotch; 2 dashes curaçao; 2 dashes Angostura Bitters; 1 teaspoonful sugar; squeeze of lemon.

WHISKY DAISY: 1 measure Scotch; 1 teaspoonful lemon juice; 1 teaspoonful orgeat. Serve on crushed ice. Fill glass with soda.

CHANCELLOR: 1 measure Scotch; ½ measure port; ½ measure Dry Martini vermouth; 2 dashes Angostura Bitters.

GOLDEN HEATH: 1 measure Drambuie; 1 measure rum; 1 measure sherry. Shake with ice. Strain.

BROWN JUG COCKTAIL: 1 measure Scotch; 1 measure Kahlua.

RUSTY NAIL: 1 measure Drambuie; 1 measure Scotch. Ice to taste.

GODFATHER: 2 measures Scotch; 1 measure amaretto; ice.

SKYE BOAT COCKTAIL (invented by Andy MacElhone of Harry's Bar): 1 measure orange juice; 1 measure Drambuie; 1 measure Scotch. Mix in a tumbler of crushed ice and add a large piece of orange peel, with a lump of sugar impregnated with malt(!) whisky.

CORONATION 1937 COCKTAIL (and this from Harry MacElhone of Harry's Bar, to commemorate the coronation of George VI and Queen Elizabeth, parents of the present Queen): 1 measure Scotch; 1 measure grapefruit juice; ½ measure lemon juice; ½ measure grenadine; 2 dashes Angostura Bitters; 1 dash peach bitters. Serve chilled with a piece of pineapple.

WHISKY MAC: 2 measures Scotch; 1 measure ginger wine.

This recipe is very commonly drunk on cold nights in Scotland (i.e. quite often). The most reputable of ginger wines is Crabbies. In the early part of the nineteenth century grocers would create a "wine" from Greek raisins and water and add spices, the most notable of which was ginger. This is, probably, according to Duncan MacElhone of the famous Harry's Bar in Paris, one of the most acceptable whisky cocktails. A must on cold nights.

BLUE BLAZER (for very, very cold nights): 2 or 3 measures Scotch; boiling water; lemon peel. Flame the whisky in a solid-silver tankard over the fire. Remove; add boiling water to taste; garnish with lemon peel.

HET PINT: ½ litre Scotch; 2 litres mild ale; 1 teaspoonful grated nutmeg; 2 spoons demerara sugar; 4 eggs. Heat ale in a pan with nutmeg until the sugar has dissolved. Beat eggs separately, add a little of the warm ale; mix. Slowly pour the beaten egg into the cooling ale. Add the whisky and again heat slowly so that the egg does not curdle.

In Scotland, Hogmanay (New Year's Eve), is accompanied by some considerable revelling. Among its traditions is that of first-footing. For luck, health and all the things that one would wish for the household, a dark-haired man should be the first to enter a house, bearing salt for wealth, coal for warmth and, no doubt, good Scotch whisky for life. A "Het Pint" may be offered to first-footers to warm them up after being out in the bitter cold, waiting, shivering, for midnight to strike.

HIGHLAND COFFEE: see *Irish Coffee* below.

SCOTCH WHISKY TODDY: 1 spoonful sugar in a warm glass; boiling water to dissolve sugar; 1 teaspoonful lemon juice; 1 very large measure hot water. Stir with solid-silver spoon. Add a little more boiling water. Add more whisky to taste.

IRISH WHISKEY

The Irish have never been ones for using their whiskey for cocktails. In general they prefer to use what to them are less exalted whiskies for such purposes.

However Harry's Bar provides two:

IRISH FIZZ: 1 measure Irish whiskey; juice of half a lemon; 1 teaspoonful curaçao. Fill glass with soda. Add lemon slice and a green cherry.

THE BLACKTHORN (named after the marvellously strong walking sticks of Ireland): 1 measure Irish whiskey; 1 measure dry vermouth; 2 dashes Angostura Bitters; 3 dashes anis.

Two more have been given to me by Bill McCourt of Old Bushmills:

THE LEPRECHAUN: 1 measure Irish whiskey; 2 measures tonic water; twist of lemon; Serve over ice.

The leprechaun is a curious green mannikin which manifests itself in the mists of Ireland, a phenomenon possibly not unconnected with the consumption of poteen.

IRISH HANDSHAKE: 2 measures Irish whiskey; 1 measure green curaçao; 1 measure cream. Shake well with ice.

There are, also . . .

WILD IRISH ROSE: 2 measures Irish Whiskey; ½ measure grenadine. Pour over ice and fill glass with soda water.

THE IRISH ROVER: 1 measure Irish whiskey; 1 measure Campari; 2 measures orange juice; dash of grenadine. Serve over ice.

IRISH DRIVER: 1 measure Irish whiskey; 2 drops crème de cacao, preferably white; 1 measure orange juice.

However, the Irish have given to a very grateful world one quite amazing drink, which, of its kind, has no equal:

IRISH COFFEE: 1 measure Irish whiskey; 2 measures strong black coffee; 2 spoons brown sugar. Thick cream.

After the end of the Second World War, when civilian transatlantic flying was resumed, flying boats and Super-Constellations were used. Not being able to make the full crossing to mainland Europe without refuelling, they stopped over at Shannon Airport. In 1952, Joe Sheridan, the airport barman, noticed that after the freezing-cold flight, some of the passengers also seemed to be very much in need of something in the way of urgent refuelling. In the past the Irish had often drunk whiskey in their tea. To please American taste he substituted coffee, added a generous portion of rich Irish cream and served the result in a stemmed glass. Such was the success of this invention that the Irish distillers set up a plaque in Joe Sheridan's honour at Shannon. The Americans took Irish coffee to their hearts. At the Buena Vista bar in San Francisco half a million Irish coffees are served every year.

Here is the true recipe, straight from the mouth of Joe Sheridan himself: Into a stemmed glass, put two teaspoonfuls of sugar, preferably brown; add one-third Irish whiskey and two-thirds really hot strong black coffee, preferably freshly brewed, not instant. The glass should be filled with this mixture to within half an inch (1 cm) of the brim. Stir well at this point to ensure all the sugar is dissolved, and then carefully float over the back of the spoon a collar of lightly whipped cream, so that the cream floats on the top of the coffee and whiskey. *Do not stir any more.* Serve the drink *without* a spoon or a straw as part of the pleasure comes from sipping the hot coffee and whiskey through the cold cream. *Slainte, agus saol agat!* ("Health and long life to you!")

If you find that you are being served Scotch in your Irish coffee, what you have been given is a beast of another colour altogether: Highland coffee. This is all right in its way but it's not quite the same thing.

Among aficionados of Irish coffee can be numbered Marilyn Monroe, Gregory Peck, John Huston, Louis Armstrong, Noël Coward, Burl Ives, John Ford, Charlie Chaplin and Princess Grace of Monaco.

JAPANESE WHISKY

YOSHITOMI NUT GRINDER (given to me by Professor Yasuo Yoshitomi at the Kyoto Cartoon Festival): 3 measures light Japanese whisky; ½ measure melon juice (cantaloupe will do); dash of lemon juice. Float a pinch of powdered green tea on top. Fill glass with crushed ice, eat a pickled cherry on the side and gaze, to the sound of a one-stringed guitar, at the lily pads floating on the moonlit pond.

BOURBON WHISKEY

These, as all American drinks, should be heavily chilled.

MINT JULEP: 2 measures Bourbon; 10–12+ leaves mint; 1 spoonful syrup; crushed ice; caster sugar. There are many approaches to make mint julep. My way is the best. Mash the mint and syrup in a tall glass. Add crushed ice halfway up the glass. Pour in the first measure of Bourbon. Stir. Add more crushed ice. Add the second measure of Bourbon. Stir. Decorate with sprigs of mint dusted in caster sugar. Some Americans prefer not to mash the mint in the syrup – more fools them! Men of taste will most likely find that the use of a silver mug is more appropriate than a glass. I have had excellent results from a late-Victorian silver mug made by Asprey. Whatever heated debate may be aroused by such important details, on one thing there is almost unanimous agreement: rye whiskey should *not* be used. H. L. Mencken, the American humorist, wrote of man who so trangressed, "Any guy who would put rye in a mint julep (and crush the leaves) would put scorpions in a baby's bed."

Even those who neither like cocktails nor are over fond of Bourbon can find nothing to quibble about this amazing refreshment on a warm balmy evening. The julep (though very much taken up in Tennessee as its native drink) is, however, like most of the best things in the United States, of British origin. The first references to it are in 1400, and in 1550 Lloyd in his *Treatise on Health* calls it "a cleare potyon made of dyuerse waters and sugar". The poet John Milton writes of: ". . . this cordial julep here/That flames and dances in this crystal bounds/With spirits of balm and fragrant syrups mix'd." In his entry for 22 June 1660, Samuel Pepys records, ". . . thence to my Lord's and had a great walk to Brigham's who gave me a case of good julep."

Other Bourbon recipes are:

THE OLD FASHIONED: 1 lump sugar saturated in Angostura Bitters crushed in a touch of water; 1 measure Bourbon. Serve with lemon peel.

Some people serve it with rye whiskey. This is an aberration which for the life of me I cannot understand. There are other modern versions of the "Old Fashioned" which I cannot recommmend. The name "Old Fashioned" means exactly that and modern versions are a contradiction in terms.

NEW YORKER: 2 measures Bourbon; ½ measure lime juice; ½ measure grenadine; zest of 1 orange. Shake with ice.

This cocktail is named not after an inhabitant of the city of New York, but after the magazine, which, since the demise of the old-time *Punch*, carries the best cartoons in the world, from such artists as Charles Addams, Peter Arno, Farris, Lou Myers, Steinberg, Searle, ffolkes, Sempé and Avoine.

CHERRY BOMB: 2 measures strong Bourbon; 1 measure cherry brandy; 1 white of egg. Shake and serve.

FOX RIVER COCKTAIL: 1 lump of sugar saturated with peach bitters; 1 measure Bourbon; 1 teaspoonful crème de cacao; zest of 1 lemon.

DOUBLE EAGLE: 1 measure strong Bourbon; 1 measure Southern Comfort; 1 measure lemon juice.

ESKIE COCKTAIL: 1 measure Bourbon; 1 dash Angostura Bitters; 1 teaspoonful Benedictine; 1 teaspoonful Sweet Martini vermouth. Add cherry, slice of orange and a slice of pineapple.

WHITE BIRD (devised by the genial Monsieur François of Harry's Bar, Munich): 2 measures Bourbon. ½ measure banana liqueur; ½ measure fresh cream.

LIBERTY: 1 measure I. W. Harper Bourbon; 1 measure Dry Martini vermouth; ½ measure lime juice cordial; ½ measure Southern Mist. To be shaken.

This cocktail was created by Duncan MacElhone, a third generation MacElhone, connoisseur, animator and master of delights at Harry's Bar, for the Franco-American Committee for the restoration of the Statue of Liberty. Part of the sale price was donated to the Committee – the recipe is donated to posterity.

Finally . . .

PINK ELEPHANT (named after the beast that will jump on you and stamp all over you if you drink too many of them): 2 measures Bourbon; 1 measure lemon juice; 2 dashes grenadine; 1 egg white. Shake with ice.

RYE WHISKEY

Perhaps the most famous rye-whiskey-based cocktail is the legendary . . .

MANHATTAN: 3 measures rye whiskey; 1 measure sweet vermouth; 2 dashes Angostura Bitters.

This makes me hum Gershwin, and, if only briefly, and try to speak with an American accent . . .

MIGHTY FINE COCKTAIL: 1 measure rye whiskey; 1 measure American Picon; 1 measure orange juice; 2 dashes orange bitters.

NINETEENTH HOLE (concocted specially for golfers): 1 measure rye whiskey; 1 measure sweet vermouth; 1 measure sherry.

BROOKLYN COCKTAIL: 2 measures rye whiskey; 1 measure dry vermouth; 1 dash Picon; 1 dash maraschino.

ROCK AND RYE COCKTAIL: 1 measure rye whiskey; 1 teaspoonful rock candy syrup; juice of half a lemon; zest of lemon.

WARD EIGHT: 2 measures rye whiskey; 1 measure orange juice; 1 measure lemon juice; 4 dashes of grenadine.

INK STREET COCKTAIL: 1 measure rye whiskey; 1 measure lemon juice; 1 measure orange juice.

ELK'S OWN: 1 measure rye whiskey; 1 measure port; 1 measure lemon juice. Add sugar to taste and a slice of pineapple.

ALGONQUIN: 1 measure rye whiskey; ½ measure Dry Martini vermouth; ½ measure pineapple juice.

The Algonquin Hotel's "Round Table", a celebrated circle of wit and bitchery in the 1920s, included such luminaries from the *New Yorker* as Robert Benchley: "Drinking makes such fools of people, and people are such fools to begin with, that it's compounding a felony"; Dorothy Parker: "One more drink and I'll be under the host" – as well as George S. Kaufman, S. J. Perelman and Robert Sherwood.

DANDY COCKTAIL: 1 measure rye whiskey; 1 measure Dubonnet Bitters; 1 dash Angostura Bitters; 3 dashes Cointreau. Add lemon and orange peel.

CAN CAN (named after the French national dance): 1 measure rye whiskey; 1 measure dry vermouth; 1 measure Pernod.

VOLSTEAD COCKTAIL: 1 measure rye whisky; 1 measure Swedish punch; ½ measure orange juice; ½ measure raspberry syrup; 1 dash anisette.

This is another invention from Harry's Bar, this time in honour of the loony Volstead who introduced the Act imposing Prohibition. Thanks to him, many Americans came to Paris and, more particularly, to Harry's Bar, in order to get a decent drink.

And finally . . .

HOLDEN TAYLOR BLIND OYSTER URGENT RESTORATIVE: 2 unbroken egg yolks in a glass; add 2 spoonfuls of Worcester sauce; 2 dashes of tabasco; 2 measures Scotch. To be drunk without ice.

This is an ideal "morning-after" drink for those who have ignored Holinshed's advice about moderation and over-indulged themselves. It was developed – for purely altruistic motives – by the celebrated poet-anthropologist Holden Taylor. It works very well indeed, on the hair-of-the-dog principle. Moreover, one very soon finds that one has abandoned the first three ingredients and is once again enjoying, nay savouring, whisky straight with water.

D I S T I L L E R Y   G U I D E

When driving through the heather and hills of Scotland or through the green fields of Ireland, through Bluegrass country in Kentucky or when gazing at a misty mountain in Japan, one of the most enjoyable side trips that you can make is a visit to a distillery, where one can not only discover actually how the local whisky is made but where one can also talk to the people who make it and discover the pride and rare pleasure they take in their work.

With the hospitality typical of those who are at one with their work, most distilleries are only too pleased to show visitors round.

Some have well-established tours and reception centres; others will just as happily and warmly show visitors the workings of their distilleries on a personal basis and offer a celebratory dram of their very best.

Opening hours for visitors are usually from about 9.30 a.m. to 4 p.m., but it is always best to telephone to make arrangements before arriving. Not only is this a question of simple courtesy, but also it must be remembered that distilleries are, after all, real places of work and not simply tourist attractions – and there may be moments when it is not entirely convenient to receive visitors. Arrangements may also have changed since the publication of this book.

Much of the fun of visiting distilleries involves discovering malts or other whiskies that are not freely found in the general specialist shops.

There is nothing quite like discovering a rare malt or a local speciality for yourself . . .

Set out below are brief notes on many of the better-known distilleries of Scotland, Ireland, Japan and the United States. An asterisk (*) indicates that further information may be found in the final section of the main text, *Pure Malt or Blend?*, pp. 159–91.

SCOTLAND

The gleaming pot stills are there waiting for you . . . The most northern is Highland Park in the Orkneys; the most southern is Bladnoch in the Lowlands; the smallest, Edradour; the oldest, Strathisla, is up in the Highlands, in the Speyside; and Glenallachie, one of the newest, is also to be found in the golden triangle of the Speyside. Islay, with its six distilleries with their deep malts, is found here, as is Campbeltown, with its two remaining distilleries. They all have stories to tell and bottles of the real thing.

The maps on page 168 will help you plan your itinerary.

ABERFELDY (Highlands)
Aberfeldy, Perthshire ☎ 0887 20330
Founded in the early 1830s high up on the river Tay, in the Perthshire resort of Aberfeldy, with its charming market, the distillery buildings date back to 1896, though there has been much reconstruction and rebuilding over the last sixty years. It is interesting in that it is a distillery built lengthways along the tracks of the old railway, rather than on the somewhat haphazard plan of some of the older distilleries. This linear plan allows the processes of the making of whisky to be very easily grasped. It has as a well-planned visitor centre.
Sweetish after-dinner malt

ABERLOUR* (Highlands – Speyside)
Aberlour, Banffshire ☎ 03405 204
There has probably been distilling here since the time of the early Christian missionaries, when St Drostan baptized his converts in the river Lour, and this was one of the first distilleries to "go legal" in 1826. The original buildings were burnt down and rebuilt in 1892. Remarkable also for St Drostan's Spring.

AUCHENTOSHAN* (Lowlands)
Duntocher, Dumbartonshire ☎ 03987 9476
All records of this distillery were destroyed in wartime bombing but there is reason to believe that there was distilling here in the seventeenth century and that a licence for distilling was taken out in the early 1800s. It is on the outskirts of Glasgow and is notable for the triple distillation of its Lowland malts.

AUCHROISK (Highlands – Speyside)
Mulben, Banffshire ☎ 05426 333
Built as late as 1974, well known for its malt, The Singleton. A fine example of a modern distillery.
Full-bodied malt

AULTMORE (Highlands – Speyside)
Keith, Banffshire ☎ 05442 2397
Built in 1895 on the road between Keith and Elgin, it claimed originally to be a "Glenlivet", a claim it has subsequently dropped in the interest of geographical logic. Its malts are used mainly for Dewar's blends.
Probably more of an aperitif malt than anything else and rather dry

BALBLAIR (Highlands)
Edderton, Tain ☎ 08628 2273
Balblair is in the heart of old smuggling country, which is riddled with streams and burns, and its history goes back to 1790. It was reorganized in 1895.
Light and aromatic malt

BALMENACH (Highlands – Speyside)
Cromdale, Grantown-on-Spey, Morayshire ☎ 0479 2569
One of the first formerly illicit distilleries to take out a licence in 1824, it is set in the undulating valleys of the Haugh of Cromdale.
Smooth sweetish malt

BENRIACH (Highlands – Speyside)
Longmorn, Elgin, Morayshire ☎ 05422 7471
Established in 1898 and vastly extended in the 1960s and 1970s. It has its own floor maltings and until recently its *dryish, rather smoky malts* were almost entirely to be found in blendings. Visitors welcome in summer months.

BENRINNES (Highlands – Speyside)
Aberlour, Banffshire ☎ 03405 215
Dating back to 1835, it is set high up in the mountains overlooking the Spey. Its *smooth and slightly smoky malts* are difficult to find in general spirit shops. Visits by prior arrangement only.

BLADNOCH* (Lowlands)
Bladnoch, Wigtownshire ☎ 09884 2233
The most southern of Scottish distilleries, it is associated with the early Christian missionaries and with Robert the Bruce, the victor over the English at Bannockburn. After a chequered history of closures, it was reopened in the 1950s. It has a good little reception centre with a very warm welcome. Hitherto its malts have been much used for the Bell's blends.

BLAIR ATHOL (Highlands)
Pitlochry, Perthshire ☎ 0796 2234
A few miles from the site of the battle of Killicrankie where yet again the Scots managed to defeat the English – and who can say whether the ancestor of its malts played a part in the victory? – it lies in the charming town of Pitlochry, six miles from Blair Castle, the seat of the Duke of Atholl, which itself is well worth a visit for its sumptuous décor, and where those with a sweet tooth can taste the Columbia Cream, a liqueur made from a blend of whisky and honey. The distillery has a large visitor centre which almost overwhelms the distillery itself and provides a very good day out. I have it on good authority that the centre will be completely revamped shortly. Another great contributor to Bell's blends as well as the producer of *a slightly peaty, well-flavoured malt*, which is more and more widely available in Scotland and England.

BOWMORE* (Islay)
Bowmore, Islay, Argyll ☎ 04968 1441
Founded in 1779, in the capital of Islay, right on the sea's edge. In some places the maturing sheds are under sea level. Its fine reception centre is housed in the rooms that the Canadian airforce used as its local headquarters during the Second World War. It has its own malting floors and is an excellent introduction to the Islay distilleries. Wheelchair access.

BRUICHLADDICH* (Islay)
Bruichladdich, Islay, Argyll ☎ 04968 5221
Established in 1881, overlooking the sea at Port Charlotte, the distillery went through hard times until its reopening in 1960. Its stills are very long necked, producing a malt that is lighter in character than most Islays. It is on the west coast of the island; the next stop is Canada.

BUNNAHABHAIN* (Islay)
Port Askaig, Islay, Argyll ☎ 04968 4646
The name means "mouth of the river" in Gaelic. The distillery was set up in 1881, and its round squat stills give body to its malts, which hitherto have been used mainly for blends, but which are now, happily, much more readily available. Down a little track along the sea, its buildings are a really fine example of the Victorian factory type, with a monumental arch more reminiscent of Lancashire cotton mills than of distilleries.

CAOL ILA* (Islay)
Port Askaig, Islay, Argyll ☎ 04968 4207
Caol Ila, the "kyle", or sound, of Islay, was first built in 1846, reconstructed in 1879, and again rebuilt in a sadly grotesque modern style in the late 1970s. This should not put off visitors to the distillery in search of this lively little malt. Do telephone before visiting.

CAPERDONICH (Highlands – Speyside)
Rothes, Morayshire ☎ 05422 7471
Sister to the Glen Grant distillery, and their malts were at one time mixed, the spirit from the Caperdonich being pumped across the main street of Rothes through a "whisky pipe". Closed in 1901 after the crash of Pattisons' blenders caused something of a depression in whisky sales, it finally reopened in 1965. Its malts have been an important element in the Chivas Regal de-luxe blend. Visitors welcome.
Peaty and fruity malt

CARDHU*, (Highlands – Speyside)
Cardhu, Morayshire ☎ 03408 204
Cardhu, the "black rock" in the heart of

Speyside, in salmon-fishing country, was established in 1824 and produces a malt which is at the heart of Johnnie Walker and which is now much more available to the general public. It was rebuilt in 1890 after a long period of rather primitive production methods, and its pagoda, reflected in the distillery dam, has featured on a thousand advertising hoardings. It has a fine little visitor reception centre.

CLYNELISH (Highlands)
Brora, Sutherland ☎ 04482 1444
Founded in 1819 by the Duke of Sutherland, the distillery is one of those originally worked to use up excess barley produced by the farmers who settled along by the coast after being evicted from their lands during the Highland Clearances. Its site was also influenced by the proximity of the Brora coalfield; the first mine was opened up in 1529.
The malt is rich and somewhat peaty for the area.

CRAGGANMORE* (Highlands – Speyside)
Ballindalloch, Banffshire ☎ 08072 202
Established in 1869, the distillery was built by the mighty giant John Smith, whose immense chair is still on exhibition. It is the home of one of the really fine Speyside malts, which has been chosen as one of United Distillers' Six Classic Malts.

CRAIGELLACHIE (Highlands – Speyside)
Craigellachie, Banffshire ☎ 0340 881212
Set in the village of Craigellachie at the meeting point of those two great rivers of whisky lore, the Fiddich and the Spey. After visiting Thomas Telford's famous and elegant iron bridge, the visitor will go on to the home of this malt, which has been such an important element of the White Horse blend. Established in 1891, the distillery was rebuilt in a perfectly tasteless modern style in the 1960s.
Pungent digestif malt

DAILUAINE (Highlands – Speyside)
Carron, Banffshire ☎ 03406 361
Founded in 1852, a stone's throw from Aberlour, and steadily expanded up to 1960, built along the now sadly defunct Speyside Railway, running from the sea to Tomintoul. Its *smoky digestif malt* is an important element in the Johnnie Walker blends.

DALLAS DHU (Highlands – Speyside)
Forres, Morayshire ☎ 0309 676 548
Though there is no longer any production at this distillery, which was originally founded in 1899, Dallas Dhu – the "black water" in Gaelic – is now run by the Scottish Historic Buildings and Monuments and is an interesting museum, not only of the distiller's traditional art, but also of local history.
The malt is a delicately flavoured after-dinner dram.

DALMORE (Highlands)
Alness, Ross-shire ☎ 0349 882362
The Dalmore distillery takes its water from the river Alness, and was built in the late 1830s. Its railway to the Cromarty Firth and the sea led to its being used by the US navy during the First World War as a mine-manufacturing base. Much of its malt goes to the excellent Harrods own and Whyte & Mackay blends.
Fine, rich after-dinner malt

DALWHINNIE* (Highlands – Speyside)
Dalwhinnie, Inverness-shire ☎ 05282 264
The highest distillery in Scotland, at 1,100 feet, nestling in a wild glen between the Grampians, the Cairngorms and the Manadhlaith mountains. Dalwhinnie, the "meeting place", at the crossroads for the oldtime cattle drovers, seems an appropriate place for a distillery. Originally called the Strathspey distillery when officially opened in 1897, it was rebuilt after fire damage in 1934. Its really excellent malt is one of United Distillers' Six Classic Malts and is also an important element in Buchanan blends such as the elegant Black & White.

The interesting visitor centre well illustrates the Buchanan link with many memorabilia of the man and his blends. The area, set in rugged scenery, is often cut off in the winter, and the workers sleep on site. This is a really first-class visit and a good stopping-off place when driving in the summer. One of my favourites.

DUFFTOWN–GLENLIVET
(Highlands – Speyside)
Dufftown, Keith, Banffshire ☎ 0340 20224
"Rome was built on seven hills,/Dufftown stands on seven stills." Dufftown is the capital of the Scotch Highland malt whiskies and this distillery was founded by the Earl of Fife. A supplier of malts for Bell's famous blends, like its near neighbour the Pittyvaich, it uses water from the famous Jock's Well, which is renowned for its purity. Established in 1896, it has been considerably rebuilt, but is definitely part of the Dufftown tour.
Light aperitif with hints of flowers

EDRADOUR* (Highlands)
Pitlochry, Perthshire ☎ 07962 095
The tiny Edradour distillery, with its supposed Mafia links during the time of Prohibition in the United States, produces only two casks of whisky per day. It is an excellent distillery for the beginner to visit as not only does it have amusing and entertaining guides of the first order but also its very smallness allows all the production processes to take place under one roof, thus allowing for an easy understanding of what is going on. Licensed in 1825, its antecedents clearly go back years beyond. It is near the Victorian spa town of Pitlochry with its many excellent hotels.

FETTERCAIRN (Highlands)
Fettercairn, Kincardineshire ☎ 0561340244
One of Scotland's oldest licensed distilleries, officially founded in 1824 in an area where many illicit stills were hidden in the forests and the glens. It was extended in 1966 and has a good reception centre.
Light fresh malt for everyday use

GLENALLACHIE (Highlands – Speyside)
Aberlour on Spey, Banffshire ☎ 0340 871315
Built in 1967 with, in front, a large warm-water dam for ducks. After some years of closure it has recently reopened.
The malt is an excellent pre-dinner dram with a long, light, sweetish finish.

GLENBURGIE–GLENLIVET
(Highlands – Speyside)
Forres, Morayshire ☎ 03438 5258
Founded in 1829, reconstructed in 1878 after a long closure and expanded in 1958. Its malts are very rarely found by the general public. This distillery is to be visited if only for this reason.
Lightly herbal aromatic malt

GLENCADAM (Highlands)
Brechin, Angus ☎ 03562 2217
Glencadam supplies malt for Ballantine's famous blends. Near the old city and market town, it was founded in 1825 and reconstructed in 1959. It has a good reception centre.
Fruity digestif dram

GLENDRONACH (Eastern Highland)
Forgue by Huntly, Aberdeenshire
☎ 046682 202
Founded as early as 1826, this stoutly built distillery is notable for its floor maltings, and has a good vistor centre. Much of its malt goes to Teacher's blends but is a *very good, sweetish after-dinner malt* either in its "Original" version, which is aged in some sherry and some Bourbon casks, or in another version, which is aged only in sherry casks. It is most instructive and of experimental interest to compare the effects of sherry wood in the maturing process.

GLEN ELGIN (Highlands – Speyside)
Longmorn, Morayshire ☎ 03438 6212
One of the important malts that go into White Horse. This was the last distillery to be built in the nineteenth century, founded in 1898 and extended in the 1960s.
Heatherish and honeyed malt

GLENFARCLAS* (Highlands – Speyside)
Marypark, Ballindronach, Banffshire
☎ 08072 257
Glenfarclas, derived from "Gleannfearanglas" ("the valley of the green grasses"), is well named, being set in a lush cattle farm. It is near the Spey, and there is barley grown in

the surrounding fields. It is typical of the distilleries that were built as adjuncts to the activities of the large farms. Family owned by that other great Grant family, the James Grants, the distillery was founded (officially, that is) in 1836 and has some of the largest stills on the Speyside, almost, to my mind, traditionally Lowland in character.

The reception centre is among the best I have seen. The shop sells many interesting bottlings of different proofs, and a prize exhibit in the well-organized museum is a confiscated illicit still, with holes bored in it, alas, to prevent any wayward nocturnal use. This still is on loan from Customs and Excise. An excellent day out.

GLENFIDDICH* (Highlands – Speyside)
Dufftown, Banffshire ☎ 0342 0373
Family-owned by the descendants of William Grant, the Grant-Gordons, the Glenfiddich distillery is renowned as one of the first and the most successful to sell its single malts to a wider general public. The whole area, including its sister distillery, the Balvenie, is excellently presented and a feature of the visit is the bottling plant. The stills are rather small for the type and the still room is arranged for easy viewing by the visitor. There is an excellent little museum, reception area and shop. Over 100,000 vistors come through each year.

This is a fine, working distillery, producing an excellent product by traditional methods and in traditional surroundings. It is simply that the Grant-Gordons have been rather cleverer than most in showing off how the whole thing works. A very highly recommended visit.

GLEN GARIOCH* (Highlands)
Old Meldrum, Aberdeenshire
☎ 0651 872706
This was established in 1797, and ox wagons were still bringing barley up the long hill at the turn of this century. It now has an excellent visitor centre within its thick granite walls and a feature of the visit is the greenhouses used to grow exotic fruits and vegetables and flowers, warmed by the excess heat produced by the distilling process. There are also the now relatively rare floor maltings. If asking the way, take note. Glen Garioch is pronounced "Glen Geery".

GLENGOYNE* (Highlands)
Dumgoyne, Stirlingshire ☎ 041332 2706
Established in 1833. Between Glasgow and Loch Lomond, in a country setting with sheep grazing and a waterfall tumbling behind it into a dam where ducks paddle, this distillery is easy to reach and well worth a visit. There is a first-class visitor centre. The malts, which are now, at last, seen more often in the shops, were an important element of the Lang's Supreme blend.

GLEN GRANT (Highlands – Speyside)
Rothes, Morayshire ☎ 03403 413
Glen Grant was established in 1840. There were considerable additions in the 1880s in a notably Victorian Scottish baronial style, which was popularized by the Queen's recontruction of Balmoral Castle. The original owners were reputedly much involved in smuggling. There is a most interesting visitor centre. The malt is widely available in Great Britain and rightly, but there seems, at the date of writing, little, alas, for export.
A great favourite – a fine, light pre-dinner dram

GLEN KEITH (Highlands – Speyside)
Keith, Banffshire ☎ 05422 7471
A new distillery, and interesting as such, it was established in 1957 and was a pioneer in the use of computer-assisted distilling. It produces a *neat, lightish aperitif malt*. Visitors welcome in the summer months.

GLENKINCHIE* (Lowlands)
Pencaitland, Tranent, East Lothian
☎ 0875 34033
Founded in 1837 and built as a model distillery, in easy reach of Edinburgh (twelve miles), with its bowling green and its redbrick buildings set in Lowland farming country, this distillery has a look that is the complete antithesis of the old granite buildings of the Highlands. But the owners have definitely insisted on some of the traditions. Until the 1960s the manager bred prize-winning cattle, which he fed on the draff. There is a good museum and a very well-planned visitor centre. The Glenkinchie is another of the United Distillers' Six Classic Malts.

THE GLENLIVET* (Highlands – Speyside)
Minmore, Banffshire ☎ 08073 427
In 1824 George Smith set up here as a young man to be the very first of the new legal distillers after the Act of 1823. He armed himself with hair-trigger pistols and had a gang of bodyguards to protect him against attacks from the bands of the great whisky smugglers. Glenlivet has been jokingly called the longest glen in Scotland, since many of the newer distilleries claimed their source of water in the Livet, in order to cash in on the great success of Smith's Glenlivet whisky. In 1880 The Glenlivet went to court successfully to support its claim to be the only whisky entitled to call itself Glenlivet. (It was this whisky, illicitly distilled at the time, that George IV so enjoyed on his visit to Scotland in 1822.) Other distilleries in the area round the Livet can append their suffix "Glenlivet" to their labels: e.g. Aberlour-Glenlivet, Dufftown-Glenlivet, Glenburgie-Glenlivet. But note well: there is only one *The* Glenlivet. The distillery was rebuilt in 1958, set in the grassy valley. Some of the original buildings remain and there is an excellent and interesting visitor centre.

GLENLOSSIE (Highlands – Speyside)
By Elgin, Morayshire ☎ 03438 6331
South of Elgin, this distillery was established in 1976 and extended in 1962. It houses among other memorabilia a fire engine last used in the 1920s – the risk of fire was always a very great preoccupation in distilleries. Its malts go mainly to the production of the Haig blends, and it is worth trying to visit this distillery if only to sample the *sweet heatheriness*.

GLENMORANGIE* (Highlands)
Tain, Ross-shire ☎ 08622 043
Established in 1843, Glenmorangie produces one of the most fragrant and popular light malts. The visitor will be quick to notice the unusually high stills, which give it its lightness and elegance. Set high up in the north, overlooking the misty Dornoch Firth, there is a large glacial boulder left in the grounds from the ice age, with an inscription to "the immortal Walter Scott". No one knows the author of this epitaph.

GLEN MORAY* (Highlands – Speyside)
Elgin, Morayshire ☎ 0343 542577
Established in 1897, on the site of a former brewery, this good, little, working distillery produces a light malt rapidly gaining favour among connoisseurs in Continental Europe. Visitors preferably by prior arrangement.

GLEN SCOTIA (Campbeltown)
Campbeltown, Argyll ☎ 03897 4154
One of the last two great Campbeltown survivors (the other is Springbank). Established in 1832 near the site of the parliament house of Fergus, the first King of Scotland. The distillery was reopened in 1989 after being shut for several years. It is almost hidden in a quiet street and the main interest lies in tasting its twelve-year-old *smoky, almost briny, malt*, a close cousin to the Islays just across the sea. Ghost-busters may be interested that there are tales of the ghost of a former proprietor who roams there at night bemoaning that he was tricked out of a large sum of money by a rival.

GLEN SPEY (Highlands – Speyside)
Rothes, Morayshire ☎ 05422 2531
Founded in 1884, worth a visit for its rare fragrant malts, the majority of which go, sadly enough, to the blenders.
Light, aperitif malt

GLENTURRET (Highlands)
Crieff, Perthshire ☎ 0764 2424
Both Littlemill and Strathisla claim to be the oldest distillery in Scotland. Likewise Glenturret. Records suggest that there was definitely distilling here in 1717 and probably much earlier. The hilly, wooded countryside and steep, inaccessible valley would have made it an ideal place for the illicit black pots. After a period of silence, it was reopened

by the excellent James Fairlie, a malt enthusiast, to preserve traditional ways of distilling whisky on an artisan scale. It has also set itself up very much as a tourist attraction, and has won awards for its Heritage Centre, tasting bar and restaurants. Its cat, Towser, who died in 1987, apparently holds the record for the number of mice caught in the barley lofts: over 27,890 all told, though who had been doing all the counting is not clear. Despite all the extras, Glenturret does remain a working distillery and produces *a really impressive malty and creamy single.*

HIGHLAND PARK* (Highlands – The Islands)
Kirkwall, Orkney ☎ 0856 3107
The furthest north of Scotland's whisky distilleries up in the Orkneys, the stamping ground of that famous smuggling minister, the Reverend Magnus Eunson. An old black pot, "poit dhu", is displayed in memory of those old freebooting days. The distillery has floor maltings and uses its own peat, which is younger and rootier than most and adds to the flavour of the malt. There is a good reception centre.

INCHGOWER (Highlands – Speyside)
Buckie, Banffshire ☎ 0542 31161
The distillery was built in 1871, but with strong smuggling antecedents. It produces a malt that is a great favourite among the fishermen from the herring fleets of Buckie, once Britain's largest fishing port. It has a good new reception centre.
Robustly flavoured, sweetish, after-dinner dram

INVERGORDON* (Highlands)
Invergordon, Ross-shire ☎ 0349 852451
For those who cannot visit a continuous still distillery in the United States, the grain distillery at Invergordon, dating in its present form from the 1960s, makes an interesting stop-over for lovers of industrial processes and landscapes. The Invergordon single grain whisky, most naturally being used in blends, is the only one at the time of writing being marketed to the general public.

JURA* (Highlands – The Islands)
Craighouse, Jura, Argyll ☎ 04968 2240
Jura, the tiny isolated island where George Orwell settled to write his last works, has just one distillery, founded in 1810 and rebuilt in 1876. Tradition has it that the island was once the lair of smugglers in the sixteenth century. Silent for some years after the Second World War, the distillery was rebuilt in the 1950s. The main geographical feature of the island are the Paps of Jura, low mountains that owe their name to some remote mammary resemblance. Jura, which can be reached only by ferry from Port Askaig on Islay, has no reception centre as such, but can lay claim to giving the warmest human reception of any distillery to those who have

travelled thus far to taste the sweet salty malt with its perfectly curious undertones of Glenmorangie.

KNOCKANDO* (Highlands – Speyside)
Knockando, Morayshire ☎ 0340 6205
Knockando, "the little black hillock", has no reception centre, but the distillery, dating from 1898, is very well worth the visit for its excellent working practices and its efficient turnout. The many aficionados of this truly great malt should flock to visit it.

KNOCKDHU (Highlands – Speyside)
Knockdhu, Knock, Banffshire ☎ 0466 86223
Established in 1893. Again, another great little visit for the amateurs and those who would wish to discover its *little, dry, gentle, single malt,* much of which is destined for the Haig blends.

LAGAVULIN* (Islay)
Port Ellen, Islay, Argyll ☎ 0496 2250
Lagavulin, "the hollow where the mill is" was established, officially, some time after 1822. The mill used for grinding barley was also the place where a great deal of illicit distilling went on. At the entrance to the distillery there is a stone with a white horse carved on it to remind us that Lagavulin adds a little something special to the White Horse blend. Another of United Distillers' Six Classic Malts.

LAPHROAIG* (Islay)
Port Ellen, Islay, Argyll ☎ 0496 2418
Established in 1815, Laphroaig, with its cult following for its phenolic malts, has a small reception centre and a very warm welcome for visitors. Overlooking the sea and bounded by low hills, it is certainly the best-kept and turned-out distillery of its size that I have ever visited anywhere. Before it was discovered that people could actually enjoy its very characteristic malts, much was "lost" to the Long John blend. The distillery has the honour of being the first to have been owned by a woman (in the 1950s and 1960s): Miss Bessie Williamson.

LINKWOOD (Highlands – Speyside)
Elgin, Morayshire ☎ 0343 547004
One of the first distilleries to be legalized in 1824, it was here that the manager forbade workers to remove spider's webs in the maturing sheds lest the quality of the whisky be impaired.
Slightly smoky, sweetish malt with no traces of spider

LITTLEMILL (Lowlands)
Bowling, Dumbartonshire ☎ 03879 4154
Another of the oldest distilleries of Scotland, established officially in 1772. It was silent during most of the 1980s but reopened in 1989, although it is silent again at the time of

writing. Largely rebuilt in the 1880s, it has the charm of a much earlier age.
Mellowish, pre-dinner dram

LONGMORN (Highlands – Speyside)
Longmorn ☎ 05422 7471
The distillery was established as late as 1894. It is said by the great whisky connoisseur and man of taste Wallace Milroy to produce one of the really outstanding malts – which should be recommendation enough to go and see how it is made. Visitors welcome in the summer months.
Truly marvellous, fragrant, nutty malt

THE MACALLAN* (Highlands – Speyside)
Craigellachie, Banffshire ☎ 03405 471
The distillery was established early in 1824, which suggests that there had been distilling going on quietly here for some time, no doubt to supply the needs of the cattle drovers who came down from the northern Highlands, driving their beasts to the Lowland markets. In recent years The Macallan had been used for finishing blends; now its malts are widely available to its many connoisseurs, who include Sir Kingsley Amis, the writer, who dubs it "the best glass", and Milroy, again, for whom it is a "masterpiece". Indeed, nowhere has that subtle fortuitous marriage between sherry wood and malt whisky been more happily celebrated and consummated.

MILTOWNDUFF–GLENLIVET
(Highlands – Speyside)
Elgin, Morayshire ☎ 0343 547 433
Also licensed in 1824 and built on the site of an ancient monastery founded by Alexander II of Scotland. Surely a great deal of distilling took place here in earlier days. Pluscarden Abbey was also well known for its beer, which "made the hearts of all rejoice and filled the abbey with such unutterable bliss, raised their devotions to that pitch which that Helden's Hills echoed to their Hallelujahs . . ." The large stills today produce an elegant malt, far too much of which goes to the blenders. The distillery has an excellent visitor centre.
Fine, fragrant, after-dinner dram

MORTLACH* (Highlands – Speyside)
Dufftown, Keith, Banffshire ☎ 0340 20318
Modernized in 1903 and 1964, and the licence dates from 1823. The highly attractive site is where Malcolm II of Scotland defeated the marauding Danes.

OBAN* (Highlands)
Oban, Argyll ☎ 0631 62110
This distillery was built in 1794, set close against the cliffs in the centre of one of Scotland's busiest holiday resorts, with its eccentric Victorian replica of the Colosseum, high above the town on the hill. The distillery has a fine visitor centre and the truly amber-coloured Oban is yet another of

United Distillers' marvellous Six Classic Malts.

ORD (Highlands)
Muir of Ord, Argyll ☎ 0463 870421
Founded in 1838 and built of pinkish stone, the distillery's malt, the Glenordie, as it now is called, usually goes to Dewar's blends. It has a really good visitor centre and there are very interesting modern maltings near by, a visit to which is a must.
Very smooth, long-tasting, fine, after-dinner malt

ROSEBANK (Lowlands)
Falkirk, Stirlingshire ☎ 0324 23325
Rosebank, stuck incongruously beside a canal in an industrial landscape, may seem a curious place to produce an extremely fine, triple-distilled malt. Established in 1841, the closeness to the canal allowing for easy transport. Definitely to be visited for its malt and the chance to see Lowland triple distillation. In my opinion far too much of this malt has been allowed to go to the George IV blends. Mothballed mid-1993.
Light but very pleasingly austere aperitif

ROYAL LOCHNAGAR (Highlands)
Crathie, Ballater, Aberdeenshire
☎ 03384 273
Established in 1845, though there was legal distilling here in 1826. Its whisky was the firm favourite of Queen Victoria, who visited the distillery from nearby Balmoral. Largely rebuilt in 1967, it has a brand new visitor centre. The church of Crathie is where the Royal Family worships when at Balmoral. The malt is what the old Queen reputedly put in her tea. Well worth a try, without the tea, for its *clean sweet maltiness.*

SCAPA (Highlands – The Islands)
Kirkwall, Orkney ☎ 0856 2071
Set up in 1885, the distillery was saved from fire by the British fleet during the First World War and was largely rebuilt in 1959. It has a reception centre and makes for a very good visit when in Orkney.
Heather and peat notes are to be found in this neat malty after-dinner dram.

SPEYBURN (Highlands – Speyside)
Rothes, Morayshire ☎ 03403 213
Built in 1897 to a typically Victorian industrial design, it is set in a landscape of breathtaking beauty. It is definitely worth a stop off here on the way from Elgin to Rothes. Much of its excellent malt, and this is one of my own favourites, goes for blending.
Deeply aromatic after-dinner dram for the musing connoisseur

STRATHISLA (Highlands – Speyside)
Keith, Banffshire ☎ 05422 7471
Established officially in 1786, another claimant to be the oldest distillery in Scotland, and

a claim I support wholeheartedly, as records very clearly show that there had been a farm distillery here on the site for many years, subsequent to earlier activities by the monks. The distillery is neatly turned out in granite and has an amusingly poky little alchemist's den of a still room. It malts are sadly scarce, much going to Chivas Regal de-luxe blends. The distillery has a very good reception and visitor centre and while their parents are sampling a dram or two of the malt and are bemoaning the fact that they cannot find it in their local spirit shop, children can dodge the cars and go across the road and look at the shaggy, russet-haired, long-horned Highland cattle.
Best after a long walk in the country on a sharp spring day; the sweetish overtones of the malt also make it a damn decent after-dinner dram.

TALISKER* (Highlands – The Islands)
Carbost, Skye ☎ 0748 42203
Established in the early 1830s, this is the only distillery on the Isle of Skye. Neil Gunn, the poetic Scottish writer and apologist for pure malt, observed of its malt, "At best it can be superb, but I have known it to adopt the uncertainties of the Skye weather." For some the sun shines clear every day on the island. Sir Ewen Fergusson, the British ambassador to Paris, considers it to be among his favourites. The distillery has good visiting facilities. Another of United Distillers' Six Classic Malts.

TAMDHU* (Highlands – Speyside)
Knockando, Morayshire ☎ 03406 221
Established in 1896. Much of its malts goes to The Famous Grouse, playing an important part in making this blend so very attractive. Tamdhu, "the black hill", has its own Saladin maltings, which makes the distillery very well worthwhile visiting. The well-planned visitor centre is charmingly set in the waiting rooms and ticket office of the disused Knockando railway station.

TAMNAVULIN (Highland – Speyside)
Ballindalloch, Dumbartonshire ☎ 08073 442
Tamnavulin, "the mill on the hill", was first built in 1865 and is an excellent example of a modern distillery using traditional methods. The very attractive visitor centre and tasting room is in a well-restored old mill.
Good, mellow, all-rounder of a malt

TOMATIN (Highland – Speyside)
Tomatin, Inverness-shire ☎ 08082 234
Established in 1897, this distillery was based on a small, fifteenth-century distillery catering for the urgent needs of cattle drovers. Today, it is owned by the Japanese. The malt is also used for Scotch blends. The single malt is rare and could provide *a clean, light, beginner's dram* to take him on the road to the even greater taste sensations waiting smilingly in their bottles. New visitor centre.

TORMORE (Highlands – Speyside)
Advie, Grantown on Spey, Morayshire
☎ 08075 244
Built in 1958, one of the first of the post-war whisky boom. Its white buildings, topped with a belfry and carillon, are set in well-tended ornamental gardens.
Golden, medium-bodied, after-dinner dram

TULLIBARDINE (Highlands)
Blackford, Perthshire ☎ 076482 252
Opened in 1949 on the site of a former brewery, it is an essential visit for its sweetish, very delicate, aperitif malt, which definitely deserves a wider public in Continental Europe.

THE SCOTCH WHISKY HERITAGE CENTRE
354 Castlehill, The Royal Mile, Edinburgh
☎ 031 220 0441
Just a minute's walk from the Esplanade of Edinburgh Castle. The visitor to this musuem is first led by the friendly guides through an exhibition showing all the processes of whisky making, starting with the raw barley up to the maturing of the distilled spirit. There is an excellent audio-visual show and a large-scale model of a distillery. The visitor will then go upstairs and take a ride in a barrel-shaped chair through some 300 years of the social and industrial history of Scotch whisky, enlivened by theatrical sets and models. The commentary is provided in several languages. The shop sells some 75 different whiskies, blends and single malts, as well as numerous books about whisky. The visit is an excellent introduction to the world of whisky, before a visit to the distilleries themselves.

IRELAND

Although Ireland's distilling has gone through hard times and the number of distilleries has been reduced to two, the quality of the product and the warmth of the welcome are unimpaired.

MIDLETON*
Midleton, Co. Cork ☎ 021 631 821
Built in 1973 on the site of the Old Midleton distillery, this is not simply one distillery but certainly the most modern distillery complex in the world. In effect, it is four distilleries in one – the home, now, of those great Irish whiskeys, Jameson, Powers, Tullamore Dew and Paddy, as well as the quite extraordinarily fine Midleton Very Rare. The distillery happily combines the most traditional and the most modern in its production processes. Behind the new buildings is the old distillery, which recently has been most imaginatively transformed into the "Jameson Whiskey Centre" where the story of Irish whiskey is told and where there is an abundance of arte-

facts, including a large water wheel, a fine steam engine, and the largest pot still in the world – of amazing capacity. There are, of course, whiskey tastings, first-class restaurants, and shops. A marvellous visit and day out.

OLD BUSHMILLS*

Bushmills, Co. Antrim ☎ 02657 31521

Near the celebrated Giant's Causeway, Bushmills is the oldest licensed distillery in the world: the licence was given in 1608. Its pagodas shine in the dam fed by St Columb's rill, encircled by trees in a picturesque setting. The distillery is gradually being enlarged, the new buildings harmonizing marvellously with the old. The visitor reception centre is certainly one of the best and most welcoming I have ever seen. Housed in the old malt kilns, it contains a wealth of old distillery tools, advertisements, photographs and memorabilia connected with the whiskey business. An ideal place to taste Ireland's only single malt.

THE IRISH WHISKEY CORNER

Bow Street, Dublin ☎ 01 72 55 66

In a street of empty, bricked-up warehouses, not without a certain Piranesian charm, the Irish Whiskey Corner is a museum where, after a vivid and highly entertaining video show (available in many languages) recounting the long history of whiskey, the visitor can wander round an excellently planned collection of artefacts and old photographs, before going to the bar for a whiskey tasting and appreciation course. The guides, soundly versed in whiskey lore, are most friendly and informative, with a deep love of their native product. The shop sells, as might be expected, all the brands of Irish whiskey in different bottlings, as well as glasses and decanters in Ireland's rightly prized Waterford crystal.

JAPAN

No doubt many visitors to Japan might well have things on their minds other than Japanese whisky distilleries but if there is one that should be visited it is the Suntory Yamazaki distillery.

YAMAZAKI* (Southern Honshu)

Osaka ☎ 075 962 1423

Midway between the commercial city of Osaka and the cultural capital of Japan, Kyoto – with its own pagodas – the distillery nests under high misty hills. It was the first built in Japan, in 1923, and has been subsequently and regularly added to since. That grand whisky buff Michael Jackson describes its pagodas as resembling "loudspeakers on a 1950s radio". However, going round the distillery, the visitor cannot fail to notice the great care that is taken in making whisky in the true Scottish way, while at the same time

taking advantage of all modern aids. Those who tend rather to scoff at Japanese whisky should come here and have their eyes opened.

UNITED STATES

Taking the Bardstown area of Kentucky as the heart of American Bourbon whiskey country, aficionados of this close cousin to the Celtic water of life should be well pleased with a visit to any of these distilleries. Those who, like myself, were originally rather sceptical about this New World spirit should come too. Perhaps they might well remain doubtful about the true qualities of American whiskeys, but they will not fail to be impressed by the care and pride the distillerymen take in their product, and, who knows, the effect of place on the tasting of this worthy descendant of the Celtic black pots might sow a vigorous seed in their minds.

ANCIENT AGE* (Kentucky)

Wilkinson Boulevard, Frankfort, Kentucky ☎ 502 223 7641

One of the oldest and largest distilleries of the States, it has been producing its highly acclaimed Bourbon in its column stills since 1869. The tour includes a video presentation, describing the history of American whiskey and its debt to the mother country of whisky, a huge nine-storey warehouse, an interesting, very modern, bottling plant where an amazing 100,000 bottles are filled capped and labelled every hour.

JIM BEAM'S AMERICAN OUTPOST* (Kentucky)

Clermont, Kentucky ☎ 502 543 9877

Some twelve miles out of Bardstown, the Beam family started distilling Bourbon whiskey here in 1795. The visit includes an old moonshine still, a museum of cooperage in the 1800s and an excellent, though naturally partisan, film on the history of Bourbon. There is also a small museum of china whiskey decanters in the excellent visitor centre. An enjoyable visit for the devotee of Bourbon.

MAKER'S MARK* (Kentucky)

Loretto, Kentucky ☎ 502 865 2099

Set in beautiful rolling countryside some twenty miles out of Bardstown. Sour-mash Bourbon whiskey has been made here since 1840 – though quaintly, like George Dickel, it is spelt "whisky". The visit to this, the smallest distillery, with its country charm and its status as a classified monument, is led by smiling guides, who rattle you through the process from still house and warehousing to bottling. Of particular note are the traditional wooden washbacks. For many, despite the cliché, Maker's Mark really is the "Rolls-Royce of American whiskeys".

WILD TURKEY* (Kentucky)

Lawrenceburg, Kentucky ☎ 502 839 4544

Some people think that American whiskey distilleries are not very pretty places. This is in the eye of the beholder. This distillery is full of steam and bustle and life, which for me is the sign of the true Bourbon whiskey distillery. No frills, perhaps, but if you want to see a nuts-and-bolts distillery, Wild Turkey is definitely the place for you – and me. There is a well-planned visitor centre. Look out also for their Wild Turkey Rye Whiskey, one of the very best rye whiskeys on the market.

For those who would still find Bourbon a touch too rich and heavy to their taste, the great Tennessee Sour Mash Whiskey might be very much more to their liking.

JACK DANIEL'S* (Tennessee)

Lynchburg, Tennessee ☎ 615 757 4221

The kindly distillerymen at Jack Daniel's are quick to point out that they are making Tennessee Sour Mash Whiskey, where the de-alcoholized fermentation from previous distillations is added to the mash to give extra body and flavour to the whiskey. The spirit distilled is then filtered through deep beds of ground charcoal. The firing of the sugar-maple staves to make this charcoal is a vivid tourist attraction, held twice a week. The buildings of the distillery are pleasantly mellowed by creepers and their visitor reception centre is well planned. In the museum there is a collection of bottles and stone whiskey jugs, but this might be slightly old hat if you have already visited the Oscar Getz Museum (see below). Lynchburg being in a dry county, at the end of the tour, the guides will give you a glass of lemonade instead of the usual dram. In part the warmth of the guides does make up for this, but many, like me, will drive as fast as possible to the county line to slake their thirst with some of that good old Jack's black-labelled Old Number 7 Tennessee Sour Mash.

THE OSCAR GETZ MUSEUM OF WHISKEY HISTORY

114 North Fifth Street, Bardstown, Kentucky ☎ 502 348 2999

In the historic heart of Bardstown, the museum has a collection of whiskey artefacts and documents dating from the earliest days of the colonies to the Prohibition period. The objects include moonshine stills and other copper distilling vessels. There is a container room displaying not only different kinds of cask, but also antique bottles and jugs. There are even mementoes of the infamous, crazed Carrie Nation, leader of the Prohibition movement, as well as tin advertising art, many novelty whiskey containers, bottles and glasses. A truly splendid visit, not only for the whiskey historian, but also an amusing one for anyone interested in past fads and fashions.

SCOTLAND

Here, as in Ireland, I have not chosen the grand hotels, which are perfectly comfortable in their own way; hotels that are a part of the huge international chains with their international décors and their cuisine (delicious, true, but owing more to the tradition of the great chefs of France than that of the Celts). I have selected smaller, more typical hotels, which for me reflect better the feeling of place, the feeling of the whisky heartlands. Nor have I chosen hotels in the great cities of the north.

It seems to me that, to be perfectly at one with the many pleasures, the myriad delights of whisky, you should leave the towns, breathe in the air – as the maturing whisky has done – and you should listen to the silence. You should be able to sit down with your glass of malt in your hand by some warm log fire, and watch the whisky glow in the light, before going in to a dinner prepared from fresh ingredients taken from the land and the hills all around you. And, then, after a late malt, a fruity Highland, perhaps, or a smoky Islay, you should be able to go up to a comfortable room looking out over the harsh moors, or across the gentle lochs or down on the wind-beaten sea. *Oidche Mhath Leibh!* From these windows, at early light you will watch the mist rise to strains of a pibroch . . . the *piobairachd*. Is it a piper or is it simply in the mind?

There are grand hotels – the finest, perhaps, Gleneagles, does not need any introduction from me – but I want to take you to country houses and old inns, places with their own unique Scottish charm, hotels where I have stayed and have not wanted to leave, hotels heartily recommended by friends – true Scots and lovers of whisky and fine food and elegant furniture, men of good taste.

These are not just any hotels, but homes from home where you will want to return again to that same warm welcome, that same Celtic smile, and that same proffered dram of fellowship. And when you stay in these houses, you will be just a step away from understanding something more of these, the most beautiful, regions of Scotland, where the castles on the crags and headlands, the crosses raised to ancient battles and the Celtic crosses of the monks, seem almost to outnumber the bustling distilleries in the glens with their pagodas shining proud through the mist, distilleries transforming earth, fire and water into the magic that is whisky.

From these hotels you will be able to cast your line across the clear waters that run down to the distillery dams, the broader waters teeming with salmon. In the evening's calm you will see lochs where the brown trout rises, sending ripples across the still waters, and the pass between the looming bulk of the mountains, where drovers have passed and battle-weary clansmen have trod. Then, when the sky is shot with purple, pink and red, you too will understand the deep affection, the love Queen Victoria felt for these glens. And then, when the wind bringing hints of the heather whistles through the rough gorse, you, too, will know why whisky, here, is truly the drink of the place.

The food, too, will delight the gourmet, send his senses dancing a strathspey of delight along paths that he had forgotten had existed. The fresh fish from the sea, the lobster, the salmon from the rivers, the trout . . . the smoked fish, salmon, again, but also the finnan haddock, the delicate dish of kippers at breakfast . . . ah, the sumptuous breakfasts . . .

And then there is the game in season, the venison marinated in whisky, the marvellous grouse, well hung, melting in the mouth, served with a jelly of moorland berries, the regal grouse . . . And then there is the beef, the Angus beef – was there ever such beef? . . . the lamb . . . and so much more . . . the cheeses . . . the oat breads . . . And the drams – the water of life . . . *Uiscebaugh!* . . . *A Dhia na Grà! a Chruitheir! a Mhuire Mhathair! . . . cead mîe fàlte! . . . fàlte do'n duthaich! Am bheil Gàdhlig agaibh?* Ah no? Then: *Slainte . . . Slainte Mhor!*

These hotels are given in alphabetical order. The maps on page 168 will help you plan your itinerary.

ALLT NAN ROS HOTEL
Onich, by Fort William, PH33 6RY
☎ 08553 210
The hotel was originally a Victorian shooting lodge. Its rooms overlook long gardens to Loch Linnhe, with wide views of mountains beyond towards Glencoe, Morvern and Mull. Log fires glow in the fireplaces in the traditionally decorated rooms. There is a good wine list, and a range of more than fifty malts add the final flourish. A warm and friendly hotel fondly remembered.

ALTNAHARRA HOTEL
By Lairg, Sutherland IV27 4UE
☎ 054 981 222
With its excellent, comfortable bedrooms, and two annexe cottages for families or parties of fishermen, this charming small hotel started life as a coaching inn. The atmosphere is warm and welcoming; the Scottish food is first class; the list of malts, impressive. Well recommended, ideal for sportsmen or simply for those who wish to admire the local flora and fauna. Its situation at the loch's edge is a pure delight.

AYRE HOTEL
Kirkwall, Orkney ☎ 0856 873001
A small simple hotel, marvellously set on the bay of Kirkwall and close to the Highland Park distillery, whose excellent golden, honeyed malt with its hints of young peat must be tried *in situ*, before taking a bottle home.

BEECHWOOD COUNTRY HOUSE
Moffat, Dumfriesshire, DG10 9RS
☎ 0683 20210
The Victorian house, in twelve acres of beechwoods, was originally a school for young ladies. They are no longer there, and in the dining room there is a menu of freshly prepared dishes made from local produce. The cheeseboard especially tempted me with its selection of Scottish cheeses, as well as the glorious cheeses from my homeland Pennines. Good drams.

BELGRAVE ARMS HOTEL
Helmsdale, Sutherland ☎ 04312 242
This well-set-up family hotel on the road north to Wick is a haven for salmon and trout fishermen. The food is good and the drams plentiful in the pub just next door. The reception and service are most kindly.

CONTIN HOUSE
Contin by Strathpeffer ☎ 0997 42 1920
Dating from the eighteenth century, the house has kept all the charm of a private residence, beautifully set on an island in this most picturesque region in good striking distance of the Speyside distilleries. I drammed with the marvellous Aberlour and followed up with the smoky Benrinnes.

CRAIGELLACHIE HOTEL
Craigellachie, Banffshire ☎ 0340 881 1204
This small hotel is set in spectacular countryside, at the meeting point of those two great rivers of whisky fame, the Fiddich and the Spey. The Quaich cocktail is excellent and most generous; the list of malts faultless.

CREEBRIDGE HOUSE HOTEL
Newton Stewart, DG8 6NP ☎ 0671 2121
Formerly owned by the Earls of Galloway, this country-house hotel offers fine country living, and is set in three acres of gardens and woodlands. The reception rooms are comfortable; no one could be disappointed in the cuisine, which uses excellent local produce, and there are over thirty malts to choose from. A very friendly place. Highly recommended.

CRINGLETIE HOUSE HOTEL

Eddleston, Peebles ☎ 072 13 233

Set in twenty-eight acres, this mansion has all the warmth and welcome of a private house. twenty miles from Edinburgh, it is a good staging house for thrusting north to the Highland whisky country or for wheeling south to take in the Lowland stills. There are very pretty views from the bedrooms and the food is prepared from produce from the gardens. Their Auchentoshan was my first choice, followed later by a very decent Knockando.

THE CROOK INN

Tweedsmuir, Tweedale ML12 6QN
☎ 08997 272

This licensed establishment dates from 1604 and was originally a stagecoach inn. Standing in the beautiful glen of Tweedsmuir and beside the banks of the river Tweed, it is well placed for fishing, in the river, its tributaries and the several lochs in the hills near by. The rooms are comfortable, the food staunchly Scottish, the talk of fishing, and the bar is well stocked with a good array of malts. A Shangri-La for fishermen who like to combine philosophical calm with a good dram.

CULLODEN HOUSE HOTEL

Inverness-shire ☎ 0463 790461

The house itself is a Georgian, Palladian-style mansion. There are high ceilings with elegant mouldings and comfortable furniture, all in excellent taste, as is the marvellous cuisine and exhaustive wine list. This historic home is part of the de-luxe Prestige Hotels chain. The welcome is of the warmest. The Scottish breakfast I had was the most delicious and generous I could remember for a long time. The list of malts and other whiskies is enormous. It was here that I first met Jim Milne, the master blender of J. & B., and the memory of our long chat, over a glass of his best, in front of a blazing log fire, was one of the high points of my whisky tours of Scotland. Culloden, the scene of the infamous battle, is near by. Loch Ness with its monster (take more than a few drams before trying to see it) is not far away, as is the fortified and moated Cawdor Castle, the dungeon of dark deeds in Shakespeare's *Macbeth*. I rank Culloden House Hotel as one of the very best of its kind that I have ever visited.

DOLPHINTON HOUSE HOTEL

Dolphinton, near West Linton
☎ 0968 82286

The building of this house started in 1801 on the site of an older home of the Mackenzie family, and in the hotel's 186 acres of parkland there are the remains of an iron-age fort. The eighteen bedrooms are appointed to a luxurious standard and the reception rooms are furnished with really fine, old fur-niture. Many specially commissioned paintings hang on the walls. The food is astonishingly good, even for Scotland, and the chef has created imaginative dishes based on traditional Scottish materials and historic recipes. Near Edinburgh, it is an ideal stopping-off point for those heading north, and for those, southbound, wishing to linger a moment longer in Scotland. An ideal place to taste the lighter Lowland drams, before, of course, mulling over a digestif of their heartier northern brothers. Very highly recommended.

DORNOCH CASTLE HOTEL

Dornoch, Sutherland IV25 3SD
☎ 0862 810216

The former palace of the bishops of Caithness; the views across the Dornoch Firth to the hills of Ross and Cromarty are quite stupendous. After being a palace, a garrison building, a courthouse, gaol and school, and private house, it has now found its true *raison d'être* as a hotel. The food is first class in the true Scottish tradition: haggis laced with whisky, salmon, game, and really fine Angus beef, the best beef in the world. The bar, set in the old courthouse, has as many malts as you could wish to try. I spent a very pleasant hour with a dram or two in my hand on the terrace overlooking the formal gardens in the still, light, northern, summer evening. The welcome and care during my stay in this picturesque old castle was most kind and warm and dispelled any thoughts of the dungeons in the foundations. Very highly recommended indeed.

THE ENMORE HOTEL

Marine Parade, Kirn Hunter's Quay, Dunoon
☎ 0369 2148

This calls itself a small luxury hotel – with reason. The sixteen bedrooms are well appointed, as are the reception rooms. The staff is most friendly and quick with a smile. The excellent five-course dinner has the true Scot's generosity and taste; the wine list is very sound, and the gardens provide gentle relaxation after a long summer's day. It has an interesting list of drams, which would take several happy days to run through. I spent several happy days here.

GLENBORROWDALE CASTLE

Acharacle, Argyll PH36 4JP ☎ 09724 266

The castle built by a Scottish magnate ninety years ago is set in truly breathtaking countryside on the Ardnamurchan Peninsula of the western Highlands. Typical of these hotels, the fourteen bedrooms and state rooms as well as the reception rooms are decorated and furnished with *objets d'art*, often of museum quality. The state rooms all have four-poster beds. The food provided from local produce is of the freshest and highest quality. Very highly recommended.

GLENFEOCHAN HOUSE HOTEL

Kilmore, Oban, Argyll, PA34 4QR
☎ 063 177 273

A turreted sandstone house rebuilt in 1875 on the remains of a seventeenth-century manor. The interior is stoutly Victorian and the accent is on comfort. The views from the windows out on to the wild Scottish country-side are remarkable and the garden has been restored after years of neglect and is a blaze of colour, with more than a hundred different rhododendrons, and a *mélange* of rich scents from flowers forgotten by the seedsman's cata-logues. Wild salmon are caught in the river Nell and on Loch Feochan and are smoked on the premises. Venison, from Jura and else-where, appears regularly on the table, together with peaches and nectarines from the large greenhouses. The hostess is a former teacher at the London Cordon Bleu School of Cookery, so the cuisine is well up to the standard expected in this type of hotel in Scotland. There are only three bedrooms; my favourite has its bathroom in the turret and a quite magnificent view. A great little stay with grand little drams.

GLENFINNAN HOUSE HOTEL

Kinlochiel, Inverness-shire, PH37 4LP
☎ 039 783 235

The old, panelled house is set in wide grounds near where Bonnie Prince Charlie raised his standard for the 1745 Rising. As soon as I said that I was writing a book about whisky, a dram was pressed into my hands – even before I went up to my comfortable, cosy room. The food was excellent in the Scottish tradition; a piper came to play in the well-decorated dining room, the bar was well stocked with the water of life. What more could I need? Altogether an excellent stay.

GRANT ARMS HOTEL

Monymusk, Aberdeenshire ☎ 04677 226

With its fifteen miles of exclusive fishing rights on the river Don teeming with salmon and brown trout, this former eighteenth-century coaching inn has been carefully and comfortably modernized, while keeping its traditional character. The hotel prides itself on its fine Scottish dishes – and with reason. They have a wide selection of malts. Yet another very friendly, small hotel, with fifteen bedrooms. An excellent choice.

THE HOLLY TREE HOTEL

Kentallan by Appin, Argyll, PA34 4QR
☎ 063174 292

Set just at the edge of Loch Linnhe, near Kentallan, the "head of the salt water" in Gaelic, this family-run hotel started life curi-ously as a railway station. The metamorphosis is complete: log fires burn in every room, the atmosphere is comfortable and informal. The ten bedrooms are charmingly appointed and look out across the loch to the mountains of

Morven while Ben Nevis looms up behind the hotel. An excellent place for setting out stalking. The food prepared from local produce is copious and very fine, though possibly a touch too much in the French style for a truly Celtic experience. On the other hand, they have very good drams indeed.

HOTEL EILEANI IARMAIN
Sleat, Isle of Skye, IV43 8QR ☎ 047 13 332
I came here for the Talisker and was given a welcome worthy of that noble gingery malt: blazing log fires, smiles of greeting from the staff, who, though they can speak English, are all Gaelic speakers – handy for those who would like to pick up a useful phrase or two. *Slainte Mhor!* Great, good health! The antique furniture develops the feeling of a traditional old Highland inn. The food – venison in season, and the local fish – was quite marvellous, and the wine list was amazingly complete and of a standard that would put many Paris and London restaurants to shame. As well as the local Talisker, there was a very catholic range of the malts, including the local vatted malt, Poit Dhubh – the "black pot". A most highly recommended visit.

KINLOCH HOUSE HOTEL
by Blairgowrie, Perthshire, PH10 6SG
☎ 0250 84 237
Built in 1840, this very fine home, set in a large parkland, is excellently appointed. The cuisine is based on first-class Scottish ingredients: beef, lamb, venison and wildfowl, and some of the best fresh fish that I have ever tasted in a long day's march. The discerning connoisseur, nay man of taste, will know that such ingredients need no frills, and here indeed they are excellently and simply prepared. There is salmon fishing on the Tay, trout fishing in the nearby lochs, and trips to Scone Place, Blair Castle, the childhood home of the Queen Mother, reputed to hold a monster in its thick walls – and, of course, the distilleries of Glenturret and Edradour are only a few shakes of a lamb's tail away. The very comfortable bar has over 130 malts of different bottlings. A very pleasant stay.

KINLOCH LODGE
Sleat, Isle of Skye ☎ 047 13 214
A former hunting lodge on the estates of the Macdonalds, this well-known hotel has been in the family for 300 years. Lady Macdonald writes books about the way of life on this island and makes bread and marvellous jam and personally supervises the memorable breakfasts.

THE LODGE ON THE LOCH
Creag Dhu, Onich near Fort William, Inverness-shire PH33 6RY ☎ 08553 237
Set on a broad bay, warmed by the Gulf Stream, which creates a microclimate with eucalyptus and palm trees flourishing in the garden. The lodge has a fine, warm atmosphere and the rooms all overlook the sea. The seafood is, as can be expected, first class and the Angus beef quite delicious. The selection of malts is most interesting and the manager a most knowledgeable chap who will take you through a tour of them, which could be a reason for staying longer in this excellent haven.

MARLEFIELD COUNTRY HOUSE HOTEL
Eckford near Kelso, Roxburghshire, TD5 8ED
☎ 05734 561
A very typical, old Scottish country house, standing proudly on the Borders. It has six spacious bedrooms, all well fitted out to modern standards and with log fires roaring in the winter and the sharp spring. The wine list is very sound and the drams include all the excellent Lowland favourites. Perhaps it is a little carping of me, given the true excellence of the table, but its Continental accent perhaps overwhelms and ignores the high quality of the local Lowland produce and cooking.

MINMORE HOUSE HOTEL
Minmore, Banffshire ☎ 08073 378
This charming family hotel, once the home of George Smith, founder of the Glenlivet distillery, is sited on the river Livet and is in the heartland of whisky country. Before and after the excellent Highland food the bar is a must with its many malts. Like me you will probably stay true to the region and plump for The Glenlivet, first, second and third – and fourth.

PITTODRIE HOUSE HOTEL
Pitcaple, near Inverurie, Aberdeenshire
☎ 046 76 444
This really first-class, country-house hotel dates back to the late fifteenth century. Burned down by the Duke of Montrose, it was rebuilt in 1675 and converted into a hotel in 1977. Set in a magnificent three-acre walled garden – my lady companion almost swooned at the scent of the summer honeysuckle – the house is dominated by the hill of Bennachie. The hotel remains at heart a country house with very many fine antiques and family portraits and there is a smoking room conveniently placed near the bar, which boasts over sixty malts. The long wine list has been carefully chosen and the cuisine relies on much local produce to provide the most delicate dishes of grouse and pheasant. Looking out over the misty garden on a moonlit night with Michael Jackson and that great buff Wallace Milroy, mulling over the glories of whisky, we chose, among others, a bottle of the very fine Balvenie. At breakfast I ate the best pair of kippers I have ever eaten in my life. Everything was just perfect, without equal. Most highly recommended.

PORT ASKAIG HOTEL
Islay ☎ 043 684 845
For those of you who just cannot drag yourselves away from the distilleries of the island, this old inn, dating from the fifteenth century, provides fine, local food and if the great Islay malts are to the front of the bar, there are many more whiskies from the other regions of Scotland as well as from Ireland, just across the water.

THE REVACK LODGE
Grantown on Spey, Morayshire, PH26 3NH
☎ 0479 82377
High on a hill on the outskirts of the town, this is one of the most warm and inviting country houses of Scotland and is the home of Lady Pauline Ogilvy Grant. It is a shooting lodge built in 1860. The hospitality is truly of the highest Scottish tradition and the perfectly delicious food is prepared from the produce of the estate. This most luxurious country-house hotel and its vast estate probably provides as many field sports as any. Lady Pauline Ogilvy Grant is reputed to be Scotland's finest deer stalker. And the salmon caught can be smoked or frozen or mounted as trophies. It has an excellent range of malts, especially from the Speyside. The lodge is, moreover, perfectly placed for visits to the distilleries in the region.

TIRORAN HOUSE HOTEL
Mull, Argyll ☎ 063 15 232
A sporting lodge set in fifteen acres of woodlands overlooking Loch Scridain, it is beautifully furnished with antiques and the rooms are most comfortable, the service charming and friendly. As so often, much of the food comes from the gardens and the estate, notably the excellent beef and lamb. The Scottish cheeses and traditional puddings are exciting discoveries for those raised solely on Continental fare. The aficionado of the excellent Tobermory malt should mull over it from the bars on the quayside of the town with its brightly painted houses. The distillery, now silent, alas, does not often receive visitors.

TULCHAN LODGE
Grantown on Spey, Morayshire, PH26 3NH
☎ 08075 200
A most attractive house dating from the beginning of the century, with huge bedrooms furnished with antiques. Marvellous drams, and a most attentive and efficient staff.

TULLICH LODGE
By Ballater, Aberdeenshire ☎ 03397 55 406
The elegant small house in the Scottish baronial style is built in pink granite, with bedrooms furnished with many fine pieces very much of the Scottish style. It has a restaurant praised by gourmets from all over the world. It has a good, if rather eclectic,

choice of malts. Like me, probably after dinner, you will opt for the Royal Lochnagar and think of old Queen Victoria.

IRELAND

There are so many charming small hotels in Ireland that my greatest regret is that, there being only two distilleries over there, the choice that I can offer you when on a whiskey tour is rather limited. Visiting Ireland, I am always struck by the warmth of the hospitality and generosity extended to me, an Englishman, coming from a country that has always dealt so harshly with the Irish. The reception at these hotels will underline this great kindness in the people of Ireland as nothing else.

ARBUTUS LODGE HOTEL
Cork, Co. Cork ☎ 021 501237
Set in a garden with an arbutus tree and full of rhododendrons and camelias, formerly the home of the Mayor of Cork, with a great view over the river. The comfort of the rooms is of a very high standard. The food relies heavily, and happily, on local produce – lobsters, fish, and game. A most comfortable stay in charming surroundings.

BALLYMALOE HOUSE
Shanagarry, Co. Cork ☎ 021 652531
This fine Georgian house, half hidden in trees, was taken over by Ivan and Myrtle Allen just after the Second World War. They have made it into something of a monument to good living. With one of the finest tables, if not *the* finest, in Ireland, it is a mecca for gourmets from all over the world. The cuisine, resolutely Irish in inspiration, uses fine produce from the gardens, and – the sea is only two miles away – the fish is perfectly delicious. The meat and game are second to none. There is croquet on the lawn and children are well catered for. Irish whiskeys are well to the fore as well as the Scotch blends and malts described in the tasting notes of this book. Highly recommended and quite perfect.

BALLYVOLANE HOUSE
Castlelyons, Co. Cork ☎ 025 3649
Set in a huge garden, the Georgian mansion was somewhat over-restored by the Victorians but is now slowly being brought back to its former glory, and already has a fine atmosphere of delicate country living. The fine, Irish cuisine is set off by a ball or two of Jameson's 1780. The teas with marvellous cakes in front of a blazing fire are the best I have ever had in Ireland. An absolutely excellent choice.

BLACKHEATH HOUSE
112 Lilleague Road, Blackhill, Coleraine, Co. Londonderry ☎ 0265 868433

In the North, well set to visit Old Bushmills distillery, the fine old house, which is a protected building, was a rectory in 1792. The furnishings of the reception rooms and the bedrooms are of the highest standard and combine the elegance of well-loved antiques with the informality of a family home. The dark-red sitting room with its log fire was a most attractive and fitting place to talk of whiskey with Dr Bill McCourt and Dr Terence Higgins from the distillery, and, down in the cellars, the Macduff restaurant served us with a meal of game and seafood that was truly memorable. There is a fine wine list and the whiskeys, which naturally include the marvellous range of Bushmills, also had the Coleraine whiskey from the now alas, silent, distillery. Very highly recommended stop-over.

BUSHMILLS INN
25 Main Street, Bushmills, BT57 8QA ☎ 02657 32339
This old inn has kept all of its old-world charm despite recent rebuilding. Situated just next door to the distillery, the menu is interesting and the Bushmills trifle, laced with whiskey, should not on any account be resisted. It would make an appropriate curtain-raiser to your visit to the distillery to take on a ball or two of their Black Bush or the Bushmills malt.

LONGUEVILLE HOUSE
Mallow, Co. Cork ☎ 022 47156
This splendid Georgian house, overlooking the Blackwater river through a line of old oaks planted to commemorate the great victory at Waterloo, was built on land ravaged by Cromwell in 1650. The welcome is friendly and warm and the house is sumptuously decorated, while at the same time maintaining a really family feel to it. The food was good and plentiful, and, in summer, meals can be taken in the delightful conservatory. My warm bedroom was huge and furnished with particularly remarkable antiques which I am sure many museums would give their eye teeth for.

MOYGLARE MANOR
Maynooth, Co. Kildare ☎ 01 286351
Some fifteen miles from Dublin, set in rich farmland, the interiors of this manor, structurally redesigned in Georgian times, are of a richness and warmth almost unsurpassed outside the pages of decoration magazines – yet the rooms maintain a cosy intimacy. The food was excellent and generously served; the night was still and the gentle early morning full of silver mists across the green land. All in all, a warm and welcoming stay.

SCILLY HOUSE
Kinsale, Co. Cork ☎ 021 772413
In the tiny harbour of Kinsale, set in a garden

packed with flowers, this charming and historic country inn has great warmth and charm. The reception and the food were of a very high standard. There are only six bedrooms, all of which give on to the gardens. A good stop-over before moving on to Midleton.

THE SHELBOURNE
St Stephen's Green, Dublin 2 ☎ 01 766471
Breaking my rule about recommending big hotels or hotels in towns, the Shelbourne ranks among the best ten big hotels that I have visited worldwide. The welcome and service are of the very highest standard, the reception rooms delightfully appointed, and the situation in the heart of old Dublin unsurpassable. My room was of a comfort that blended old-style furniture with the very best of modern convenience. Nothing was too much trouble for the staff; the food was delicious, especially the breakfast; the bar was well stocked with a fine selection of the whiskies in the Celtic tradition as well as the finest selection of Bourbons and ryes that I have ever come across in Europe – though, naturally, true to the spirit of the place, I stuck to those great favourites, the whiskeys of Ireland. The Shelbourne has maintained a tradition of care, quiet, polite and friendly service, fine cooking and elegance of appointment and attitude that so many big hotels have sadly lost today. Most highly recommended, indeed it would be absolute madness for the man of taste not to stay here when in Ireland, if he can.

UNITED STATES

When travelling through the whiskey country of Kentucky and Tennessee, the driver will not be short of a choice of boarding houses, these being advertised regularly along the roadside. One near Jack Daniel's distillery is a must:

MISS MARY BOBO'S BOARDING HOUSE
Lynchburg, Moore County, Tennessee ☎ 615 759 7394
In 1908, Miss Mary Bobo took over the former Salmon Hotel, orginally built in 1867, and a great legend was born. The building has been carefully preserved to maintain its character and is a pleasant whitewashed place shaded by one big tree. The food is in the traditional southern downhome style and includes such delicacies as fried chicken and home-grown vegetables, as well as an amazing variety of meats, remarkable cornbread and biscuits, and the best pies this side of Tockholes. Miss Mary seemed to have thrived on her fare, dying a month short of her hundred and second birthday in 1989. Miss Lynn Tolley took over and most charmingly carries on the traditions of hospitality, in this dry county, started by Miss Mary.

S H O P S   G U I D E

This list is clearly not exhaustive. I have confined myself to those shops which have consistently updated and expanded their range of whiskies over the past twenty-five years and which have always been more than helpful in finding difficult or rare bottles for me and for friends who feel very passionate about their whisky buying. Indeed, most of these shops are run by people who can not only offer advice about the whisky you want to buy but will also be happy to take time to develop your knowledge of whisky and to point you in the direction of more and more exciting whisky sensations.

Using this list you should be able to buy probably all of the four hundred or so whiskies I tasted in preparing this book and end up, rather like me, wishing that more were readily available to taste and enjoy. But then, the voyage is without end and this is the great pleasure of the whole pursuit.

ENGLAND

BIRMINGHAM

Connolly's
110 Edmund Street, Birmingham
☎ 021 236 9269

BLACKPOOL

The Wee Dram
5 Queen's Square, Blackpool
☎ 0253 751935

BRIGHTON

The Brighton Malt House
North Road, Brighton
☎ 0273 601060

BRISTOL

Reid Wines
The Mill, Marsh Lane, Hallatrow, Bristol
☎ 0761 52645

CHESTER

Chester Fine Wines
15 Watergate Street, Chester
☎ 0244 310455

FALMOUTH

Constantine Stores
34 Fore Street, Falmouth
☎ 0326 40276

GRASSINGTON

The Wine Shop
The Square, Grassington, Nr Skipton,
BD23 5AQ
☎ 0756 7552468

HAWES

J. & E. Hogg
Market Place, Hawes
☎ 0969 667213

LINCOLN

The Whisky Shop
87 Bailgate, Lincoln
☎ 0522 537834

LONDON

Berry Bros and Rudd
3 St James's Street, London SW1A
☎ 071 839 9033
The home of the Cutty Sark blend, which was created in 1923. The shop has elegant panelled décor and sells its own blends and whiskies in many different and interesting bottlings.

The Bloomsbury Wine and Spirit Company
3 Bloomsbury Street, London WC1B 3QE
☎ 071 436 4763

Fortnum and Mason
181 Piccadilly, London W1A 1ER
☎ 071 734 8040
Established in 1701, Fortnum and Mason reinforced their reputation as a fine food and spirits shop during the Crimean War when they sent out food hampers to officers struggling to uphold civilization in the mud. A hamper from Fortnum's is still, today, one of the most welcome of Christmas gifts. Their list of whiskies runs to some eighty well-chosen malts and blends as well as a very sound selection of the best American and Canadian whiskies. The list also gives some interesting notes on the different regions and types. Though Fortnum's was packed, the assistant in charge of the whisky section was happy to give me a good run-down on the whiskies on sale, and this developed into an amusing and well-informed conversation between connoisseurs. Of special note is a good selection of Strathisla malts of different ages, and the Fortnum and Mason "Choice Old" blend is more than satisfactory. The haggises – puddings crying out for the accompaniment of a dram or two – are probably the best on the southern side of the border.

Harrods
Knightsbridge, London SW1X 7XL
☎ 071 730 1234
Perhaps because Harrods has become such a tourist attraction, there are some who feel that things are not as good here as they used to be. Banish the idea. Harrods does have a perfectly excellent selection of over a hundred whiskies and, perhaps after strolling through the food halls with their marvellous tiled walls, the experienced drinker of whisky will certainly be able to find more than a few whiskies very much to his taste. Particularly interesting is their "As we get it"(a Macallan at 57.2°) and their Sheep Dip.

Justerini & Brooks
61 St James's Street, London SW1A
☎ 071 493 8721
The most royal of addresses – J. & B. have been the royal wine merchants since 1749 – this elegant shop sells a very fine selection of whiskies, including, of course, the fine market leader J. & B. Rare and the marvellous, pale-gold, flowery Knockando single malt. The shop in Edinburgh (George Street) has an even wider selection of malts.

Milroy's
3 Greek Street, London W1V 6NX
☎ 071 437 0893
The true whisky buff will know that Soho, despite its seedy reputation, is much more famous as being the location of Milroy's, run by the grand whisky connoisseur Wallace Milroy's brother Jack, whose knowledge of whisky is well up to the family tradition. Just off Soho Square, Milroy's is a tiny unpretentious palace of delight with more than three hundred different whiskies, at my last count, in various packagings, ages and strengths.

They range from 60.7° Springbank bottled in 1966, via a forty-two-year-old Balvenie, a fifty-year-old Dalmore and a 1939 Pride of Strathspey, to the regular bottlings of all the malts you may care to mention, as well as the whiskeys from Ireland, a good handful of the better Bourbons, and the regular blends of whisky, including such comparative rarities as Te Bheag Nan Eilean and Pig's Nose.

This is the true mecca for whisky lovers in London. Hardened whisky buffs drool at the mouth at the fine selection and spend hours trying to make up their minds, tearfully rediscovering lost favourites and reminiscing fondly about distillery visits of long ago. But the newcomer to whiskies should not be put off by such erudition. Jack Milroy and his staff are most attentive and kindly.

Milroy's do whisky tastings from time to time, and it would be advisable for serious tasters to telephone and find out just when.

Milroy's even sell mineral water from Drumnadrochit taken from the spring of Fionnar (Gaelic for "cool and fresh") for those who want to be absolutely sure that nothing could possibly interfere with the true Celtic delights held in their bottle.

If you cannot get up to Scotland to explore whiskies *in situ* – or even if you can – go to Milroy's; it is a must. If shops were awarded stars, Milroy's would get seven on a rating system of five.

Oddbins

Head Office: 31–3 Weir Road, London
SW19 8UG
☎ 081 944 4400

"Its range, its spirit of innovation, its staff and the ambience of its shops make it a role model for almost all of Britain's other wine merchants." (*The Sunday Telegraph Good Wine Guide*, 1992.)

For over thirty years Oddbins has been selling wines and spirits in the high streets of the capital and the provinces, and its success has as much to do with the excellence of staff as to its very wide and interesting list of products on sale. The list of single malts and blends is definitely impressive, and more than well worth a visit. The staff, usually young, friendly and enthusiastic, are most helpful and will guide the new amateur of whiskies carefully round the different regions, tastes and flavours.

Highly recommended; Oddbins has too many shops to be listed here, so it is worth looking the shops up in the telephone directory when making a visit to England. Alternatively, write to the Head Office for lists – much more than simple lists, rather they are free magazines devoted to the Oddbins product range. These are amusing, informative and excellently presented, as one would expect from this great British institution. They provide not only good tasting notes on whiskies but also on some exciting and distinguished wines. Ralph Steadman, one of England's leading cartoonists, provides illustrations and embellishments as well as his own idiosyncratic and highly informative texts.

Soho Wine Market

3 Greek Street, London W1
☎ 071 437 9311

Sotheby's

Hester Road, London SW11
☎ 071 924 3287

Though, unlike Christie's, the auctioneers Sotheby's do not have sales exclusively devoted to whiskies, from time to time old malts will be put on offer during sales of wine. In a recent auction, for example, they had some fifteen lots, including an interesting bottle of The Macallan distilled in 1938.

The Vintage House

42 Old Compton Street, London W1V 6NX
☎ 071 437 2592

As well as a good selection of wines, this Soho highspot has some hundred and fifty malts on offer with good, informative service.

St Ives

Wadsworth

The Broadway, St Ives, Cambridgeshire
☎ 0480 63522

Shrewsbury

Tanner's

26 Wyle Cop, Shrewsbury
☎ 0743 66389

Tavistock

N. H. Creber

Brook House, Tavistock
☎ 0822 612266

Thetford

T. & W. Wines

51 King Street, Thetford, Norfolk
☎ 0842 765646

SCOTLAND

Aberdeen

The Still Man

54 Holborn Street, Aberdeen
☎ 0224 210323

Aviemore

Cairngorm Whisky Centre

Inverdruie, Aviemore
☎ 0479 810574

Edinburgh

Cadenhead's Whisky Shop

172 Canongate, Edinburgh
☎ 031 556 5864

A William Cadenhead, described as a poet and grocer, first set up shop in Aberdeen in 1842. Independent bottlers, they bottle from casks from distilleries whose products are otherwise available only in the neighbourhood, and consequently their stock is never constant, since they buy only in small, very select, lots, usually at cask stength (approx. 44° to 65.5°). They have an impressive list of some ninety-odd fine malts. All visitors are given a kindly and well-informed tour of the malts for sale, and this could be the high spot of any visit to Edinburgh.

Lambert Brothers

9/11 Frederick Street, Edinburgh, EH2 2HA
☎ 031 225 4642

Royal Mile Whiskies

379 High Street, Edinburgh, EH1 1PW
☎ 031 225 3383

The Scotch Malt Whisky Society

81 Giles Street, Edinburgh, EH6 6BZ
☎ 0931 554 3452

Phillip "Pip" Hills set up the Society in 1983 to develop and promulgate the many joys and delights of Scotch malt whisky. Today the Society membership, developed largely by word of mouth, numbers some 14,000 and includes among its members former prime ministers (among them Edward Heath) and such figures as Sean Connery, Charles Dance and the writer and whisky buff Sir Kingsley Amis. The Society selects casks of special merit which it bottles at cask strength for purchase by its members. Regular newsletters with tasting notes are sent out with price lists. The malts the member can buy are of a quality that is rarely available to the general public. Details of membership can be had from the Society and first-time membership includes an introductory bottle. This excellent society is not only the perfect way for the aficionado to develop his or her knowledge and love of malts, but also allows the relative beginner to start off with only the very best. Most highly recommended.

The Scotch Whisky Heritage Centre Shop

354 Castlehill, The Royal Mile, Edinburgh,
EH1 2NE
☎ 031 220 0441

A museum containing a fine selection of more than eighty vatted and blended malts. The staff are more than willing to advise on the best whiskies for your particular tastes. A good address.

Elgin

Gordon and MacPhail

58—60 South Street, Elgin, Moray, IV30 1JY
☎ 0343 545111

In 1895, the independent bottlers James Gordon and J. A. MacPhail opened their first business in Elgin, one of the "capitals" of Scotch whisky. The firm was one of the first to sell single malts on a wider scale. Still in Elgin, the firm now produces blends under its own label. They buy their whisky at source, and stock it in their own warehouses at Elgin and this is bottled when they feel the moment of perfection has been reached. They also sell whiskies that are rare, either because they are produced in very small quantities or because the producing distillery has closed down – such as the St Magdalene. The single malts, some fifty of them, are sold with the label "Connoisseur's Choice" and are aged from ten to thirty-five years, and notable are the whiskies of the years 1940 to the early 1950s, which are relatively very rare, due to restrictions on grain production for distillation. I have particularly appreciated their bottlings of Benrinnes, Bladnoch, Ardbeg and Glendronach.

Christie's

164–6 Bath Street, Glasgow, G2 4TG
☎ 041 332 5759
The fine-art auctioneers Christie's hold auctions for collectors of fine and rare bottles of

whisky. Though I have my doubts about buying bottles to collect and not to drink, the list of bottles sold recently is most impressive. Serious collectors should contact the quiet and helpful Martin Green, the man in charge, with a charming and inexhaustible fund of whisky lore, who will provide catalogues.

B A R S   G U I D E

"I like bars just after they open for the evening. When the air inside is still cool and clean and everything is shiny and the barkeeper is giving himself that last look in the mirror to see if his tie is straight and his hair is smooth. I like the neat bottles on the bar back and the lovely shining glasses and the anticipation. I like to watch the man mix the first one of the evening and put it down on a crisp mat and put the little folded napkin beside it. I like to taste it slowly. The first quiet drink of the evening in a quiet bar. That's wonderful."

I agreed with him.

"Alcohol is like love," he said. "The first kiss is like magic, the second is intimate, the third routine. After that you just take the girl's clothes off."

"Is that bad?" I asked him.

(Raymond Chandler, *The Long Goodbye*)

LONDON

Athenaeum

116 Piccadilly, London W1V
☎ 071 499 3464
The bar of this first-class hotel has nearly sixty single malts, and a vast selection of other whiskies. The barman is a true whisky buff and will guide his clients through the list. If you can drink your way through them all (though not at one sitting), during his advanced *ad hoc* courses on whisky tasting, you will be awarded a bottle of your favourite.

PARIS

Bar le Forum

4 boulevard Malesherbes, 75008 Paris
☎ 42 65 37 86
In 1918 the old Restaurant de la Poste became the Bar le Forum, and gentlemen have been quietly applauding ever since. I first came here with my grandfather in 1956. Their claim to be "the most English of American bars" is no mere advertising puff. The comfortable armchairs, the relaxed

atmosphere, a general feeling of quiet contentment, a politeness and friendliness of service, and a truly well-established range of whiskies – there are seventy-one – all support this claim. At the well-appointed bar, old English ex-patriots are to be seen discussing Paris life with young French businessmen or writers, old local French residents will bandy the names of Parisian tailors and shirtmakers with the young English newcomer to Paris, and all with that gentle feeling of equals among equals that is to be seen nowhere else except in the great clubs of London. Their cocktails vie with those of Harry's Bar (see below) – I cannot declare a winner between them. The genius of the establishment is Jean Biolatto, the only Frenchman with an Italian name who can wear a kilt as to the manner born. What he cannot tell you about whisky is not worth knowing. The distillery he has not visited in his search for excellence in whisky is yet to be built.

La Closerie des Lilas

171 boulevard de Montparnasse, 75006 Paris
☎ 43 26 70 50
Particularly out of the tourist season — when Paris is full of Americans seeking out the bars where Hemingway drank — this is an excellent place to select a whisky from the interesting and extensive list.

Harry's Bar

5 rue Daunou, 75002 Paris
☎ 42 61 71 14
Established in 1911, Harry's Bar has been admirably run by the MacElhones since 1923. Hemingway drank here; so did the Prince of Wales (the Duke of Windsor) Gene Kelly, Marguerite Duras, Pierre Brasseur, Jeanne Moreau, and many others. The list of whiskies is truly impressive, and the whisky cocktails superbly made. A collection of old bottles of whisky in display cases emphasizes long devotion to the dispensing of the water of life. In the afternoon, with the sombre, dark-wood panelling, this is a place for meditative

drinking. In the evenings, especially after the Opéra, it is a pleasantly crowded place for meeting friends and indulging in long and happy conversation. On the evening of 4 July or Thanksgiving Day, this is the place where all true American Parisians and their friends congregate. This is a real bar for whisky, or whiskey, and if, in the service, the first nosings are rather austere, over the years the follow through becomes sweeter and sweeter, developing into a marvellous crescendo.

Kitty O'Shea's

10 rue des Capucines, 75002 Paris
☎ 40 15 00 30
No one who has been to Ireland can come away without taking a little piece of it in his heart. This is the little piece of Ireland in the heart of Paris. Even the Irish come here. Perhaps you would like to sip a little draught Guinness to lay a base for the proud whiskeys of Ireland. This is the place where James Joyce may have written, "the light music of whiskey falling into a glass . . . a most agreable interlude". Some of their simply perfect smoked salmon with, say, a ball of Tullamore Dew is one of the truly great pleasures of life. As the evening draws on a convivial atmosphere develops, soft Irish songs may be sung, you may be swept up by wilder music and, when you come away, you come with the feeling that the world is a better, dare I say, more Celtic place – and the names Jameson, Power's, Paddy and Tullamore and Bushmills will ring gently up to the stars.

Pub Winston Churchill

5 rue Presbourg, 75016 Paris
☎ 40 67 17 37
Set up in 1965, and inaugurated by Winston Churchill's daughter, the wife of the then British ambassador to Paris, this was one of the rash of designer pubs created in Paris during the 1960s which seemed to the Englishman almost certainly destined to oblivion within five years. Rightly, the Winston Churchill is a great survivor. The

downstairs bar l'américaine, with its soft lights, suave decoration, and gently strumming piano, serve a vast range of whiskies, as well as a selection of more than forty English-style sandwiches.

UNITED STATES

ALASKA

Simon & Seafort's
420 L Street, Anchorage, Alas.
☎ (907) 273–3502

ARIZONA

Arizona Biltmore Hotel
Phoenix, Ariz.

CALIFORNIA

Kincaid's Bay House
60 Bayview Place, Irvine, CA
☎ (415) 342–9844

Skate's on the Bay
Berkeley Marina, 100 Seawall Drive, Burlingame, CA
☎ (415) 549–1900

Stepp
350 Hope, Los Gatos, CA
☎ (213) 626–0900

COLORADO

Scotts-Doubletree Hotel
Aurora, Colo.

FLORIDA

Bern's Steak House
1208 S. Howard Avenue, Tampa, FL
☎ (813) 251–2421

HAWAII

Ryan's Grill
Ward Center, 1200 Alamoana, Honolulu, HI
☎ (808) 523–9132

ILLINOIS

Buckingham's
Chicago Hilton, 720 S. Michigan Avenue, Chicago, ILL
☎ (312) 922–4400

Duke of Perth
2913 N. Clark Street, Chicago, ILL 60614
☎ (312) 477–1741

MASSACHUSETTS

Rowe's Wharf Bar
Boston Harbor Hotel, 70 Rowe's Wharf, Boston, MA
☎ (617) 439–7000

MINNESOTA

Kincaid's Steak, Chop and Fish House
8400 Normandale Lake Boulevard, Bloomington, MN
☎ (612) 921–2255

NEW YORK

Keen's Chophouse
72 W. 36th Street, New York, NY
☎ (212) 947–3636

OREGON

Hall Street Bar and Grill
3775 S.W. Hall Boulevard, Portland, Oreg.
☎ (503) 641–6161

PHILADELPHIA

Cutter's Grand Café
2005 Market Street, Philadelphia, PA
☎ (215) 851–6262

WASHINGTON

Cutter's Bay House
2001 Western Avenue, Tacoma, WA
☎ (206) 448–4884

Stanley and Seafort's
115 E. 34th Street, Tacoma, WA
☎ (206) 473–7300

G   L   O   S   S   A   R   Y

As we get it   name of a malt whisky sold at cask strength (usually c. 65°).
Ball of Malt   a glass of whiskey (Ireland).
Bead   bubbles that form at the surface of heavier American whiskeys.
Beer   in distilling, the wash, the fermented wort (USA).
Blend   to combine various malt whiskies, up to 40–50°, with grain whisky to produce a blended whisky.
Blended de luxe   blended whiskies produced with a higher proportion of older malts.
Blended whiskeys   American or Irish whiskeys produced in the same way as the following entry.
Blended whiskies   whiskies made from a blend of malt and grain whiskies.

Bourbon whiskey   whiskey distilled at no less than 160° US proof from a fermented mash containing no less than 51% corn (maize).
Bootlegger   American smuggler of whisky particularly during Prohibition. The term originates from the hiding of whisky bottles in the tops of boots.
Bottled in bond   American whiskeys aged for at least four years, without being reduced, and bottled under US excise control. The excise on these whiskeys is levied only after bottling.
Campbeltown   whisky-producing region of Scotland, now comprising two distilleries in part-time production. In the late nineteenth century there were over thirty distilleries in the area.

Coffey still   the "Patent", "continuous" or "column" still; a system of continuous distillation in two columns, the analyser and rectifier, to produce "grain spirit", usually from a fermented mash of mixed grains containing some malted barley.
Column still   see *Coffey still.*
Continuous still   see *Coffey still.*
Diastase   in germination, the embryo of the barley secretes diastase, which makes the starch in the barley soluble and breaks it down. This process is then halted by drying.
Dram   a small glass of whisky. Originally one-eighth of a fluid ounce, this simply came to mean a small drink. When we speak of "having a dram", this in no way implies taking it in a dramglass – with a capacity of

one-eighth of a fluid ounce – as this would prevent the addition of water, without which no true connoisseur of whisky would taste his malt.

Draff the residue of grain left over after mashing; used for cattle feed.

Double marriage see *marriage*; a second marriage of the malts in the blending process.

Exciseman British government officer responsible for the collection of duty on whisky and the prevention of illicit distilling.

Feints during the second distillation in pot stills, the final part of the distillate, which contains unpleasant-tasting higher alcohols. These are separated off and redistilled.

Fermentation the conversion of sugars into alcohol.

Flask small bottle for whisky, often made of silver, to be put in the pocket or sporran, usually by sportsmen, for drinking outdoors.

Foreshots the first part of the second distillate; rejected and redistilled.

Fusel oil undesirable elements in the new spirit eliminated by maturation in used oak casks (German: *fusel* = "rotgut").

Keepers of the Quaich elective society of men and women in and connected with the whisky business, or eminent connoisseurs enjoined to forward the cause of Scotch whisky.

Hogshead an oak cask containing 250–305 litres, the most common size employed for the maturing of whisky, previously used for either sherry or Bourbon.

Highlands whisky-producing region north of an imaginary line drawn from Greenock in the west and Dundee in the east, developed originally by the Wash Act (1784), legislating on duties levied on whiskies. The Highland whiskies are very variable in type but in general are broader and fruitier than the Lowland. The Speyside is the only accepted subdivision of the region, mainly because of the number of distilleries sited in this north east corner of Scotland. The Islands, without being an accepted subdivision of the Highlands and mainly a figment of the marketing man's imagination, are a purely geographical concept, and include all the Islands except Islay (see below).

Islands see *Highlands*.

Islay whisky-producing region of Scotland centred on the island off the west coast, and producing rather heavy, peaty, seaweedy malts, which are also an essential part of the better Scotch-whisky blends.

Lowlands whisky-producing region of Scotland south of an imaginary line drawn from Greenock in the west to Dundee in the east, developed originally by the Wash Act (1784), legislating on duties levied on whiskies. As a general rule the stills in this area were larger and long-necked, producing a lighter whisky, of which much went to London in the early nineteenth century to be rectified into gin. Some triple distillation is practised here, somewhat similarly to Irish practice.

Low wines the distillate from the first distilling in pot stills from the wash. These are distilled a second time in the low-wines still to produce spirit for maturing into whisky.

Malting floor floors where the damp, germinating barley is turned to prevent heat or moulds developing.

Malt whisky whisky without the addition of grain whisky, from one single Scottish distillery using malted barley in pot stills.

Marriage in blending, the malts are brought together, thus producing a "vatted malt", and given a further maturation before proceeding, in some cases, to a second marriage, where more malts are added and matured for a further period before being married with the grain whisky before further maturing and bottling.

Mash the dried, ground, malted barley mixed with hot water in the mash tuns to produce wort, a sugary liquid.

Middle cut the spirit produced in the second distilling, with the undesirable foreshots and feints eliminated; also called the "heart".

Moonshine illicit spirits (USA).

Pagodas ventilators of the kilns, so named for their distinctive shape.

Patent still see *Coffey still*.

Phylloxera (vastatrix) beetle that attacks certain strains of grapevines.

Pot still rounded copper vessel with swan neck used for distilling malt whiskies. There are usually two stills, the wash still and the low-wines still. Sometimes, in the Lowlands and Campbeltown, there is a third distillation similiar in some ways to practice in Ireland.

Poit Dhubh the black pot, the illicit still producing poteen. Today, the name of a vatted malt produced on Skye.

Poitin see *poteen*, below.

Poteen spirits distilled illicitly (Ireland).

Proof the term by which the strength of alcohol is measured. In early days this was done by adding gunpowder to the spirit. If there was enough alcohol in the distillate to allow the gunpowder to light it was deemed to be proof. NB: 50° proof = 100° US proof.

Pure malt a term that is sometimes used somewhat loosely; in this volume it denotes a whisky that has no added grain whisky. Thus vatted malts, single malts and single-single malts are all "pure malts".

Quaich early Celtic drinking vessel with two handles.

Rye Whisky whisky made using at least 51% rye in its mash (Canada and the USA).

Saccharify to convert into sugar – when the diastase converts the starch in the grain to sugar.

Sassenachs southerners, the English (Scottish).

Shiels shovels made of wood which does not bruise the grain; used to turn malting barley.

Single malt malt whisky produced by a single distillery.

Single-single malt whisky produced from a single distillation from a single distillery, and usually from a single cask.

Single whisky malt or grain whisky produced by a single distillery.

Sour mash an American whiskey for which part of the de-alcoholized fermentation is used to start the next mash.

Speakeasy illicit bar selling whiskies during Prohibition (USA).

Speyside see *Highlands*.

Spirits distilled alcohol that has been matured for less than three years and thus cannot be called "whisky".

Spirit safe device that allows for the inspection and manipulation of the young spirit without giving direct hands-on access.

Still room working area where the stills are found, worked by the stillman.

Straight Bourbon Bourbon produced without the addition of neutral spirits, usually in one single distillery and from one single distillation.

Tumbler flat-based cylindrical glass most often used for drinking whisky.

Uisce beatha the Gaelic word for "water of life", the ancestor of whisky.

Vatted malt an assemblage of malt whiskies, usually from the same region but not exclusively so, which has no added grain whisky.

Wash the liquid obtained when the wort is fermented in the washbacks.

Whiskey corruption of *uisce beatha*; Irish and usual American spelling.

Whisky corruption of *uisce beatha*. Scottish, Canadian and Japanese spelling.

Wort the sugary liquid produced from the malted barley in the mash tun.

c. **800 BC** Arrack is distilled in India. Egyptians use distillation to produce fards.

584 BC Aristotle born; later refers to distilling in his *Meteorology*.

AD 356 Some forms of distillation known in Wales.

AD 432 St Patrick, of Scottish origins, sent to Ireland as a missionary. Monks distilling water of life in Ireland.

Sixth century AD The Welsh bard Taliessin refers to the distillation of mead.

1170 Anglo-Norman troops encounter whiskey in Ireland.

1494 Scottish Exchequer Rolls mention Friar Coll making *aqua vitae* for the king.

1505 Barber Surgeons in Edinburgh given the right to produce *aqua vitae*.

1620 The Pilgrim Fathers arrive in North America with distilled spirits.

1640 The first recorded distillery in North America set up on Staten Island.

1644 Charles I raises taxes on "everie pynt of aquavytie sold within the country".

1707 The Act of Union joins the parliaments of England and Scotland. Taxes raised on malt whiskies.

1715 The Old Pretender's uprising. Malt tax withdrawn.

1725 Malt taxed again in Scotland, provoking riots.

1745 Bonnie Prince Charlie's uprising. Highland clans are crushed, and whisky distilling becomes more and more clandestine.

1750 Samuel Johnson refers to whiskey in his dictionary.

1775–85 The earliest large distilleries set up in Kentucky.

1780 Jameson sets up the first large commercial Irish-whiskey distillery in Dublin.

1784 The Wash Act defines the "Highland Line" as running from Dundee to Greenock for tax purposes.

1788 Duties again increased on whisky.

c. **1790** Whiskey distilled in Bourbon County, Kentucky.

1791 Powers establishes his distillery in Dublin.

1791 Washington attempts to raise tax on whiskeys, which –

1794 – leads to the "Whiskey War" in the United States; this in turn causes farmer distillers to move westward.

1811 Kentucky is said to have some 2,000 small distilleries.

1822 George IV visits Scotland for reconciliation celebrations and enjoys contraband Glenlivet.

1823 A new Act establishes a standard £10 licensing fee on stills and duty of 2s 8d per gallon distilled.

1824 With the support of the Duke of Gordon, George Smith establishes the first distillery in the Highlands licensed under the new rules.

1831 Aeneas Coffey develops his patent still.

1845 The potato famine in Ireland encourages mass emigration to the United States, where the new settlers give an impetus to Irish whiskey sales.

1846 John Dewar, one of the first of the great Scottish whisky barons, sets up in the whisky business.

1848 Queen Victoria discovers the delights of Scotland and visits distilleries.

1853 Andrew Usher introduces the first whiskies to be blended with grain whisky.

1854 Hiram Walker distils rye whisky in Canada, setting up as a leading producer of whisky and one of the first great whisky barons.

1870 *Phylloxera vastatrix* hits the vineyards of France.

1877 The Distillers Company is formed.

1880 Johnnie Walker sets up offices in London.

1882 Hiram Walker's Canadian Club appears.

1906 Islington Council brings the "What is Whisky?" case.

1908 A Royal Commission decides that both grain and malt whiskies are "true".

1909 Whisky is defined as a "spirit obtained by the distillation of a mash of cereal grains saccharified by the diastase of the malt; that Scotch whisky is, as above defined, distilled in Scotland". Lloyd George raises taxes on whisky.

1914 The First World War brings restrictions on the sales of alcohols.

1916 The Easter Rising in Dublin, followed by difficulties in the Irish-whiskey trade.

1918 The war ends. Masatake Taketsuro, the father of Japanese whisky, visits Scotland.

1920 Prohibition is imposed in the United States.

1919–21 Civil War in Ireland. The Irish trade war with the British Empire hinders sales of whiskey.

1921 Taketsuro sets up first whisky distillery in Japan with Shinjiro Torii.

1929 The Great Depression.

1932 The repeal of Prohibition by Roosevelt.

1945 The end of the Second World War. Mainland Europe develops a taste for whisky.

1947 A sharp increase in taxes on whisky imposed by the Socialist government.

1960 The Scotch Whisky Association is given legal status in non-British courts to protect whisky. "Bourbon" whiskey is recognized as a whisky-type by European distillers.

1973 Britain joins the European Economic Community; this causes a slight easing in whisky duties.

1988 Irish Distillers is taken over by the Pernod Ricard Group.

1990 A new Welsh whisky distillery is established in Ffrwdgrech, after an interruption of some ninety years in the production of whisky in Wales.

1991 EC regulations enshrine the concept that Scotch whisky is spirit elaborated from a grain alcohol, matured for at least three years in casks in Scotland and marketed at at least 40°. This closes the door on many younger bogus alcohols containing some Scotch whiskies and sold at 30° as Scotch in Continental Europe.

BIBLIOGRAPHY

Of the titles listed, the author particularly recommends the books by Wallace Milroy, Derek Cooper and Michael Jackson, which are essential reference books.

Amis, Kingsley, *On Drink*, Cape
—*Memoirs*, Hutchinson
Andrews, Allen, *The Whisky Barons*, Jupiter Books
Arnold, Wendy, *The Historic Hotels of Ireland: A Select Guide*, Thames and Hudson

Barnard, Alfred, *The Whisky Distilleries of Scotland*, Northern Books
Barr, Andrew, *Wine Snobbery*, Faber and Faber
Bell, Brian, *Scotland: Insight Guide*, Apa Publications
Bell, Colin, *Scotch Whisky*, Auld Lang Syne Publishing
Boulogne, Jean-Claude, *Histoire morale et culturelle de nos boissons* (in French), Robert Laffont
Brander, Michael, *The Original Scotch*, Hutchinson
—*A Guide to Scotch Whisky*, Johnson and Bacon
—*An Introduction to Scotch Whisky*, Spurbooks
—*The Essential Guide to Scotch Whisky*, Canongate
Bruce-Lockhart, Robert, *Scotch*, Putnam
Bunn, Mike, *Ireland: The Taste and the Country*, Anaya Publications

Cooper, Derek, *A Guide to the Whiskies of Scotland*, Pitman
—*The Whisky Roads of Scotland*, Norman and Hobhouse
—*Enjoying Scotch*, Cassell
—*A Taste of Scotch*, André Deutsch
Carson, Gerald, *The Social History of Bourbon*, Kentucky
Critchley, Julian, *Westminster Blues*, Hamish Hamilton
Crowgey, Henry, *Kentucky Bourbon*, Kentucky

Dagouret, Pierre, *Le Barman universel* (in French), Flammarion
Dumay, Raymond, *Guide des alcools* (in French), Stock
Dunnett, Alastair, *The Land of Scotch*, SWA

Edwards, Graham, and Sue Edwards, *The Dictionary of Drink*, Alan Sutton

Fairley, Jan, Jack Gillon, Charles McMaster and Michael Mass, *Scottish Drink Book*, Chambers
Fleming, Susan, *The Little Whisky Book*, Piatkus
Forbes, K. J., *A Short History of the Art of Distillation*, Brill

Gunn, Neil, *Whisky and Scotland*, Souvenir Press

Hallgarten, Peter, *Spirits and Liqueurs*, Faber and Faber
Hammer, Richard, *The Illustrated History of Organized Crime*, Courage
Hills, Phillip, *Scots and Scotch*, Mainstream
House, Jack *et al.*, *Scotch Whisky*, Macmillan

Jackson, Michael, *The World Guide to Whisky*, Dorling Kindersley
—*Malt Whisky*, Dorling Kindersley

Keegan, Alan, *Scotch in Miniature*, Famedram

Lamond, John, *Scotland's Malt Distilleries*, Benedict Books
Lichine, Alexis, *Encyclopédie des vins et des alcools* (in French), Robert Laffont
Lord, Tony, *The World Guide to Spirits, Liqueurs, Aperitifs and Cocktails*, Macdonald and Janes

Macdonald, Aeneas, *Whisky*, Porpoise Press
Macdonald, Claire, *Claire Macdonald's Scotland: The Best of Scottish Food and Drink*, Little, Brown
MacElhone, Harry, and Andrew MacElhone, *Harry's ABC of Mixing Cocktails*, Souvenir Press
Mackenzie, Compton, *Whisky Galore*, Penguin
Mackie, Albert, *The Scotch Whisky Drinker's Companion*, Ramsey Head Press
Maclean, Fitzroy, *A Concise History of Scotland*, Thames and Hudson
Macleish, Martin, *The VIP Guide to Scotland 1989–1990*, Kensington Publications, in association with the Scottish Tourist Board
Magee, Malachy, *1000 Years of Irish Whiskey*, O'Brien
McCreary, Alf, *Spirits of Age*, Old Bushmills

McDowell, R. S. J., *The Whiskies of Scotland*, John Murray
McGuire, E. B., *Irish Whiskey*, Gill and Macmillan
McNulty, Henry, *Vogue Cocktails*, Flammarion
Milroy, Wallace, *Malt Whisky Almanac*, Lochar
Morrice, Philip, *The Schweppes Guide to Scotch*, Alphabooks
—*The Whisky Distilleries of Scotland and Ireland*, Harper
Morrissey, James, *Hot Whiskey*, Kerryman
Moss, Michael, *Scotch Whisky*, Chambers
—*The Story of Scotch Whisky*, SWHC
Moss, Michael, and James Hume, *The Making of Scotch Whisky*, James and James
Murphy, Brian, *The World Book of Scotch Whisky*, Collins

Nugue, Christian, *Les Cinglés du whisky* (in French), Hermé

Robb, Marshall, *Scotch Whisky*, Chambers
Ross, James, *Whisky*, Routledge
—*Scotland's Distilleries: An Illustrated Visitor's Guide*, Famedram

Schumann, Charles, *Schumann's Barbuch* (in German), Wilhelm Heyne
Sillet, S. W., *Illicit Scotch*, Beaver Books
Simpson, Bill *et al.*, *Scotch Whisky*, Macmillan
Skipton, Mark, *The Scotch Whisky Book*, Hamlyn
Smout, T. C., and S. Wood, *Scottish Voices*, Fontana
Steel, Tom, *Scotland's Story*, Fontana
Stenekey, Fred, *Whisky: the Complete Whisky Book*, Macmillan

Taylor, Iain Cameron, *Highland Whisky*, An Commun Caidheadlach

White Kenneth, *L'Ecosse* (in French), Arthaud
Wilson, John, *Scotland's Malt Whiskies*, Famedram
—*Scotland's Malt Distilleries*, Famedram
Wilson, Neil, *Scotch and Water*, Lochar
Wilson, Ross, *Scotch Made Easy*, Hutchinson
—*Scotch, the Formative Years*, Constable
—*Scotch: Its History and Romance*, David and Charles

A C K N O W L E D G E M E N T S

The author would like to thank friends and connoisseurs in and around the whisky business for their help in writing this book, and most particularly: in Great Britain, the Earl of Elgin and Kincardine K. T., David Boyd, Michael Burkham and Tom Thomson of United Distillers, Dr. Sean Feadragh, Dr. R. B. J. Gadney, Martin Green of Christie's Scotland, Dafydd Gittins of the Welsh Whisky Distillery, Ross Gunn and Mark Lawson of the Chivas and Glenlivet Group, Alexander Grant-Gordon, Sally Grant-Gordon, and Mrs. Roberts of William Grant and Sons, Iain Henderson of Laphroaig, Phillip Hills of the Malt Whisky Society, Stuart Hodkinson of Auchentoshan, Michael Jackson, Katie MacAulay of Oddbins, Jim McEwan of Bowmore, Dr. William McCourt and Dr. Terence Higgins of Old Bushmills, Gordon McIntosh, Secretary of the Keepers of the Quaich, Mr. and Mrs. Christopher Matthew, Sheridan Morley, Jim Milne of Justerini and Brooks, John Milroy, Wallace Milroy, Ian Mitchell and Sandy Fraser of Aberlour, Innes Shaw of Knockando, Anthony Tucker of The Scotch Whisky Association, Conal Walsh, Chris Willis of Campbell Distillers; in Ireland, John and Jane Ryan; in France, Sir Ewen Fergusson, the British Ambassador to Paris, and Richard Wilkinson and Robin Kealey at the Embassy, Olivier Beytout, Georges Benitah of the Maison du Whisky, Jean Bialatto of Bar le Forum, Jean Castel of the Club Princesse (Castel's), Robert Courtine, président, and Jacques Faizant and André Pousse, of l'Académie du Pure Malt Scotch Whisky, Michel Couvreur, Michel Creignou, Marielle Darwen, Peters Day, Agnes Debret of the British Tourist Authority, Irène Duret and Florence Valette of the Irish Whiskey Information Bureau, Pierre Coussen of Nicolas, Philippe Jeannier of Carrefour France, François Ladoux, Eric Ledoigt, Duncan MacElhone of Harry's Bar, Michel Mazuet, Bruno Raphaelli, Patrick Ricard of Pernod Ricard, Olivier Vialard, Anne Zeimour of the Irish National Tourist Office, as well as the cartoonists who so ably and determinedly helped me with my tasting notes: Avoine, Jy, Mose, Nicoulaud, Soulas and Wozniak; in Japan, Professor Yasuo Yoshitomi, Masahiro Miyasaki, Keiko Tonegawa; in New Zealand, Colonel James Holden Taylor; in the USA, Anne Lewis-Loubignac, Cultural Attaché at the French Embassy in Washington, Tim Culver of the Kentucky Travel Development, and Don Williams. And my thanks to Sabine Greenberg for her excellent, extensive and painstaking documentary research, and to Ghislaine Bavoillot, and her assistant Anne Fitamant-Peter, at Flammarion, who sagely followed the long maturing of this book, and whose patience and attention to detail would suggest that they were ideally suited to setting up their own whisky distillery.

Harold Starke Publishers Ltd are very grateful for the advice and assistance of Campbell Evans of The Scotch Whisky Association.

P I C T U R E   C R E D I T S

The maps on pages 167, 184, 185 and 187 were drawn by Léonie Schlosser.

Photographic credits: Alpha: p. 24 (bottom); Peter Aprahamian: p. 20 (top); Arqué Collection: pp. 11, 12 (bottom), 21 (top), 24 (top), 44, 68 (top), 69 (centre), 181 (bottom), 186 (bottom right); Baumgartner: p. 176 (bottom); Ian Berry: p. 137; Bettmann Archive: pp. 14 (bottom), 15, 16, 17 (bottom), 30 (bottom), 33, 34–5, 37 (top), 53, p. 80 (centre and bottom), 81 (top), 83 (bottom), 84 (top and right), 85 (bottom), 86, 87, 89, 90 (right and bottom), 91 (bottom), 92, 93, 94, 153, 164 (top); Olivier Beytout: pp. 110, 112 (bottom), 114 (bottom), 116 (top), 117 (bottom), 122 (top), 127, 129 (bottom), 130 (right), 145, 152, 170 (bottom), 171, 173; C. Boisvieux: p. 45; Klaus Bossemeyer: pp. 39, 112 (top), 128 (top), 129 (top), 161; Jacques Boulay: cover, pp. 1–7, 11, 43 (top), 49 (centre), 56, 57, 105, 130 (bottom), 140, 142–3, 158, 160, 163, 164 (bottom), 165, 166 (bottom), 167, 176 (top), 178 (bottom), 183, 190, 192; Bill Brandt: p. 19; Martin Breese: pp. 41, 72, 73, 95, 97 (left), 182, 187 (top); Bridgeman Art Library: pp. 25 (top), 27, 46, 59, 60, 61 (bottom), 62 (top), 63 (bottom), 64; British Film Institute: p. 13; British Library: p. 58; British Museum: pp. 43 (bottom), 61 (centre); Cahiers du Cinéma: p. 17 (top); Campbell's Distillers: p. 146; Henri Cartier-Bresson: p. 31; Casterman: p. 166 (top); C.E.D.R.I.: p. 169; Dave Chancellor: p. 24 (bottom); Cherrier: p. 114 (top); Chivas Glenlivet Group: p. 66; Christie's: pp. 67 (right), 71 (bottom), 151, 191; Cinémathèque française: p. 12 (top); Cinéstar, pp. 14 (top), 32, 54 (bottom), 90 (top); Cosmos: pp. 74, 75, 76; Crown Copyright: pp. 25 (bottom), 26 (top); D.R.: pp. 10, 38, 49 (bottom), 52 (top), 62 (centre and bottom), 63 (top), 67 (bottom), 107 (top), 117 (top), 126 (right and bottom), 159, 180, 181 (top), 189; Mary Evans Picture Library: p. 30 (top), 37 (bottom), 61 (top); Explorer: pp. 30 (top), 37 (bottom), 42, 45, 61 (top), 99, 101 (top), 176 (bottom); Daniel Faure: pp. 77, 97 (top), 98, 115, 121 (top), 128 (bottom), 136, 138 (bottom), 141 (top), 144 (bottom), 186 (top); Fay Godwin: pp. 119, 177 (centre); Goodwood Collections Trustees: 65; Marc Gouby: pp. 22–3, 28 (top), 40, 106, 108–9, 113, 118, 124–5, 132–3, 139, 144 (top), 170 (top), 174–5, 187 (bottom), 188 (top); P. Gould: pp. 121 (bottom), 131, 155, 156, 157, 162; Susan Griggs: p. 120; Hergé: p. 166 (top); P. Hinous: pp. 80 (top), 81 (bottom); Ian Howes: pp. 48, 52 (bottom), 67 (top), 78, 82, 83 (top), 84 (bottom), 85 (top), 96 (top and bottom), 111, 123, 130 (top), 134 (bottom), 148, 154, 172 (bottom), 188 (right); Hulton Picture Library: pp. 18, 19, 33, 47, 55 (bottom); L'Illustration: p. 91 (top); Image Bank: pp. 179, 188 (bottom); Irish Distillers: pp. 51, 55 (top), 126 (top), 138 (top); C. Karnow: pp. 74, 75, 76; Keystone: pp. 8, 88, 91 (top); Maja Koene: p. 99; Guillaume de Laubier: pp. 28 (bottom), 147, 177 (bottom), 178 (top); Magnum: pp. 29, 31, 116 (bottom), 134 (top), 137; Colette Masson: p. 21 (bottom); Fred Mayer: pp. 29, 116 (bottom); E. Meo: p. 188 (bottom); Metropolitan Museum of New York: p. 166 (right); Milroy's (London): p. 36; J.-P. Nacivet: p. 101 (top); Network: pp. 119, 177 (centre); Michael K. Nichols: p. 134 (top); K. Okada: p. 103 (bottom); Package Design Japan No. 3: p. 103 (bottom); Paddington: p. 181 (right); A. Pistolesi: p. 179; Punch: p. 54 (top); Ian Quémère: p. 169; Rapho: pp. 119, 177 (centre); Retrograph: pp. 41, 72, 73, 95, 97 (left), 182, 187 (top); Rikuyo-Sha: p. 103 (bottom); Martin Rogers: p. 120; Scope: pp. 77, 97 (top), 98, 115, 121 (top and bottom), 128 (bottom), 131, 136, 138 (bottom), 141 (top), 144 (bottom), 155, 156, 157, 162, 186 (top); Scotch Myths Archive: p. 26 (bottom), 68 (bottom), 69 (right), 149; Seagram: p. 96 (left); Ralph Steadman: p. 172 (top); William Strode: p. 79; Studio X: pp. 39, 112 (top), 128 (top), 129 (top), 161; Suntory: pp. 101 (bottom), 102, 103 (top), 122 (bottom), 141 (bottom); Sygma: p. 91 (top); Pierre Tetrel: p. 42; Eric Thorburn: p. 107 (bottom); Top: pp. 80 (top), 81 (bottom); United Distillers: pp. 20 (bottom), 49 (top), 50, 70, 71 (top), 104, 150, 177 (top); Woodfin Camp: pp. 74, 75, 76.

216